FROM HANNAH
FATHER'S DAY
JUNE 21, 2020

Hopi Runners

CultureAmerica

ERIKA DOSS

PIIILIP J. DELORIA

Series Editors

KARAL ANN MARLING

Editor Emerita

Hopi Runners
Crossing the Terrain between Indian and American

MATTHEW SAKIESTEWA GILBERT

UNIVERSITY PRESS OF KANSAS

Published by the University
Press of Kansas (Lawrence,
Kansas 66045), which was
organized by the Kansas
Board of Regents and is
operated and funded by
Emporia State University,
Fort Hays State University,
Kansas State University,
Pittsburg State University,
the University of Kansas, and
Wichita State University.

Library of Congress Cataloging-in-Publication Data

Names: Sakiestewa Gilbert, Matthew, author.
Title: Hopi runners : crossing the terrain between Indian
and American / Matthew Sakiestewa Gilbert.
Description: Lawrence : University Press of Kansas, 2018. |
Series: CultureAmerica | Includes bibliographical
references and index. Identifiers: LCCN 2018027422
ISBN 978-0-7006-2698-4 (cloth : alk. paper)
ISBN 978-0-7006-2700-4 (ebook)
Subjects: LCSH: Hopi Indians—Social life and customs. |
Indian athletes—United States. | Long-distance runners—
United States.
Classification: LCC E99.H7 S264 2018
DDC 305.8997/458—dc23.
LC record available at https://lccn.loc.gov/2018027422.

British Library Cataloguing-in-Publication Data is
available.

Printed in the United States of America

10 9 8 7 6 5 4 3 2 1

The paper used in this publication is recycled and contains
30 percent postconsumer waste. It is acid free and meets
the minimum requirements of the American National
Standard for Permanence of Paper for Printed Library
Materials z39.48-1992.

For my wife,

Kylene,

and our children,

Hannah, Meaghan,

Noelle, and Luke

Contents

Illustrations

Preface

My path to complete this book has taken me beyond Hopi ancestral lands to cities and towns across America. Along my route I met many individuals, shared my research with them, and learned from their experiences. On other occasions I ran alongside people, literally and figuratively, and I listened to their stories about running, a topic all cultures and societies have in common. My experiences on this journey will forever mark me as a scholar and as a member of the Hopi community. Written at a moment when interest in running in America is at an all-time high, this book will appeal to those interested in running and sport in general. But I also hope that it will prove especially meaningful to Hopi runners of the past and present, and those young harriers who now have the responsibility to continue this tradition into the future.

Over the years I had several opportunities to share my scholarship on Hopi runners with people back home. Early on, when I was still a graduate student, I published articles on Hopi runners in the Hopi Tribe's newspaper, the Hopi Tutuveni. I knew that while the majority of people on the reservation would not be able to access my research in scholarly journals, they could access it in the tribe's newspaper. Working closely with the Hopi Cultural Preservation Office (HCPO), I also shared my research on my blog, Beyond the Mesas, and used this platform to make my scholarly publications available to Hopis and the greater public.[1] More than anything else, my posts on Hopi runners received the most traffic and comments. On one occasion, after I published a post about a Hopi runner named Harry Chaca (Chauca) from the village of Polacca, Arizona, I received a comment from his granddaughter Cheryl Chaca (Appendix D). She remarked how pleased she was to learn about her grandfather's running accomplishments and wished "he could have read" the post himself. Cheryl's response reminds me of the reasons why I publish and produce scholarship. While I am expected to research as a member of the academy, I have a responsibility to make my research meaningful and useful to my people. I want to give a voice to Hopi people and share that voice widely.

In addition to making my work available on the internet, I often shared my research back home in person. On two occasions, Sam Taylor and other members of the Louis Tewanima Foundation invited me to present on Hopi runners at the annual Louis Tewanima Memorial Footrace pre-race dinner held at the village of Songòopavi (Shungopavi), Arizona, on Second Mesa. As a professor at a large research university in the Midwest, I rarely if ever have the chance to share my scholarship with such an informed audience, most of whom knew more than me about the essence of Hopi running. It was a humbling experience, but it further grounded me as a Hopi person and in my connection and responsibility to my community. The following community-based research highlights the voices of Hopi people and places our history and culture at the focal point of the narrative. It is first and foremost a Hopi story, but a story that is closely tied to the world beyond the mesas.

In the years that followed my presentations at the Tewanima footraces, Hopi runner and organizer Wendi Lewis of We Run Strong asked me to talk on Hopi footraces and American marathons at their Native running forum at my village of Upper Munqapi (Moencopi), Arizona. Here I met Hopi runners Caroline Sekaquaptewa, her brother Wayne Sekaquaptewa, and Trent Taylor and learned from them as they shared about their experiences running in Ironman triathlons and the coveted Boston Marathon. Returning home to give back in this way will always be a highlight of my career, and my experiences at home demonstrate how the Hopi community values knowledge gained from within and beyond the Hopi mesas. Not long after this experience, my research also hit the airwaves (and internet live-stream) when Bruce Talawyma interviewed me and my father, Willard Sakiestewa Gilbert, on the Hopi radio station KUYI (88.1FM) about making our research meaningful to the community. It was a thrill to see the phone lines light up the second I started talking about Hopi runners, a small demonstration of how important this topic is to our people. My experience with radio helped prepare me a year later when Scott Harves of ESPN interviewed me for a documentary he was producing on Hopi running and the Hopi High School cross-country team. During our two-hour conversation, he asked me about Hopi culture and society, but most of his questions focused on our long history of distance running. The thirty-minute film began airing two months later on ESPN2.

While I have had the privilege of presenting my work with people back home, I also had opportunities to share my research with different Native-related organizations in the Southwest. In summer 2013, Navajo organizer and runner Dustin Quinn Martin of Wings of America asked me to present at the organization's annual Indian Running Coaches Clinic in Santa Fe, New Mexico. Founded in the late 1980s to "enhance the quality of life of American Indian youth" through running, Wings of America exists to foster the next generation of Native "leaders, thinkers, and teachers of tomorrow." On the day that I spoke, the audience was full of young Native running coaches, and some older ones, including our famous Hopi High School cross-country coach Rick Baker, whom Hopis affectionately refer to as "The Legend." Two years later, I returned to the Southwest and spoke on Hopi running as a guest at the Tohono O'odham Nation Cultural Center and Museum in Topawa, Arizona, and then at the Amerind Museum in Dragoon, Arizona, the next day. These talks, organized by Christine Szuter and Eric Kaldahl, were part of the museum's exhibit on Indigenous runners that I was fortunate to help with.

Celebrated distance runner Amby Burfoot once remarked that "running clarifies the thinking process as well as purifies the body. I think best—most broadly and most fully—when I am running."[2] I could not agree with him more. The following book is the result of a lot of thinking, taking place during a lot of running. Trekking my way through the streets of Champaign, Illinois, or on an indoor running track at the University of Illinois, I formulated sentences in my mind, sharpened my arguments, and contemplated my approach to telling or analyzing a particular story. And about those stories . . . there are so many of them involving the great Hopi runners of the past. Some of these accounts I have retold here, but several others have yet to be shared. Every reader should know that this is not a comprehensive book on the history of Hopi running. That history would require multiple volumes and need to rely more on Hopi religious discussions on running and oral interviews, especially from those of older and younger generations. While providing a window into Hopi running from the early 1880s to the 1930s, I did not intend to cover everything in this book. Instead, I attempted to add to the existing scholarship on Hopi long-distance running during a specific period and to provide my people with a written history from one of many Hopi perspectives.

Acknowledgments

This book would not have been possible without the support of my family. I am especially grateful to my wife and best friend, Kylene, and our beautiful children and Hopi runners, Hannah, Meaghan, Noelle, and Luke. They sacrificed more than I could have asked or imagined as I wrote and finished this manuscript. Many individuals at the University of Illinois also provided much encouragement as I completed this book. I extend a heartfelt thanks to my colleagues in the Department of History, including Clare H. Crowston, Adrian Burgos, Kenneth M. Cuno, Antoinette Burton, Frederick E. Hoxie, Jerry Davila, Peter Fritzche, Ralph W. Mathisen, Harry Liebersohn, Kristin Hoganson, Leslie J. Reagan, Kevin Mumford, Craig M. Koslofsky, Berooz Ghamari-Tabriz, Augusto F. Espiritu, Tamara Chaplin, Rana A. Hogarth, Robert Michael Morrissey, Dana Rabin, Kathryn J. Oberdeck, Tariq Omar Ali, Roderick Ike Wilson, Mauro Nobili, James R. Brennan, John W. Randolph, Claudia Ruth Brosseder, Poshek Fu, Erik S. McDuffie, Marc Adam Hertzman, Ikuko Isaka, Theresa Barnes, Mark D. Steinberg, Marsha E. Barrett, Eugene M. Avrutin, Dorothee Schneider, Sundiata-Cha-Jua, and Carol Symes. A great amount of support also came from my colleagues in the American Indian Studies Program and the Native American House, including Dustin Tahmahkera, Jenny Davis, Kora Maldonado, Silvia Soto, Shanondora Billiot, Courtney Cottrell, Robert Dale Parker, Brenda Farnell, John McKinn, Dulce Talavera, Nichole Boyd, Beverley Smith, and Jamie Singson. I also thank my colleagues in the College of Liberal Arts and Sciences, namely Dean Feng Sheng Hu, Martin Camargo, Karen Carney, Kelly Ritter, David Tewksbury, Barbara Hancin-Bhatt, Joan Volkmann, Matthew Ando, Randy McCarthy, Derek Fultz, Brad Peterson, Jennifer Jorstad, Amy Elli, Carol Hartman, Donna Hulls, Staci Wagers, Audrey Ramsey, Leisha Beasley, Rayme Ackerman, Amy Scott, and Paula Hayes.

At Illinois, I am fortunate to be surrounded by many wonderful students who sharpened my thinking as I worked on this book. They include Raquel Escobar, Christopher Green, Stetson Kastengren, Beth Eby, David Horst Lehman, Christine Peralta, Issac Akande, Terry Foster, Logan Mullins, Emma Kosnik, William Kozlowski, and Deonte Harris. I am also extremely grateful for Josh Levy, who served as my graduate research assistant as I completed this project. Other support came from various Native studies scholars whose works greatly influenced my own, including K. Tsianina Lomawaima, Robert Warrior, Brenda J. Child, Margaret Connell-Szasz, Peter Nabokov, David Wallace Adams, Jon Reyhner, Jacqueline Fear-Segal, Ned Blackhawk, Jean O'Brien, Jennifer Nez Denetdale, Simon Ortiz, Cathleen Cahill, David Shorter, Kent Blansett, Jodi A. Byrd, Tiya A. Miles, Adrea Lawrence, Alyssa Mt. Pleasant, Shelly Lowe, Vicente M. Diaz, Christine DeLisle, William J. Bauer, Jr., Joseph P. Gone, Coll Trush, Kevin Whalen, John R. Gram, Keith Camacho, LeAnne Howe, Joy Harjo, Debbie Reese, Manu Vimalassery, Stanley Thangaraj, Erika Doss, Annie Gilbert Coleman, Donald L. Fixico, Peter M. Whiteley, Wesley Bernardini, Justin B. Richland, Barbara Landis, Rebecca "Monte" Kugel, Michelle Raheja, Brian S. Collier, Jill Doerfler, James F. Brooks, Christine R. Szuter, Thomas E. Sheridan, Eric J. Kaldahl, Stephen Kent Amerman, Jill Doerfler, Louellyn White, Christina Ackley, Brianna Theobald, Lindsey Passenger Wieck, Paul McKenzie-Jones, Farina King, Maurice S. Crandall, Kathleen Whiteley, Kris Klein Hernandez, Matthew Villeneuve, Kate Rennard, Barry Walsh, Carolyn O'Bagy Davis, J. Gregory Behle, film directors and producers Allan Holzman and Scott Harves, and my former graduate advisor and mentor Clifford E. Trafzer, who graciously gave this book a "once over" prior to publication.

I am also grateful to a handful of people who accompanied me on this journey in other meaningful ways. I am especially thankful for Philip J. Deloria and C. Richard King, who participated in a writer's workshop involving my book at the University of Illinois. I owe them a debt of gratitude for their support and for providing me with very helpful feedback. I also thank Kim Hogeland at the University Press of Kansas for her constant encouragement and for never losing patience with me even when I missed more than one deadline. And I thank my copyeditor, Martha Whitt, whose edits and astute observations helped ready this book for publication. I am also appreciative of Ranjit Arab, former acquisitions editor at the University Press of Kansas, for first chasing after this project for the press. Furthermore, I am grateful to my relative Neil Logan, who created several drawings for this book, including the book's jacket cover. Neil is a highly accomplished sculptor living in the Southwest, and I am honored to include his art in my book. And I am thankful for Lorene Sisquoc, director of the Sherman Indian Museum. Lorene was the one who introduced me to all the many wonderful archival records of Hopi and other Indian runners at Sherman Institute.

Several Hopi individuals also helped me along the way and offered guidance and valuable information on the long tradition of running among our people. They include Sheilah E. Nicholas, Victor Masayesva, Jr., Benjamin H. Nuvamsa, Wayne Taylor, Jr., Patty Talahongva, Bonnie Talakte, Caroline Sekaquaptewa, Catherine Talakte, Sam Taylor, Taavi Honahnie, Nick Brokeshoulder, Wendi Lewis, Justin Secakuku, Angela Gonzales, Lomayumtewa C. Ishi, Sahmie Wytewa, Justin Hongeva, Juwan Nuvayokva, Bucky Preston, Coach Rick Baker, Coach Arvis Myron, Romalita Laban, Jeremy Garcia, Trevor Reed, LuAnn Leonard, Ivan Sidney, and Leigh J. Kuwanwisiwma, as well as Stewart B. Koyiyumptewa, Lee-Wayne Lomayestewa, and Terry Morgart of the Hopi Cultural Preservation Office. Finally, I thank members of my immediate family, including my parents, Willard and Christine Gilbert; my siblings Chris and Angela and their spouses, Chrissy and Mitch; my nephews Justin (Daca), Bradley, and Isaac and niece, Alyssa; my So'o (grandmother), Ethel Sakiestewa Gilbert of Upper Munqapi; my grandfather, Tio A. Tachias; and other extended family members, including those belonging to the Sakiestewa, Honahnie, Warner, Hopewell, and Carl families.

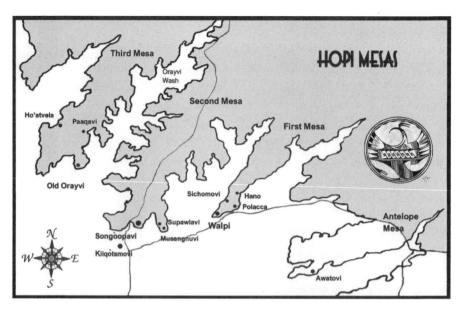

Map of Hopi Mesas and Villages, *by Neil Logan.*

Hopi Runners

Standing on the southernmost point of Third Mesa near the village of Orayvi, looking in a southeast direction. Photograph by author.

On the southernmost point of Third Mesa, near the ancient village of Orayvi on the Hopi Reservation in northeastern Arizona, one can stand on the mesa edge and see for miles in all directions. To the south, the land extends beyond the Hopi mesas, and the silhouette of Nuvatukwia'ovi, or the San Francisco Peaks, is visible in the distance. In the valleys below, corn, melon, and bean fields stand out as green patches against a backdrop of earth and sandstone. From on top of the mesa, one can enjoy the sweet smell of burning cedar, hear and feel the wind blowing over the mesa edge, and behold a breathtaking landscape surrounded by a canopy of deep blue sky. Looking east toward the village of Songòopavi on Second Mesa, running trails stretch from Orayvi like veins that connect and bring life to each of the Hopi villages. The trails near Orayvi give testimony to the tradition of running in Hopi culture and the continuance of running among today's Hopi people.

To the Fence and Back

When I was writing this book I had an opportunity to run with Victor Masayesva, Jr., a well-known Hopi filmmaker and farmer from the village of Ho'atvela (Hotevilla) on the Hopi Reservation in northeastern Arizona.[1] He had come to the University of Illinois to work with me and my colleagues in American Indian Studies on a film called *Maize*, about the corn of Indigenous people.[2] During our short, three-mile run at the Crystal Lake Park in Urbana, we talked about our film project, and I asked him several questions about his life, but the majority of our conversation centered on the topic of running. "Has anyone ever told you about how Hopis once mimicked the movements of animals to make them better runners?" he asked me. "No," I replied, a bit embarrassed that I had no idea what he was talking about. "I'm surprised people back home haven't told you," he said to me. He then proceeded to describe the movements of deer and antelope and the lessons that Hopis, or Hopìit,[3] of long ago learned from studying these magnificent runners.[4]

While we made our way around the lake I became self-conscious about my sloppy, unrefined running form. At times I struggled to maintain his pace, but like most runners I worked equally as hard not to show it. There was something about his running that both intrigued and impressed me. His stride was quick, and his shoes tapped the pavement, whereas mine pounded it. He seemed to run effortlessly, as though he was gliding along on a cushion of air, exemplifying what distance runners Danny Abshire and Brian Metzler once said: "No matter how fast you're running, your body is in harmony with the ground beneath you, moving freely and eas-ily, springing almost effortlessly with each footstep."[5] Then in his early sixties, Victor had fine-tuned his running stride, and he knew it. To him, I was but a young scholar who spent his time writing about Hopi running, while he had lived his life as a runner. And it soon became apparent to me that I had much to learn from him.

My advanced degrees and faculty appointments are no substitute for the lived experiences of others. In Hopi culture, men such as Victor serve as "uncles," teachers of younger men such as myself. We are instructed at an early age to respect and honor our elders and to listen to their advice.[6] And we are taught to value their life experiences and to place those experiences above our own. Shortly before we approached the last quarter-mile of our run, I asked Victor one final question. "So when you run back home, how many miles do you usually cover?" I thought perhaps he would say five, eight, or even ten miles. I wanted a figure, something to gauge what we had just done to the distance he normally covers at Ho'at-vela. And I wanted to know how my running compared to Victor's daily jaunts. But he gave me an answer that I did not expect. He smiled, chuckled a bit, and said to me, "Oh, you know, to the fence and back."[7]

Many American runners today are obsessed with two factors in their running, distance and time. Open any issue of *Runner's World* magazine, and you will see advertisements for products that promise to improve these two areas.[8] Today's runners resemble moving laboratories of gadgets and gauges. With the help of digital trackers and other audio devices, runners can escape the natural noises around them, including the sounds made when they breathe and the rhythmic pounding of their feet. Companies such as Apple and Garmin have engineered running watches with GPS and built-in heart-rate monitors. Some watches have the ability to track your position, distance, pace, and other bits of information and send the data wirelessly to your home computer or mobile device.[9] Through social media platforms such as Facebook and Twitter, people can now run anywhere on the globe and remain connected to the world. But this kind of running, and the mentality behind it, was not the kind of running that Victor spoke of when he and I ran loops around Crystal Lake Park.

Victor's brief description of running "to the fence and back" speaks to a cyclical aspect of traditional Hopi running that is often not reflected or practiced in today's society. For Victor, and other Hopi runners of his generation, running was not always meant to be measured in miles, or timed in increments of hours, minutes, and seconds. And it did not always involve modern gadgets, shoes, sport drinks filled with electrolytes, or the latest running attire.[10] Hopi messenger runners of long ago routinely ran barefoot and navigated their high plateaus and deserts, sometimes in the darkness of night, by studying their mountains, valleys, the moon, and the stars.[11] They ran to nearby villages or American towns and often returned to Hopi in the same day. Their "fences," metaphorically speaking, were the Hopi villages of Songòopavi and Walpi, or the Arizona towns of Flagstaff and Winslow, to name a few. Other times their "fences" were located far beyond Hopi ancestral lands and included the Pueblo villages of New Mexico, the Indigenous communities of central Mexico, and the coastal lands of Native California. They ran with a purpose and a destination (the fence) in mind, but they always returned to their villages (and back). They always returned home.

In his book on the lure of distance running, marathon runner Robin Harvie remarked that "getting back home lies at the heart of understanding one of the fundamental instincts of why we run."[12] The concepts of migration, mobility, and "home" also serve as an important lens for understanding the ancient and modern world of Hopi long-distance running. Since the beginning of Hopi time, Hopis have been in a constant state of movement to and away from home. Similar to many other Native peoples, Hopis have explained these movements in very detailed origin and emergence accounts. The stories connect the people to the land and give Hopis a worldview to understand and interpret their past, present, and future. From a very early age, Hopis have been taught about the great migration stories of long ago.[13] Well before Europeans set foot on this continent, Hopis learned that their people once divided themselves into clans and migrated in all four cardinal directions.[14] According to Hopi beliefs, the clans traveled to the Pacific Ocean, Central America, and occupied lands in present-day New Mexico and Colorado.[15] During these migrations, the people experienced different climates and terrains and learned to survive by hunting, gathering, and planting. But as Hopi cultural historians Stewart B. Koyiyumptewa and Leigh J. Kuwanwisiwma, and anthropologist Thomas E. Sheridan and others once noted, Hopi migration was "not a single migration but a complex series of journeys, many of which followed river valleys including the Colorado, Verde, the San Pedro, and the Membres."[16] And one of these journeys, to a place nearly two hundred miles east of their mesas, tells of a time when the people ran footraces and established running in Hopi culture.

At Chaco Canyon in the San Juan Basin of New Mexico, Hopi clans cleared trails that extended to the ancient settlement of Mesa Verde in Colorado. Used by the Flute Clan for ceremonial purposes, the running trails at Chaco Canyon are among the earliest evidences of running in Hopi society. Hopi clan runners who competed at Chaco Canyon did so to bring rain to their "family's fields." When they returned to their original lands in the place we now call northern Arizona, the Flute Clan continued its ceremonial races and established running in Hopi culture. Hopi runners, or warik'aya as they are referred to in Hopi, of the distant past ran as representatives of their clans and believed that their swiftness of foot would benefit their people with much-needed rain and a bountiful harvest.[17] Tuwangyam, or Sand Clan, runners regularly ran to shrines or other sacred sites far beyond Hopi ancestral lands to entice rain clouds to follow them back to their mesas. The ceremonial runners believed that the faster they ran on their return journey, the quicker the clouds would arrive on Hopi lands to water their fields.[18]

But the migrations to distant locations, and the complexities that surrounded them, did not cease when the Flute or other clans returned to their present mesas and established villages. Many years after those initial clan migrations, Hopis participated on a second wave of migration as their world intersected with the one beyond the mesas. With the establishment of the railroad, opportunities for Hopis to venture outside of their ancestral lands slowly increased. For a number of years, Hopi runners who had been hired by white individuals to deliver messages from Hopi villages to American towns such as Winslow or Holbrook often witnessed the arrival and departure of trains. The ancient running trails of their people brought them to the steel tracks of the Atlantic & Pacific Railroad. And although they had witnessed these marvels of modernity from a distance, they soon became their passengers and traveled from one end of the country to the other.

One of the first examples of this came in the early 1890s. At this time, government officials carefully planned a trip for Hopis, all of whom were runners, by train to the East Coast to show them modern civilization, the supposed superiority of American ways, and the power of the US military. During this trip, officials brought the people to American cities known for their industry, federal Indian boarding schools, and military forts. They also had them witness the "acres and acres" of corn and other agricultural fields throughout the Midwest.[19] They did so to convince the people to adopt Western methods of farming back home, to stop resisting US government mandates, and to embrace Western forms of schooling for their children. When the people returned to their villages, they argued among each other about how to respond to these outside forces of colonialism and contemplated their future in an ever-changing American society.

The accounts of Hopi leaders who traveled by train to the East and West Coasts connect to the larger story of Hopi running in important ways. Prior to the early 1890s, Hopis rarely, if ever, boarded trains to travel across the United States. Instead, trains brought visitors to the Hopi mesas, many of whom came to survey the region or to see and record Hopi religious ceremonies. These visitors returned home by rail with stories about footraces that they had observed on Hopiland and published them in American newspapers and other forms of literature. But when the Hopi delegation departed by rail for the nation's capital, or when a group of Hopi runners and prisoners left Arizona in the same fashion for Alcatraz Island in the San Francisco Bay, they foreshadowed a new era for Hopi running in American society. The delegations, whether voluntary or forced, point to a time when government officials required the people to board locomotives for places such as the "land of oranges," a term Hopis used to refer to the many orange groves surrounding Sherman Institute, an off-reservation Indian boarding school in Riverside, California.[20] Others boarded trains to travel far east to the Carlisle Indian Industrial School in Pennsylvania.[21] Although Hopi youth arrived at the schools to receive an academic and industrial education, some used the opportunity to join the school's track and cross-country teams. They signaled toward a future when school and other government officials sent Hopis by train to compete in cities across the United States, including Los Angeles, Seattle, and New York, and to when these same runners traveled by rail back to their villages as modern athletes, only to be confronted with deeply rooted cultural beliefs about running in Hopi society.

In my book I rely heavily on this concept of leaving and returning to understand and tell the story of Hopis who left their villages to compete at off-reservation Indian boarding schools. In the late 1870s, US government officials began creating these schools to help assimilate Native people into American society and to teach them trades that would be useful to tribal and nontribal communities. At the schools teachers and other officials taught the students to read and write English and instructed them in several other disciplines. In addition to teaching them subjects most commonly found in American grammar schools, school officials trained female students in domestic education and provided male students with opportunities to learn trades including blacksmithing, plumbing, and leatherwork.[22] "All the ordinary mechanical occupations likely to be useful in the future life of the pupils are taught at the Phoenix Indian School," wrote the *Arizona Republican*. The "girls learn housekeeping, cooking, [and] sewing" while the "boys have ample chance to find their natural bent in the bakery" and in the "machine and tailor shops."[23]

Although focused on academic education and industrial training, Indian schools offered students the chance to participate in several extracurricular activities including music, drama, and sports. In his book *To Show What an Indian Can Do*, historian John Bloom keenly observed that sports at Indian boarding schools "provided a popular image of modern Native Americans that the promoters of the Indian boarding school system used to promote their cause."[24] School officials encouraged athletic competitions to reinforce the values of team effort, competition, and the benefits of hard work. Students joined athletic teams as a result of their desire to compete, to improve their athletic skills, and to demonstrate to each other and white audiences that Indian athletes—if given the chance—could compete against white members of American society. Furthermore, sport teams increased the visibility of Indian schools and taught athletes the Western concepts of competition and what non-Native people deemed to be fair play.

While Hopis participated in several sports, including basketball, football, and even boxing, their greatest success came as members of track and cross-country teams. Sports at off-reservation schools provided Native athletes opportunities that did not exist for them on their reservations. When Hopis joined cross-country teams at Sherman Institute, or the Indian school at Carlisle, they experienced for the first time different regions of the country, life in modern cities, and a new way of running footraces. And Hopis used these opportunities to learn and interact with people from other parts of the United States and the world. While competing in marathons, Hopis ran with runners from Ireland, Germany, Sweden, and Japan, and although from vastly different cultures, they spoke a common—and perhaps universal—language of competitive running.[25]

Having come from a society that valued long-distance running for ceremonial and practical purposes, Hopi youth transferred this cultural mindset with them when they entered these faraway schools. Hopi runners who competed at Indian schools had come from a tribe of racers. While none

Runners at the Oraivi Footrace, Orayvi, Arizona, 2009. Photograph by author.

of these athletes needed to be taught the essence of long-distance running, coaches nevertheless trained them in modern running techniques and rules to compete effectively in American track and cross-country events. The dirt trails on the reservation did not resemble the paved roads or clay tracks used in many American running competitions. And so in their first year on a school's cross-country team, Hopis learned about running in different locations, climates, and elevations. And they had to develop mental and physical strategies for running in cities, on mountain roads, or in front of thousands of cheering spectators in a stadium.

When Hopis ran on trails back home, they did so in a relatively quiet and peaceful environment, far from the sounds of locomotives arriving and departing towns such as Winslow. Running on or near the mesas, Hopis became attuned with their bodies and surroundings, becoming one with their environment. They listened to their own breathing, the sound of their feet tapping the trail as they danced on Mother Earth. They felt the rhythmic pounding of their heart telling them to adjust or steady their pace.[26] And they listened to birds singing and the sound of the wind cutting through the canyons. And often they ran alone, experiencing physical ailments that all distance runners endure. "He was alone and running on," Kiowa poet N. Scott Momaday writes of a Jemez Pueblo runner named Abel. "All of his being was concentrated in the sheer motion of running on, and he was past caring about pain."[27] In the high desert of Arizona, Hopi runners also beheld beautiful landscapes, greeted majestic sunrises and sunsets, and had unobstructed views for miles in all directions. Running with no distractions from the outside world, Hopis ran with "good hearts," prayed silently for the well-being of their people, and sang songs to their katsina spirits to entice the rain clouds to follow them home to their villages.[28]

However, the tranquil environment that encompassed the trails back home did not reflect the fast pace and at times chaotic life in large modern American cities. In Los Angeles, for example, Hopi runners had to learn to navigate through crowds of shouting spectators and endure the piercing sound of honking automobiles. Most of these automobiles lined the race path alongside the spectators, but others, accompanied by newspaper reporters, drove ahead of the runners and fumigated them with their exhaust. As one reporter for the Associated Press remarked, "life in the clean-up land of the Hopi reservation with their own people is far different from the gasoline laden sphere of the white man's out of doors."[29] For some Hopis and non-Indians who raced in Los Angeles and in other cities such as New York, the exhaust caused severe breathing problems that required them to quit. No longer running back home where the air was clean, the Hopi runners learned to endure the smell and ill effects of toxic automobile smoke and adjusted to this new way of running in modern American cities.

But toxic fumes from automobiles was not the only issue Hopi runners had to contend with when they ran in American races. Most competitive runners at this time wore leather-and-rubber shoes specifically designed for distance running.[30] However, back on the reservation, the people either ran barefoot or wore moccasins made by members of their village. To compete in American events in the early 1900s, Hopis often had to replace their traditional footwear with modern running shoes. Many Hopis found them to be cumbersome and uncomfortable, and at times attributed their less-than-stellar performances to the shoes that race officials required them to wear. While some Hopi runners competed in at least one American race wearing moccasins made from the hide of a deer,[31] most had to adopt the American-style shoes and adjust their strides accordingly.[32]

But as Hopi runners accepted, sometimes begrudgingly, Western forms of running in US races, newspapers and the sporting communities had to also rethink how they understood Hopis in this new American sport context.

When Hopi people competed and won American running events, newspaper writers seemed surprised that the "little Hopis" had the ability to defeat top runners in the nation. In their articles, authors and their illustrators focused on the Hopi runners' short stature and quiet demeanor and wondered how the runners could perform so well in the nation's prestigious marathons. Some writers attempted to explain their running success on Hopi religious customs, forces of colonialism, and exercise they received from trekking up and down cliffs to tend to their corn and melon fields below the mesas. With little or no familiarity with Hopi history or culture, newspaper writers informed their readers on Hopi running accomplishments, explained why Hopis did so well in cross-country events, and situated Hopis in what they perceived to be their place in American society. Often accompanied with illustrations and photographs, newspaper accounts of Hopi running victories created tremendous excitement for American sport enthusiasts, and solidified—at least for the time being—Hopi running in American sport society.

While sport enthusiasts praised Hopi runners for their victories, they also became disappointed in them when they lost races and fell short of their expectations. For years, newspaper and other writers had published glowing accounts on the running accomplishments of the Hopi people. At times describing the runners in mythic terms, newspapers built them up in the minds of their readers to succeed, and not to fail. But Hopis competed in hundreds of track and cross-country meets throughout the country, and won only a portion of them. Regardless of their Native identity or cultural upbringing, Hopi runners faced physical and mental handicaps that every runner experienced in the early twentieth century. They suffered fatigue, sprained ankles, sore knees, and blistered feet. Running long distances, whether on soft or hard surfaces, took a toll on their bodies and often shortened their careers. After trotting through the hot Mojave Desert in the late 1920s, limping his way through the mountain region of northern Arizona with sprained ankles and battered knees, one acclaimed Hopi runner not only quit the race but used the occasion to exit competitive American running entirely.[33]

In addition to enduring physical handicaps, those Hopi runners that competed at Indian schools suffered in other ways. Government officials established the schools to instruct youth in grammar, math, science, history, and various occupational trades. However, for students to properly learn these subjects, they needed to be present in the classroom. Students who ran for the school's cross-country and track teams devoted large amounts of time to practicing, conditioning their bodies to function at the highest levels. Early in the morning, while their schoolmates slept, the teams ran the city streets and paths of Riverside, Phoenix, and Carlisle, to name a few. Those who ran for Sherman Institute also trained on long stretches of dirt roads that ran parallel to the many orange groves in Southern California, stopping now and then to quench their thirst and replenish their energy with the sugary fruit. And after their training, while experiencing physical and mental fatigue, they sat in their classrooms and attempted to learn their daily lessons. Having once run freely up and down their mesas as young children, the Hopi youth, and even their running, had become "institutionalized," a term used by runner and writer James F. Fixx to describe the constraints imposed on running and movement when youth enter schools.[34] Then, in the late afternoon, as their peers relaxed in dorm rooms or visited with each other under the shade of a palm tree, the runners often hit the streets again, a cycle that continued for months during the school year.[35] And some accomplished Hopi runners participated in so many meets that they spent much of their time away from school, and their education and grades suffered as a result of it.[36] But fatigue and subpar grades at Indian schools did not compare to other, more culturally problematic, issues awaiting the runners when they returned to their village communities.

While a select few Hopis at Indian boarding schools received honors and notoriety for their feats of endurance, others back home remained unimpressed with their running accomplishments.[37] When Hopis returned to their villages after their boarding school days, they came home to a society with a long tradition of distance running and great runners. However, the vast majority of these runners, many of whom were much older than the student athletes, never had opportunities to compete at Indian schools, marathons, or for city athletic clubs. Since they did not attend an off-reservation school, they never demonstrated before newspaper writers their abilities in American marathons or international events. Therefore, they remained virtually unknown to those outside of the Hopi community. But people back home knew of these runners and regularly reminded the young Hopi track stars about the long tradition of running in Hopi society and culture. They reminded them that long before Hopis won medals and trophy cups in American marathons, or had their names grace the pages of American newspapers, Hopi clan runners competed against each other on and below the mesas, and when *they* won footraces, *they* received rain.[38] Furthermore, younger Hopis often came home from Indian boarding schools with a heightened sense of accomplishment and pride. Fellow pupils treated certain Hopi athletes with celebrity status at their schools, but when they returned to the reservation, their national and international fame failed to impress the older Hopi runners, who continued to run according to the Hopi way. Hopi runners at Indian schools realized that many runners remained on the reservation with "better wind and faster legs,"[39] and this reality created tensions with the older Hopi runners when the proud and accomplished athletes returned home.

The tensions between older and younger runners often centered on issues of identity and how Hopis understood running according to Hopi culture. At off-reservation Indian boarding schools, the cultural reason for running races at times conflicted with certain values reinforced at Indian schools. Officials at Sherman, for example, routinely told the students that the "determination to win" was the "epitome of American sport."[40] People in US society participated in sports to win, and not to bring wellness or health to their team. Historically, Hopi clan runners ran footraces as a way to express their culture as Indigenous people, to elevate their clan status, and to bring much-needed rain to their dry and arid fields. School officials believed that students' athletic achievements should stem from personal loyalty to the school, and competitive successes would in turn enhance the runners' own sense of institutional fidelity and allegiance. This understanding encouraged Hopi students to set aside their practice of running according to Hopi culture, in order that it might be replaced with values esteemed by American society. No longer in an environment or among a people who ran according to Hopi clanship loyalties, the Hopi runners learned to compete on behalf of the school and for their peers who cheered them to several marathon victories.[41]

American understandings of sport also differed greatly from Hopi clan beliefs about long-distance running. In the early twentieth century, politicians, educators, philosophers, and others believed that sports unified the nation, strengthened the ideals of American citizenship, and demonstrated to foreign nations the superiority of US culture and democracy.

Sport historian Mark Dyreson noted that during the early twentieth century, figures such as Theodore Roosevelt, A. G. Spalding, and Price Collier believed that sport would "restore civic virtue," promote an understanding of "fair play," dictate "American economic and social relations," and "serve as a crucial institution for creating a twentieth-century American republic."[42] While the ideals of nationalism greatly influenced sport competition at the turn of the century, not every athlete competed in sports to strengthen and promote the American republic. Ralph C. Wilcox once remarked that some Irish immigrants competed in US sports to foster pride in the "Land of Erin" and to "ensure that their fellow countryman's Irish roots were never forgotten."[43] Marathon historian Pamela Cooper noted that "immigrant groups" participated in sports as an "expression of ethnic cohesion." Cooper observed that immigrant runners "ran as representatives" and that the "success of a single runner was all that was necessary to enhance the honor of an entire group."[44] While Hopis and other Indians have never considered themselves to be immigrants in North America, Native athletes shared similar understandings of representation and community with Irish, German, and other immigrant runners.

Although individuals such as Roosevelt, Spalding, and Collier emphasized the role sport had in the furtherance of American nationalism, others focused on the power of sport to transform into better individuals.[45] At this time, many Americans still considered Hopi adults and other Indians to be dirty, lazy, and to have the mental capacity of children.[46] But in their participation in athletics, even Indians could be lifted to a higher moral and virtuous state. "Take a class of boys and give them proper instruction in cross-country running," Coach Lewis of Sherman Institute once remarked, and it "will develop [them] into good strong youths" and "will do more for the temperance cause and to do away with cigarettes than anything else that I know of."[47]

In addition to running for sport programs at Indian schools, some Hopi runners also ran for teams under the auspices of city athletic clubs and competed alongside people from many nationalities. Prior to 1900, sport enthusiasts strategically developed athletic clubs in cities such as Los Angeles, New York, and Philadelphia.[48] Although colleges and off-reservation Indian schools created their own sport programs, athletic clubs in American cities influenced sport in US society in significant ways. "Nearly all contemporary sports evolved, or were invented, in the city," sport historian Steven A. Riess observed, for the "city was the place where sport became rationalized, specialized, organized, commercialized, and professionalized."[49] City athletic clubs competed against each other and emphasized fair play and gentlemanly conduct.[50] For the Hopi runners, representing athletic clubs in large cities also gave them opportunities to race against top runners and to compete in more meets. It also provided them with financial backing needed for their race entry fees and other expenses.

While Hopis ran beyond the mesas for various reasons, school administrators, government officials, sport promoters, and a host of other individuals had their own agendas for Hopis to compete and succeed in national and international competitions. School superintendents and coaches saw the success of Hopi runners as a way to bring recognition to their schools and athletic programs. City officials saw Hopi running success as a way to promote their towns and attract business to their cities. Government bureaucrats used Hopi runners to bolster pride in America and to demonstrate to the world the superiority of American culture and society. Race promoters and other organizers viewed Hopi running success as an opportunity to earn money and to advance their personal and financial interests. And newspapers published thousands of articles on the accomplishments of Hopi and other Indian runners to increase their sales and to heighten interest in sporting news throughout America.[51]

This book examines Hopi runners who left their villages in the early 1900s to compete in cities across the United States. It examines the ways Hopi marathon runners navigated between tribal dynamics, school loyalties, and a country that closely associated sport with US nationalism. It calls attention to Hopi philosophies of running that connected the runners to their village communities, and to the internal and external forces that supported and strained these cultural ties when Hopis competed in US marathons. This work pushes the notion that between 1908 and 1936, the cultural identity of Hopi runners challenged white American perceptions of Natives and modernity and placed them in a context that had national and international dimensions. This broad perspective linked Hopi runners to athletes from around the world, including runners from Japan and Ireland, and caused non-Natives to reevaluate their understanding of sport, nationhood, and the cultures of Indigenous people.

Over the years, scholars and other writers have published modest amounts of material on Hopi runners. Beginning in the late nineteenth century, anthropologists such as Alexander M. Stephen and Jesse Walter

Fewkes made several trips to Hopiland to study certain aspects of Hopi life, including running. In his two-volume ethnography *Hopi Journal*, Stephen provided brief observations on the religious significance of Hopi kickball races and offered short commentary on Hopi clan runners.[52] Around the same time, Fewkes published his essay "The Wa-Wac-Ka-Tci-Na, a Tusayan Foot Race" on competitions between Hopi clan runners and Hopi katsinas and clowns.[53] These and other anthropological expeditions to Hopi paved the way for other scholars and academics to conduct research on the mesas, including a Ukrainian anthropologist named Mischa Titiev, who published an essay on Hopi clan runners at Orayvi.[54] "The Hopi believe," Titiev wrote in this essay, "that the faster a man runs, the faster the clouds will come."[55]

For the next several years, written accounts of Hopi running mostly appeared in newspapers, children's books, or in venues intended for public audiences.[56] In the early 1980s, however, Peter Nabokov, then a graduate student in anthropology, rekindled scholarly interest in Native and Hopi runners by publishing a comprehensive account of Indigenous runners entitled *Indian Running*.[57] In this study, Nabokov wrote at length about Hopi runners of the past and present. He was the first scholar to situate Hopi running within a contemporary American sport society.[58] Eight years after Nabokov released *Indian Running*, Dick and Mary Lutz published a nonscholarly but well-cited account of Tarahumara Indian people of northern Mexico and dedicated an entire chapter to their running legacy and abilities. Written for the general public, *The Running Indians* provides an intimate glimpse into the lives of the Tarahumara based on two trips the authors took to Copper Canyon in Mexico to live among the people.[59]

While much of what authors wrote in the 1980s and 1990s centered on the running traditions of tribes, journalists and other writers soon began publishing biographical works on individual Native runners. In 2006, musician and amateur historian Michael Ward published a biography on Narragansett runner Ellison "Tarzan" Brown, who is perhaps best known for twice winning the Boston Marathon and for competing in the Olympic Games in Germany in 1936.[60] The following year, historian Brian S. Collier wrote a remarkable account of Steve Gachupin, a Jemez Pueblo runner who amazed America's running community for his six consecutive victories of the Pike's Peak Marathon in Colorado during the late 1960s and early 1970s. Basing much of his essay on oral interviews that he conducted with Gachupin, newspaper accounts, and works by Pueblo and non-Indian scholars, Collier highlights the cultural significance of running for the Jemez runner and his village community.[61] At the same time that Collier published on Gachupin, an editor for the *Colorado History Now* newsletter named Ben Fogelberg published a brief article on Hopi runner Saul Halyve of Musangnuvi (Mischongovi) and his short-lived success competing at the Teller Institute in Grand Junction, Colorado.[62] And although not writing on a specific runner, Christopher McDougall, an avid distance runner himself, two years later published a highly popular book entitled *Born to Run* wherein he explores Tarahumara running by focusing on the people's health, cultural beliefs, and environment.[63]

Building upon this rich body of literature, I place Hopi long-distance runners within a larger American sport context. I seek to accomplish what Dyreson did with his wonderful article "The Foot Runners Conquer Mexico and Texas." In it he situated Tarahumara runners within international dimensions, challenged notions of their Indigenous identities in the print media, and demonstrated their influence on people's understandings of Mexican nationalism.[64] While I situate Hopi running within a broad American sport context, I do not offer a comprehensive account on the topic. Instead, I provide a window for one to see a particular time in American history when Hopis competed simultaneously for their tribal communities, Indian schools, the nation, and even for themselves. Much has yet to be researched or written on Hopi runners, especially works on contemporary runners, and the many runners who are lesser known outside of the community and who have received little to no attention.[65] I am, of course, also reminded of this whenever I speak to other Hopi individuals about this topic: "Oh, have you heard of [so and so]?" they ask me; "he was a great runner."

Although it has been some time since I ran laps around Crystal Lake Park with Victor, his comment "to the fence and back" still resonates with me as a Hopi person. It helps me understand my people's history as a continuous cycle of leaving and returning, of going away and coming back. It causes me to consider the ancient ones who ran to sacred sites far beyond Hopi ancestral lands to entice the rain clouds to follow them back to their mesas.[66] And it reminds me of messenger runners who used a network of trails to deliver information to other Hopi villages and to people in faraway lands. Hopi clan and messenger runners of the past foreshadowed a new era in Hopi society when the people left their villages to visit American cities and returned to tell about what they experienced and saw on their journeys. And it points to a time when Hopi youth and older adults continued the cycle of leaving and returning when they departed on trains for off-reservation Indian boarding schools, competed on cross-country teams, ran for race promoters or city athletic clubs, and then migrated back to their villages as modern Hopi athletes.

They are for the blessings of the cloud people, for the rain, for the harvest, so we have a good life, a long life. That's what these ceremonial runners do. They bring this positiveness to the people.

—Leigh J. Kuwanwisiwma, *Village of Paaqavi*

Ascending First Mesa at Walpi, *by Neil Logan*.

CHAPTER ONE

A World Unlike Their Own

On an autumn morning in 1899, a group of male Hopi runners began ascending a mesa edge near the village of Walpi on First Mesa. The race, and the ceremonial dance that accompanied it, attracted onlookers from across the United States. Among them were "Mormons, be-pistoled cowboys, prospectors, army officers, teachers, scientists, photographers, and tourists," all eager to catch a glimpse of the "fleet" runners. When the runners approached the village, the spectators witnessed "dark forms" coming toward them, resulting in a "murmur" that passed "through the crowd." Children, there to welcome the runners and to express their gratitude for their efforts, ran alongside them waving "wands of cornstalk" to announce their grand entry. When the lead runner entered Walpi, he passed over the roof of the underground ceremonial chamber of the Snake kiva, signaling to all that the "day of the Snake dance [had] begun." One by one the other runners reached the village, each carrying "melon vines, corn and other products" from their fields below the mesa. And when they arrived at the kiva, they deposited their gifts with the priest to ensure that their running and prayers resulted in bountiful harvests for their clans and village community.[1]

In the late 1800s, relatively few white Americans ventured to the Hopi mesas in present-day northeastern Arizona. Although the Atlantic & Pacific Railroad had by this time carved its way through the high desert region, only a small number of people visited the villages and buttes of Hopiland.[2] Those that did most often arrived by wagon or horse to witness one of several Hopi ceremonies, including the well-publicized and highly fantasized Snake Dance.[3] In 1895, for example, American sculptor Hermon Atkins MacNeil traveled to the reservation to see the Snake

Dance and the footraces that went with it. A year later, after having been so moved by this experience, he created a bronze sculpture, *The Moqui Runner*, of a muscularly toned Hopi ceremonial runner sprinting with snakes in his hand. He casted a small number of these sculptures, one of which has remained at the Art Institute of Chicago.[4] To grab the attention of their readers, newspaper writers of the late 1890s also described the Hopi ceremony in barbaric images and terms. A "Horrible Rite of the Moki Indians," proclaimed a headline from the *Columbus Journal*, "Who Dance with Live Rattlesnakes Dangling from Their Hands and Mouth."[5] While journalists conveyed barbaric and racist images with their words, cartoonists did so with their sketches and drawings.[6] They drew pictures of Hopis, often with frowns on their faces, dancing hysterically with rattlesnakes hanging from their mouths.[7] The stories, and the drawings (and sculptures) that accompanied them, ignited the curiosity of readers across America and contributed to a steady but small wave of visitors to the Hopi mesas at the turn of the twentieth century.

When the visitors came to Walpi to witness the Snake Dance, they wanted to experience a world unlike their own. Newspapers often emphasized the otherworldliness of Hopi society, and they portrayed this society as one that had yet to be influenced by Western ways and ideals. In this regard, white Americans did not need to trek to faraway lands to witness a world of so-called savagery and primitive customs. They instead only needed to travel to the American Southwest. For in this region of their own country, they encountered a people still practicing their ceremonies in the tradition of the ancient ones. "Untouched by modern civilization," explained a writer for the *Times*, "still clinging to the religion and customs of their forefathers, in far Arizona dwells a race of people which offers scientists an unsurpassed field for research and to the tourist unrivaled attractions."[8]

Prior to European contact, Hopis spent more than a thousand years adhering to their ceremonies and living according to Hopi principles. They cultivated crops on and below their mesas and performed many rituals to appease their katsina spirits to send rain to water their fields. They made pilgrimages to the Pacific Ocean and frequently visited shrines and other sacred sites throughout the Southwest.[9] They traded with other Indigenous people, including the Pueblo Indians of modern-day New Mexico, and ventured far south to exchange goods with Native communities in northern and central Mexico. Hopi clan runners also practiced their cer-

emonial races without the imposition of colonial pressures or other influences. Living upon their mesas in the dry and arid region of northern
Arizona, the Hopi lived far removed from the reach of European practices
and values. They held tightly to their spiritual beliefs and understood
them to have a constant influence on their lives.[10] And even when colonial
forces eventually arrived on their land, they remained committed to their
religious ways and practices. "The Moqui have withstood alike the tyranny
of the Spanish army and the persuasions of the missionaries," a white
visitor to the Hopi mesas once remarked, "clinging with singular tenacity
to their old religion and customs."[11]

By the sixteenth century, the world of the "Moqui" no longer only consisted of Hopis and other Indigenous people in the Americas. In July 1540,
a group of seventeen Spanish explorers led by Pedro de Tovar arrived un-
invited on Hopi land at the base of Antelope Mesa seeking gold and other
riches. They had been told that a city existed in Hopi country, or *Tusayan*
as the Spanish called it, of immense gold.[12] At first the Hopi did not welcome the Spaniards or their horses on their land. They approached the
Spaniards with "bows, and shields, and wooden clubs" and drew lines
in the sand and instructed de Tovar and his men to not cross them. But
when a Spaniard made a sudden move to disobey their wishes, one of
the Hopi men struck his horse and confusion erupted among the people. Some Hopis ran back to their village of Kawaioukuh, while others
returned with gifts seeking peace and for the Spaniards to simply go on
their way.[13] However, after the explorers realized that the Hopi possessed
nothing of value for the Spanish monarch, they continued west on horseback to the Grand Canyon, more than a hundred miles away.[14] This brief,
yet intense, encounter between the Hopi and Spanish explorers became
a turning point in Hopi history and set in motion a wave of other visitors
to the region including Christian missionaries, white explorers, school
superintendents, Indian agents, academics, and military personnel.

Many years after Pedro de Tovar encountered the Hopi at the foot of Antelope Mesa, federal government troops on occasion visited the Hopi mesas and often remarked about the running abilities of the people. In 1858,
the US Army sent topographical engineer Lieutenant J. C. Ives out West to
conduct a survey of the Colorado River from its mouth in present-day Baja
California to the "Moqui villages." In May of the same year, Ives and his
crew of engineers left the Colorado River, perhaps at or near present-day
Lee's Ferry, and journeyed east by mule to the Hopi mesas. After returning

briefly to the river for water, the convoy of men and mules pressed on over the "deserted and ghastly region" before arriving in the valleys below First and Second Mesa. From this location, and with the help of a "spyglass," Ives caught his first glimpse of the structures that constituted two or three of the Hopi villages. "The outlines of the closely packed structures," he wrote in his diary, "looked in the distance like the towers and battlements of a castle, and their commanding position enhanced the picturesque effects."[15]

Ives recalled that when he and his men approached the mesa, two Hopi men riding the same horse "charged suddenly" upon them, shouting words of welcome, and "insisting upon shaking hands with the whole company." Once Hopis who remained on top of the mesa observed Ives's peaceful intentions, they ran down the mesa cliff "at the top of their speed" to greet them and surrounded their mules. Ives noted that after startling his animals and shaking their hands, the Hopis joined the company until they eventually made their way to the village of Musangnuvi on Second Mesa. When they arrived at the village, Ives met the village chief, "a pleasant looking, middle-aged man, with a handsome shell suspended from his neck." Using Ives's incomplete map, the chief informed the lieutenant about the locations of the other six Hopi villages, including the village of Orayvi, located nearly fourteen miles northwest from their present location. Upon hearing the chief's description of the village, Ives asked the chief to provide him with a guide to Orayvi. The chief agreed to Ives's request and even offered to lead the way. The next morning, Ives and his men departed for Orayvi, but the chief had been delayed. "Concluding to pursue a northwest course," Ives recalled, "the chief appeared over the brow of a hill, running, as the Indians had done on the day before, at full speed." When the chief reached the company of men, he told Ives that he needed to "go back to his house, but would soon overtake" them by a "shortcut." He then instructed a young Hopi boy "nearby" to act as a guide in his absence, and then sprinted toward his village and "disappeared as rapidly as he had approached."[16]

Taking place at a time when American newspapers rarely published stories on Hopi runners, the account provides an example of a Hopi running narrative that did not correspond with a footrace or other religious ceremony. When Ives and his men arrived on the Hopi mesas, they did not come as ethnographers, reporters, or tourists. They did not traverse through Hopiland to witness or experience a world of so-called savagery and primitive customs. Belonging to a company of soldiers, the men arrived to create a map for the US government, not to witness a dance or other ceremony. In this brief moment, the men experienced a long tradition among the Hopi of running up and down the mesas to serve their interests and the interests of others. For the Hopi runner chief, he used his ability to run swiftly to greet Ives and to better understand his intentions. And he relied on his fleetness of foot and knowledge of the landscape to serve Ives as his guide and to remain in communication with others back at his village.

Nearly ten years after Ives and his men traveled through Hopiland, other explorers arrived on the mesas and later told of the remarkable abilities of Hopi runners. In summer 1869, Major John Wesley Powell, a highly regarded naturalist and Civil War veteran, led a major expedition through the Green and Colorado Rivers to map canyons, including the Grand Canyon, of the Colorado Plateau.[17] Known as the Powell Geographic Expedition of 1869, the exploration followed Powell's two other preliminary expeditions of the region. The expedition began "as an exploration," he later recalled, but soon "developed into a survey, embracing the geography, geology, ethnography, and natural history of the country."[18] On this trip out West, Powell, along with nine other men, journeyed through present-day Wyoming, Colorado, Utah, Arizona, and Nevada, traveling mostly by boat. During his visit to the Hopi mesas, Powell and Charley A. Behm, a "prominent Yavapai citizen" who was in charge of Powell's pack train,[19] observed a race at one of the Hopi villages. He recalled that early in the morning, before the sun rose, crowds of people in the village climbed to their rooftops to witness boys and young men run naked to a water tank at the bottom of the mesa. Some of the runners wore cow and horse bells "strapped around their waists." The runners believed that the loud noise of the bells ringing and clanging as they ran down the mesa "scared off any evil spirit that might be lurking about."[20] Once the runners reached the tank they got in and bathed for several hours. Behm noted that he witnessed this race more than once, and that there were a "few cold days and ice formed on the tanks an inch thick. I know of them breaking the ice and taking their bath just the same."[21]

In the early 1880s, Captain John Gregory Bourke of the US Army spent time on the Hopi mesas while visiting the nearby Zuni Pueblo in New Mexico. During his stay with the Hopi, Bourke kept a detailed diary and wrote at length about Hopi ceremonies and other customs. One of the ceremonies that he observed was the Hopi Snake Dance at Walpi, which included a series of sacred events that lasted for several days. Bourke recalled that on the first day of the ceremony, at four o'clock in the morning, sounds of excited children awoke him from his sleep. When he went outside, he saw that a group of Hopi youth had "assembled at the foot" of the mesa to begin a much-anticipated footrace. However, before they set off for their race, they sang a beautiful song "whose notes" reached "perfect distinctness" and that could be heard by all in the village. Once they finished their song, perhaps a song to their katsinas to bless their efforts with much-needed rain, the children began their race. Describing them as a "convoy of rabbits," Bourke noted that from his vantage point, the children "could scarcely be made out," for they "looked so small in the dim light of early dawn." But while he had difficulty seeing them, he could hear the bells each runner wore as they spread throughout the valley below. During the race, Hopi elders also positioned themselves at various points along the trail. While Bourke described them primarily as "Umpires" and "station-keepers," they more than likely stood at strategic points on the path to encourage the runners to run strong, to thank them for their efforts, and to remind them to run with good hearts.[22] And similar to the experiences of other harriers, running with good and happy hearts also likely made them better runners, as British marathoner Ian Thompson once explained: "When I am running well I am happy, and when I am happy I run well."[23]

The idea of running with happy and joyful hearts is an important aspect of Hopi cultural understandings of running, and over the years visitors to Hopiland often mentioned it in their reports. In the early 1900s, Mennonite missionary Heinrich Richert Voth wrote at length about a race at Orayvi that took place between runners of the Snake and Antelope societies. He noted that just before the race began, a messenger runner positioned the other runners behind a starting line made of cornmeal, most likely at or near the center of the village. After rubbing clay on the palms of each runner, the messenger runner addressed the men in Hopi, saying: "Now we shall race joyfully. Hence you strong young men do not once detain each other! Whomever comes out ahead on his account we shall drink when the sun has not yet come up half-way. Being concerned (about this) to these our mothers and our fathers, to the village, we shall ascend, we shall enter it happily, courageously. Now we go!"[24] Exhorting them to run with joyful hearts, the messenger runner encouraged the young men to see themselves as part of a larger group, and he warned them to not hold one another back. He called on them to run strong and to honor the one

Village of Old Orayvi, circa 1890s. Photograph courtesy of the Hopi Cultural Preservation Office, Kiiqòtsmovi, Arizona.

who ultimately won the race. Finally, he reminded the runners that they ran for their relatives, and that each one of them, regardless of their place, needed to "ascend" the mesa and enter their village with happiness and courage.[25] Voth's account is similar to Ruth DeEtte Simpson's retelling of a footrace that was part of a Snake Dance at Walpi: "At midnight the Antelope Priest calls from the roofs, asking all Hopi men who are swift runners and of good heart to go with him and take part in the traditional race from the valley to the mesatop."[26]

Hopi children were not the only ones racing with good hearts in the early morning hours at Walpi. Bourke also observed that just before the last child completed the race, a group of male adult runners began their footrace six or seven miles in the distance. Running as "hard as they could," the Hopi men raced toward the foot of the mesa with "bewildering speed," while the children, who had just finished their own race, waited for their arrival with much excitement. When the men approached the foot of the mesa, the children cheered and called out to them, perhaps their fathers, brothers, uncles, or grandfathers. As the men crossed the finish line, the children clamored to see the runners. And when the two "parties came together, a regular Northern war-whoop rent the air" along with the sound of jingling bells. In addition to the children, a "delegation of young women was expecting them and ran with them at full speed up the steep trail, crossing sand dunes and climbing the rocky precipices" six hundred feet to the top of the mesa edge. Bourke recalled that the trail "ascended by the racers was, if anything, more steep and arduous than the usually travelled one, which we had climbed; yet none of them paused a moment in an upward and onward incline which would have caused an American, unused to ascending and descending these rugged paths, to die of palpitation of the heart."[27]

While the majority of Hopi running accounts at the turn of the twentieth century center on male participants, a small number of them involve Hopi women and their participation in clan races on and below the mesas. In the early 1890s, Alexander Stephen observed women at the village of Walpi who ran a footrace as an act of prayer for the community.[28] Before the race began, women leaders from various Hopi societies and others walked through Walpi in single file down the mesa until they reached a spring cared for by the Sun Clan. After the women "deposited water prayer sticks" in the spring, they gathered to begin the race, which started with a drop of a basket. Although Stephen was "late to witness the [start of the] race," he saw a woman named "Nū´īsi, the wife of Ka´ kaptī, carrying the standard, running breathless, well in the lead, followed by all the women and maids running as best as they could for the kiva." He further remarked that "there, on entering, they passed along the [corn] meal trail on the north side of the main floor, took a pinch of meal and prayed on it and cast it upon the altar." Then the runners "passed along the meal trail on the south side; and about three feet from the altar, a Sun chief named Kwa´chakwa held a crook vertical upon the trail. Each woman in passing stooped down and grasped the crook or pressed her palm upon it and passed on and sat down or went home."[29]

Over the years Hopis have also told oral accounts of women runners who competed at two villages called Tikuvi and Payupki. In the late 1960s, a Hopi woman and pottery maker from Munqapi (Moencopi) named Tsakaptamana told a story about a race between a Hopi girl from Payupki and a boy from Tikuvi. On the day of the race, people from the villages placed their bets, including "grinding stones" or "anything that could be used in the home." Acting as a race official, the chief from Tikuvi gathered the runners at the starting line and signaled for the race to begin. Tsakaptamana remarked that not long after the race started, "the people saw that she could run" and that she "flew along" and "finished ahead of the other runner." They raced two more times, and on the third race a spiritual being called Spider Woman crawled inside the girl's ear and instructed her on how to defeat her male opponent. "Jump, my daughter," Spider Woman told the girl, "Now, there isn't anything more [to worry about]." As the girl approached the village, the people clamored to see her, but the other runner was lagging behind. Then Spider Woman, a wise old woman who appeared at many races before, gave the girl one final set of instructions. "Run past the finish line," Spider Woman told her, "up to that pile of rocks, and then come back the way Tikuvi runners do." Seeing that the girl completed the race, the chief from Tikuvi sent men to check on their runner, and when they "reached him" he was exhausted, and they scolded him saying: "Hurry up, the girl is up to the finish line already. You are beaten." When the boy eventually crossed the finish line, the people of his village expressed displeasure in him, and they were extremely disappointed in his performance.[30]

Mvskoke Creek historian Donald L. Fixico once remarked that "oral accounts contained parables and lessons, and the young people learned from them; morals of stories told by their elders enlightened them as to virtues, values, and the importance of respecting taboos."[31] The story of the race between the Tikuvi and Payupki runners teaches several lessons about running and its connection to the spiritual world of Hopi culture. In Hopi society, villages did not typically host races between female and male participants. Most, if not all, ethnographic or newspaper accounts of running on Hopiland before the twentieth century involved races conducted along strict gender lines. Boys ran against boys, and girls ran against girls. In this story, the two villages hosted a race between the sexes, and none of the village members objected to it. Instead, the people expressed great confidence in their runners, although some doubted that the girl had the ability to outrun her male counterpart. When the girl won the first race, the boy and his people may have thought that it was an anomaly, but then they raced a second time and she beat him again. After the second race, however, Spider Woman saw that she needed help from the spiritual world of her people, and so she offered the girl assistance in her time of distress. The girl could have rejected Spider Woman's offer and relied solely on her physical strength and endurance. But having been raised in the Hopi society, she knew from an early age to revere the Old Woman and to listen to her counsel.

Hopi stories about races of long ago evoked pride in the people, placed emphasis on the well-being of the community, and produced knowledge about the Hopi and non-Hopi world. In his work on oral accounts of the Hopi people, Harold Courlander recorded an additional story of a race that took place between runners of the same two villages.[32] One of the stories begins by recalling that long ago the chief from Payupki looked across the mesa and saw that the people from Tikuvi were preparing to have a race. Wanting to gather information about the runners in the nearby village, the chief instructed his best runner to enter their race. "The people of Tikuvi are racing today," he told the young runner, "and I would like to know how good their runners are. You are the best runner we have in Payupki. Go down and join them. Run with them. Let me know what you learn." As he competed against the other runners, the runner from Payupki hoped to win the race, but he remembered that his chief had instructed him only to gather information, so he did not compete to his full potential. Upon returning to his village, the chief told him to train for the next race against Tikuvi. Obeying his chief, the young runner "ran across the mesa, he ran on the low ground, he ran in the hills," and with this training his legs became stronger. One day, while the chief from Payupki was smoking tobacco in the village kiva, a sacred underground chamber, the chief from Tikuvi entered the kiva and both men smoked. "We are glad you have come," said the chief from Payupki. "What is on your mind?" The chief from Tikuvi told him that in four days their village would be hosting another race, and that he had come to invite the best runners of Payupki to participate.

The chief from Payupki eagerly accepted this invitation and once again called on his best runner to represent the village.[33] That night, the men of Tikuvi gathered in their kiva and talked about the upcoming race. Aware of the situation, Spider Woman, the female creator deity, came to the men and told them that she had brought special medicine to help their runners run fast. But the men refused Spider Woman's help. Their runners had defeated the runner from Payupki in the past and they were confident in a second victory. Spider Woman then went to Payupki and spoke to the men in the kiva and offered her assistance. The men at Payupki respected Spider Woman, and they welcomed her into the kiva and accepted her help. She rubbed a special ointment made of water and magic powder on the runner's legs to protect him from evil spirits.

The men of Payupki considered Spider Woman to be a wise old woman, and so they listened to her every instruction. On the day of the event, the people from both villages placed bets of "moccasins, belts, shawls, kilts, and even bows and arrows." Word quickly spread to the surrounding villages about the race, and Hopis from each of the three mesas came to watch the runners compete. As the people looked on with much excitement, the runners set forth on the running trails. With the help of Spider Woman, the runner from Payupki won the race, and he collected all that he had earned and gave much of it to the wise old woman and to his community.[34] By accepting Spider Woman's help, the Hopi runner from Payupki did not rely entirely on his physical abilities to win the race. And similar to the girl who ran against the boy from Tikuvi, the runner from Payupki listened to his elder, he drew upon the strength of his culture, and he received power from the spiritual world of his people.

At around the same time that Stephen observed women clan races at Walpi, a middle-aged ethnologist named Jesse Walter Fewkes arrived in Hopi country as part of an expedition to Zuni Pueblo. Director of the Hemenway Southwestern Archaeological Expedition, Fewkes visited Hopi twice, once in 1890 and then again in 1891. In his first expedition he studied ancient petroglyphs that told the story of when Ute Indians had once attacked the Hopi. He also made observations on the insides of Hopi kivas and took care in detailing Hopi ceremonies, including the Hopi Snake Dance.[35] Reflecting on his work among the Hopi, Walter Hough recalled that Fewkes "saw the importance" of recording these ceremonies and provided the world with a "body of scientific knowledge of inestimable value."[36] While Fewkes preserved a wealth of knowledge on Hopi ways and customs, his interest in and comments about Hopi running are perhaps most striking. Among the "customs of the Indians of Tusayan [Hopi]," Fewkes once remarked, "there are none more suggestive from an ethnological standpoint than the games and races of these people."[37]

During this period, ethnographic interest in Native running extended well beyond the Hopi mesas in northern Arizona. In early 1896, Professor W. J. McGee of the Bureau of American Ethnology at the Smithsonian Institution conducted extensive research on Indians of the Southwest and northwestern Mexico. Although his research was primarily intended for a scholarly audience, he occasionally shared his findings with the nation's major newspapers, including the *New York Times*. In March of the same year, McGee told the *Times* that during a trip to this region, he witnessed a kickball race among the Papago Indians of southern Arizona. "In spite of the blazing heat of the sun," McGee remarked, "these Indians will run for a long time in the desert without seeming to feel any ill play in their hours of leisure." Describing the race in detail, McGee explained that the race began when one of the Papago runners placed "a ball on the top" of his "foot" and caught it "again before it touche[d] the ground." He observed that "in the afternoon, when the sun is low, they will have races around their tracks, at which no white man could attempt to compete with them even under more favorable conditions of temperature. I have seen them in the afternoon go six or eight times around a five-mile track, running all the time—not at a trot, but at a fine rate of speed."[38]

Further south, near the town of Chihuahua, runners of the Tarahumara also began receiving attention in American newspapers for their abilities to run long distances. Located in a secluded region of northwestern Mexico in Copper Canyon, the Tarahumara fascinated the world with reports of their endurance races, often running more than a hundred miles for each event. In summer 1901, a writer for the *New York Sun* observed one of their kickball races and recalled that before the race began, members from the surrounding villages contributed prizes for the runners, including "bows, arrows, sandals, goats, chickens and sheep," and "two wooden ploughs" for the top finishers. But when "American visitors added a cupful of copper coins, a gaudy lithograph, and a water color painting of a cross surrounded with flowers," all prizes that had never been offered in the past, the runners concluded that it would be the "race of their lives." Describing the runners as "long-limbed and slender," and with the appearance of having been "created for speed," the writer noted that the race began at five o'clock in the afternoon when twenty runners, each with their own clay ball, ran at top speed out of the village. The writer further remarked that the runners ran a course that was twelve miles long and that the runners had to make the "circuit" ten times, a total distance of a hundred and twenty miles. Similar to the rough physical contact allowed in American football, the Tarahumara runners tripped, crowded, blocked, and used other strategies to prevent their opponents from "reaching or throwing the ball."[39] The race ended fourteen hours after it began. [40]

Northwest of where the Tarahumara are located, another group of Indigenous people from Mexico received notice and praise for their abilities to run long distances. Up to this point, the Seri Indians had lived an isolated life on Tiburon Island in the Gulf of California (Sonora). Although few individuals outside of this community had ventured to visit or study them, Professor McGee led an American expedition to Tiburon to research their lives and customs in 1895. Less than five years after McGee visited the Seri, a lecturer and writer of the American West named George Wharton James also began researching and writing on the little-known Mexican tribe. While James described the Seris as "bloodthirsty and treacherous," he also commented at length about their physical strength and ability to run long distances. In "physique," he wrote, "there is no people on the American continent who is their equal." He described the Seri as being "Tall of stature, gifted with phenomenal strength and capable of marvelous prowess." Even Seri women, he remarked, are nearly as "strong as the men, and both sexes are runners of extraordinary speed and staying quality." "In this regard," he concluded, "they are rivaled only by the desert Yuma Apaches and the centuries-trained Hopituh or Moki."[41]

Reports written and published by McGee and James ignited a flame of interest in and fascination of the Seri Indians. In August 1903, the *St. Louis Post-Dispatch* published a sensational story on the Seri Indians and their highly anticipated appearance at the 1904 St. Louis World's Fair. Prior to this, American newspapers circulated false reports that the Mexican government had accused the Seri people of practicing cannibalism.[42] McGee wanted to bring representatives from various Native communities from the continent to the St. Louis World's Fair. When word spread that he planned to transport a group of Seris to the fair, local newspapers wrote about their upcoming visit with grotesque and highly racialized commentary that portrayed the Seris as ruthless cannibals. With a headline that read "Will Prof. M'Gee Bring His Cannibals Here?," the *St. Louis-Dispatch* warned people, especially those who were "fat and edible," about the dangers the Seris represented for them if they came to the fair. "There will be something worse than street car killings going on in St. Louis next year," the newspaper writer remarked. "Does anybody think the cannibals of Tiburon Isle are going to live in St. Louis six months and subsist on Schweickhardt's sandwiches?"[43]

While the story in the *St. Louis-Post Dispatch* attempted to attract readers by building on their fears of cannibalism and Native people in general, the cartoons accompanying the piece also provided a visual representation of the dangers that awaited residents of the city. One drawing by cartoonist Oscar Charles Chopi depicted a pair of Seri runners chasing down a St. Louis streetcar, threatening to punch the "head of the motorman" who refused to allow them to board. Another cartoon described two "blood-thirsty" Seris running after one of the city's "fat emissaries of Harry Hawes" to kill him, and cook him in a large black kettle—a not-so-subtle warning to the city's obese police officers.[44] A third drawing, which was part of a "Prospective picture of the camp of the Seri cannibals at Forest Park," depicted a lone Seri chasing two white visitors with a dagger in his left hand.[45] Portraying the Seri as predators running after their prey, the cartoonist's barbaric drawings dehumanized Native people, furthered racist stereotypes, and spread fear of Indians among white Americans.[46]

Although the *St. Louis-Post Dispatch* attempted to instill fear in its audience, many other American newspapers provided readers with more factual, thoughtful, and accurate accounts between Indian runners and the non-Indian world. While most of the traditional or tribal races on reservations at this time involved competitions between Native people, non-Natives on occasion competed against Indian runners. More than ten years before the *New York Sun*'s account of the Tarahumara kickball race in Copper Canyon, two military officers named Lieutenant Chauncey B. Baker of the Seventh infantry and Lieutenant John J. Pershing of the engineer corps, who would become a highly regarded general of World War I, traveled to the Hopi mesas and the Navajo reservation with Commissioner of Indian Affairs Thomas J. Morgan. While visiting with an encampment of Navajos, Baker told the Navajos that he questioned reports of their remarkable abilities to run long distances. His statements offended the Navajos, and they responded by turning the conversation back on Baker and suggested that he race against one of their horses. Baker rejected their proposal but recommended instead that the race involve him and one of their runners.

The Navajos eagerly accepted the challenge and "swiftly gathered up their valuables," including "beautiful garnets," animal skins, and "silver girdles" to wage for their bets. After the two runners agreed on a course, the Navajo runner entered the race naked, while the lieutenant shed only some of his clothes. In spite of the Navajo runner's confidence, the military officer won the race and consequently all the bets went to him. A report in the *Wyandott Herald* noted that the Navajos were "sadly disappointed in their man but the bets they never gave a second thought." However, the lieutenant did not keep his winnings for long. When the two military officers showed their "plunder" to their fellow soldiers, they sent for the Indians to come so they could give "everything back." "It was quite a difficult matter," the writer for the newspaper recalled, "for them to explain to the Indians that an army officer could not gamble with Indians, and certainly could not justly win from them." The Navajos, however, refused to endure further humiliation by taking "their things back."[47]

The race between Lieutenant Baker and the Navajo runner happened at a time in American history when the US military often arrived on Indian lands and attempted to subdue Native people into compliance. It also speaks to a time when military personnel did not always see Indian running as a harmless activity of sport and recreation. In an editorial published in the *Coleman Voice*, a small semi-weekly newspaper in Coleman, Texas, the author explained that "one of the problems of the soldier in the West is to overtake the Indian when that fellow wants to get away." Allow a "band of Indians to commit a depredation and start to run and it is one of the greatest difficulties to catch them," he observed. Recalling stories about how difficult it was for the US Cavalry to catch Geronimo and his band of Apaches once they "reached the mountains," the author explained that not only did the Apaches know the "land thoroughly, but they could run so rapidly that you might have them safely located in one place, bring your attachment up, only to find they had gone, bag and baggage, hours and hours before."[48]

In the early 1900s, reporters and other writers of American newspapers increased their coverage on the accomplishments of Indian runners. Their interest in Hopi runners stemmed from a fascination with American Indian culture and a deep-seated belief that Native people belonged to a "vanishing race." "The once noble red man is disappearing from the American continent," wrote one reporter for the *San Francisco Chronicle*, and the "remaining aboriginal peoples of this country are gradually lapsing into a condition of non-entity, the warlike ones having been slain, and the tamer ones herded upon isolated reservations."[49] To address, and perhaps even combat, this supposed "vanishing race" epidemic in North America, museum curators, university scholars, and photographers set out to uncover and preserve Indian artifacts and record the life and especially the ceremonies of Native people.[50] For the Hopi, the ceremony that the world beyond the mesas wanted to witness and record, whether in written form, drawings, or photographs, was the Hopi Snake Dance.[51]

In autumn 1902, a curator named Charles P. Wilcomb of the California State Parks Museum in Sacramento traveled to the Hopi mesas to collect objects for the museum and to witness the Hopi dance. While satisfied with what he had secured for the museum, he was most impressed with the footrace that accompanied the ceremony.[52] In an op-ed piece that he wrote in the *San Francisco Chronicle* entitled "Are Moqui[53] Runners World Beaters?" (Appendix B), Wilcomb provided a detailed and colorful account of the race that surely delighted and intrigued his readers: "Look way down there on the desert plain," he began his story, "five miles to the eastward. Isn't the morning air of Arizona wonderfully clear? Can you see that little dark patch, there? Take the field glass. Now you can make it out. That is five miles from here. Cattle? No, those are Indian footracers," and they are "preparing for the start" of a five-mile race. Wilcomb then explained to his readers that while the distance of five miles is a "long race for any athlete," the desert terrain and high rugged cliffs made it especially difficult for the Hopi runners.

Wanting to contrast the leisurely lives of his readers with the disciplined and dedicated lives of the Hopi, Wilcomb continued: "At 3 o'clock this morning, while you were sleeping profoundly and restfully, as a man will in such an atmosphere, a pueblo priest proclaimed this race from the top of one of those queer, laddered adobe houses on the mesa." Wilcomb recalled that an hour later thirteen or so runners gathered at the start line, and when a ray of sun "touched a certain cliff top in the middle mesa," a priest signaled for the race to begin. "They're off!," Wilcomb explained, "Can you see them move? . . . Keep the glass on them and I'll tell you how these Moquis came to be such great marvelous runners." Wilcomb told his readers that the Hopis ran "naked, bare feet and all" to "travel as light as possible." "Look behind you at their houses. See the ascending ladders leading from lower to upper stories. Now glance down this trail to the level of the plain. Doesn't it look like a life of climbing? Think of the constant training these Indians get. . . . The tribe is in unconscious training to produce a race of runners with great staying powers."[54]

While Wilcomb's editorial informed his readers of the remarkable running abilities of the Hopi, he also forced them to consider that in the high desert of Arizona Indians existed that could outpace and outdistance the most esteemed white runners in the nation, and perhaps even the world. He reminded his readers that up to that point English runner J. White of London held the world's record of running five miles in twenty-four minutes and forty seconds. The American record for the same distance was held by an amateur runner named Mullen in twenty-five minutes and twenty-two and one-half seconds. And in 1902, the world record for the mile was held by a runner named George of London who completed the distance in four minutes and twelve and three-quarters seconds. Wilcomb noted that even if George could have kept that pace for five miles, he would have been a minute slower than the Hopi runners he witnessed on the reservation. "What would college athletes think of running on a course like that?," asked Wilcomb, "It would create a sensation to have these Moqui runners at an intercollegiate field day. Let them have a good track and run to beat the world's record for three, four, or five miles."

Around the time that Wilcomb witnessed the footrace at Orayvi, a writer for the *New York Sun* recalled a story about a Hopi runner named Talashyatua from the same village who left his home at sunrise for Tuba City, a small town some forty miles to the northwest.[55] According to the writer, Talashyatua, whom he considered the "finest" runner "among the Hopis," reached Tuba City and returned to Orayvi by three o'clock in the afternoon. In addition to noting that Talashyatua completed eighty miles "in less than nine hours," the writer mentioned that the runner was "credited with having run 50 miles through the sand in five hours." And even though the runner ran over terrain that was "uneven and in some places extremely rugged," Talashyatua never slackened his pace no "matter how steep the grade."[56] The writer's observation about the runner's ability to run through sand is noteworthy for different reasons. Unlike when Hopis competed in American races on pavement or other hard surfaces, the Hopi runner from Orayvi ran fifty miles on a surface that gave him great resistance. Every step he took, his feet sunk into the sand, which caused each of his strides to be a fraction of a second slower than if he had run on an even surface.[57] Throughout the duration of his run, the fractions of time turned into seconds and then minutes. His feet and leg muscles had to adjust to the constant jarring of his body, the sand's density, and the inclines or declines of his path.[58]

In the early 1900s, newspaper writers such as Wilcomb and the writer for the *New York Sun* often remarked on the "rugged" landscape of the reservation. In contrast to the paved streets and clay tracks that many white athletes competed on during this period, the topography at Hopi helped reporters and other writers to better understand the accomplishments of Hopi runners. And as they reflected on the running conditions on the Hopi mesas, they doubted, as far as "long-distance runners" were concerned, that the Hopi had "equals in any other of the Indian tribes of the United States." One newspaper writer summed up his comments by saying: "The

Hopi cornfield in valley below Third Mesa. Photograph by author.

character of the country in which they live renders walking a slow method of progress, and they have developed an ability to run through heavy sands with the expenditure of far less energy than walking would consume; and their fields are situated at so great a distance from their villages that they are obliged to run in order to get to them, accomplish their work and return in the same day."[59] The resistance provided by the soft sand, the steep grades of their running trails, and their dependence on running to accomplish work all conditioned Hopis to excel in long-distance races and helped give them an advantage over white American runners.

A month after Wilcomb witnessed the Snake Dance footrace at Orayvi, a reporter for the *New York Sun* traveled to the reservation to witness an Antelope Clan footrace at the same village. The reporter noted that the race began with a yell from on top of the mesa, a signal for all of the spectators to do the same. As the runners dashed from the starting line, they tore "across the desert" at nearly "full speed" on a four-mile uphill course that ended back again at Orayvi. Twenty minutes later, the lead runner entered the village and made his way to his clan's kiva. The reporter observed that the winner of the race was a "graceful youth, with deep, full chest and heavily muscled legs." Once at the kiva, the people presented him with his reward, a "handful of flour for his field, to appease the rain god and to insure good crops for the ensuing year."[60]

On occasion, visitors arrived on the Hopi mesas to witness ceremonies other than the Snake Dance. In the late 1920s, anthropologist Julian H. Steward, known for his work on the "scientific theory of culture change," journeyed to Hopiland to observe the Wöwöchim (Naashnaiya) ceremony at the villages of First Mesa.[61] Usually held in the month of November, the ceremony represented a ritualistic rite of passage where Hopi children became initiated into various clan societies. An important part of the ceremony included a race involving the youth and elder members of the community. According to an account given to Steward by a Hopi Tunwub katchina at Walpi, the prerace ritual began when a Horn Society leader named Alosaka accompanied the runners down the mesa to the south. Once at the bottom of the mesa, Alosaka gently poured a line of cornmeal on the ground to distinguish the start of the race. "What is your name?," Alosaka asked each of them in the Hopi language. After they answered, he told them "Now boys, if you catch me before we get to that mountain, Sistávatekwin (a butte twenty miles or so to the south), we shall come back again. If you do not catch me, we will run all the way there. You must stay here until I get to that point." He then pointed to a location a mile or so away.

After Alosaka explained the rules and parameters of the race, he began running toward the mountain. Once he reached the designated point, the youth ran after him and attempted to pass him, which most did after ten or fifteen miles. As each youth ran by, Alosaka grabbed on to them and kept them until every runner arrived. At that point, Alosaka told the youth that he was simply warming up, and then he sprinted again toward the mountain. When the young runners overcame him a second time, Alosaka then conceded, ended the race, and invited them to eat with him a lunch consisting of "sweet cornmeal dough which one of the boys [had] carried" and water that a "man on horseback" brought to them. After the young runners and older men ate their lunch, they began their trip back to Walpi, running the entire way, stopping only to pick up "soap-weed as they go." Although Steward remarked that the boys ran "even though exhausted," their fathers and uncles accompanied the young runners and took care of them. As the boys gathered up the soap-weed they handed it to their elders, who then rolled it up and returned it to them to "tie around" their waists. When the runners returned to the bottom of First Mesa, they picked up the ears of corn they had left at the start line and took them to their kivas at Walpi. Inside the kivas, the youth continued their ritual ceremonies of clan initiation.[62]

Two days after the race to gather soapweed, other younger runners from the Agave Society at Walpi participated in a race "to secure wood." The race also began at the bottom of the mesa, but on the east side of the village. Standing behind a line of cornmeal to mark the start, young runners and their "fathers," or older clan relatives, waited for the race to begin. While waiting, the older runners held onto each of the younger runners, and once the race started, the older men released the young runners and immediately the elders attempted to "catch" them over a distance of fifteen or twenty miles. After the elder runners caught all of the younger runners, they walked back to Walpi together, collecting greasewood along the way. When they eventually arrived at the starting point below the mesa, they ascended "by way of Toreva" and then "proceed[ed] directly to Goat kiva." Later on, the Agave Society used the wood that the runners had collected on the race to build a fire in the center of the village for their ceremonial dance.[63]

While a majority of the published stories about Hopi running first appeared in American newspapers or scholarship of ethnographic reports, on occasion the topic also appeared in literary works. In the early 1900s, a writer named Samuel Travers Clover published a novel entitled *On Special Assignment*, which told of a young newspaper correspondent named Paul Travers and his adventures out West. One of his assignments included a trip to the Hopi mesas to witness and report on the Hopi Snake Dance. While at Hopi, Travers remarked at length about Hopi customs, the matriarchal aspect of Hopi society, and the physical appearance of Hopi women. He also observed the remarkable running abilities of the Hopi people. While talking with an individual only referred to as Professor Winans about the "queerer style" of Hopi girls' hair, a "young fellow clad only in a breech-cloth passed" their "wagon at an easy trot."[64] For a moment both individuals stopped talking and "turned to watch him cover the ground with his soft, regular pat-pat, never tiring, never varying gait." Travers then told the professor that he had heard that the "Moqui runner has marvelous staying-powers." He recalled that back on the mesas, the people had "pointed out" to him a "wiry little fellow" who had "covered ninety miles from dawn to dark in one day." Attributing their running abilities to the dry and arid climate, Travers also remarked that people on the mesas proudly noted that their runners regularly run sixty miles "in a day." While Travers emphasized the climate to explain Hopi running success, he was also astonished by the Hopi runner's fitness and physical endurance. "What I admire about them," said the professor, is their fine heart action. Just think how we puffed climbing to the top of Oraibi, yet these youngsters will keep up a swift trot in the valley and maintain it clear to the summit of the mesa, the eight hundred feet of precipitous trail at the finish seeming not to bother them at all."[65]

Works by Clover and others only increased American interest in Hopi running. And as more non-Hopi people began to visit the Hopi Reservation during the early 1900s, they provided additional accounts of running among the people.[66] In May 1904, for example, a white entrepreneur named W. Maurice Tobin visited the Hopi mesas and described a footrace that he organized for the community. Tobin was one of the founders of The Cliff Dwellers, an exposition that toured the nation for white audiences to experience a romanticized portrayal of ancient Southwest Indian cultures. Wanting to witness for himself the remarkable abilities of Hopi long-distance runners, Tobin offered cash prizes to all first-place winners for the twenty-five-, fifty-, and one-hundred-mile races. In an interview for the St. Louis Sunday Star, Tobin claimed that when a Hopi runner named Peeho Hopi won the one-hundred mile race, he did so in "something less than six hours." Noting that the runners completed this course at an elevation upwards of 7,000 feet above sea level and that the course was not ideal for distance running, he remarked that the Hopis were "wonderful runners, and no people on earth [could] equal them for long distances."[67]

While the accounts retold by Spanish explorers, American academics, and newspaper reporters give testimony to the long tradition of running among the people, they do little to help situate Hopi runners within a modern American sport context. In the same year that Jesse Walter Fewkes visited the Hopi in 1890, life for the people had increasingly changed. New railroad lines had been built throughout northern Arizona and the West, and with them came additional visitors to Hopi country. But the railroad also provided Hopis with opportunities to leave their villages, sometimes by force, to cities far beyond Hopi ancestral lands. Within a relatively short period of time, Hopis began leaving the reservation for regions and cities on the East and West Coasts, and many places in between. They went as ambassadors for their people or as prisoners of the US government, and many youth left their homelands to attend one of several off-reservation Indian boarding schools.

Prior to this, however, US government officials worked tirelessly to subdue Hopi and other Indian people throughout the Southwest. Constantly fearing that tribes would uprise against the government, officials paid close attention to reports provided by non-Native Indian agents stationed on various reservations. "The Navajo Indians in New Mexico are becoming troublesome," explained a report in the *Record-Union*, "and fears of general outbreak are expressed."[68] But years earlier, Walter Clement Powell, first cousin of John Wesley Powell, remarked that the Hopi treated him with "civility" and welcomed him into their homes.[69] And shortly thereafter, another individual offered a similar observation by noting that during his visit to the Hopi villages, the people "appeared to be delighted with [their] visit and showed great hospitality."[70] Describing the Hopi as peaceful, civil, and hospitable ran contrary to newspaper accounts that portrayed the Navajos and Apaches as savages, raiders, and troublesome. Referring to the Hopi as "partially civilized," a correspondent for the *Saint Louis Globe-Democrat* remarked that the Hopi are "quiet and inoffensive in their habits" and yet "tenaciously cling to their old traditions and superstitions."[71] At this time government officials had greater patience with the Hopi. They believed that the people could be convinced of the supposed superiority of Western culture and American society. And they were sure that the Hopi would slowly abandon their backwards superstitions and religious ceremonies if they saw and experienced the world beyond the mesas.

CHAPTER TWO

Dirt Trails and Steel Rails

Near the turn of the twentieth century, a hotel clerk in Winslow, Arizona, received a message that an "Indian" was waiting outside and requested to "see a leader of an exploring party."[1] When the leader stepped outside, he found the man "sitting on the curbstone, mouth agape with wonder" as he watched the trains pass on the Atlantic & Pacific Railroad.[2] The Indian was a Hopi runner from the village of Orayvi who had been commissioned to deliver a letter to the party leader in Winslow. The runner informed the leader that he had left Orayvi at four o'clock the previous afternoon and arrived in Winslow during the middle of the night. When the hotel clerk and party leader realized that the path between Orayvi and Winslow was sixty-five miles, and that the runner "ran over a country with which he was not familiar" with, they concluded that he ran until darkness fell and then finished his "journey by moonlight."[3]

The Hopi runner's fascination with the locomotive, and the clerk and party leader's amazement of the runner's accomplishment, tells of a time in Hopi and American history when ancient practices of running intersected with modern advancements in transportation. It signals to a moment in history when the Hopi people met and confronted the evolving world around them with their abilities to run long distances. At a time when the US Postal Service regularly used horses, wagons, and trains to transport its mail throughout the West, the Hopi runner's ability to quickly deliver a message by foot astonished the men standing in the entrance to the hotel.[4] While the Hopi runner sat in awe of the locomotive, the hotel clerk and the leader of the exploring party stood in amazement of him.

In this brief moment, modern America intersected with the ancient world of the Hopi.[5] Steel railroad tracks converged upon dirt trails. The

A Meeting Point of Cultures, by Neil Logan.

roar and whistle of the locomotive transcended the sound of horses hitched to wagons and the chatter of people conducting their daily business. Here, in the high desert of north central Arizona, the small and dusty town of Winslow had become a meeting point of cultures. White Americans had come to this cultural intersection by train, but Hopis and other Native people arrived using the running trails of their ancestors, routes long established in the distant past. For the Hopi runner who arrived at Winslow to deliver his message, he had come as a runner from Orayvi, while guests at the hotel arrived from cities on the East and West Coasts, and everywhere in between.

This cultural intersection, however, reflected more than America's diversity and technological advancements. For the Hopi, it signified a rapidly changing world, and it represented a way for them to experience this world with other non-Indian people in the late nineteenth and early twentieth centuries.[6] While Hopis used their trails to enter the periphery of this world, few Hopis at this time had ventured beyond their ancestral lands in northeastern Arizona. And fewer still had visited the nation's large metropolises in California, New York, or elsewhere. But not long before the messenger runner had confronted the railroad in Winslow, trains such as the Atlantic & Pacific Railroad had significantly altered Hopi mobility in American society. With their feet the people traveled hundreds of miles, while the train allowed them to cover thousands of miles. Hopi runners had witnessed these modern marvels from a distance, but soon these runners, and others like them, would become their passengers and turn Winslow and other small towns along the railroad line, including Holbrook, into points of departure for the outside world.[7]

While the newspaper report suggested that the Hopi messenger ran on unfamiliar terrain, the land surrounding Winslow had cultural and historical significance for him and his people. Anthropologist E. Charles Adams once observed that long ago Hopis established settlements near Winslow called Homol'ovi, a name referring to the mound-like "buttes and hills that dot the region." For nearly a thousand years, Hopis have considered Homol'ovi to be a place of "cultural crossroads" and have used the Little Colorado River's close proximity to the region as a waterway to trade with other Native people and to participate in various ceremonies. Long after Hopis had left their homes at Homol'ovi in the 1400s, white Americans furthered these cultural exchanges with Native people by constructing the railroad line that cut through the town and region.[8] During the late nineteenth and early twentieth centuries, Hopis saw Winslow as a gateway to the world beyond their mesas. They routinely left their villages for Winslow to buy items from white Americans, and white Americans and others used the town to trade and sell goods with the surrounding Indian communities. At the turn of the century, Winslow also served as a strategic town for the US government's dealings with Hopi and other Native people.

The first significant opportunity for runners from the Hopi community to experience the outside world by train took place in the summer of 1890. At this time, government officials struggled to force Hopis to comply with their wishes regarding the mandatory enrollment of Hopi children in government schools, Hopi religious customs, and various land disputes. To help weaken this resistance, government officials orchestrated a carefully planned trip for five Hopi leaders, all of whom were runners, to travel east to Fort Defiance, Arizona, and then board a train in Gallup, New Mexico, for Washington, DC.[9] The delegation was to be led by Indian Agent C. E. Vandever in charge of the Navajo Agency, and accompanied by a white trader who lived and worked among the Hopi named Thomas V. Keam. Government officials had hoped that the trip would help broaden Hopi understanding of the world beyond their mesas. They wanted Hopis to be impressed with modern cities and agricultural practices, and certain technological advancements in white society. But there was a deeper, and perhaps more culturally destructive, reason why government officials wanted Hopis to see the wonders of modern America. As historian Philip J. Deloria observed: "Every moment of contact in which Europeans sought to impress the natives by firing a gun, demonstrating a watch, predicting an eclipse, or introducing mirrors and steel set expectations about the backwardness of indigenous people and their seemingly genetic inability to understand and use technology."[10]

In his report to the Commissioner of Indian Affairs, Vandever described how the Hopi delegation responded to their first train ride and told of their initial perceptions of the outside world. The "swift motion of the railway train whirling them through an ever changing scenery overpowered them with amazement," Vandever remarked, and "almost completely stunned their every sense." While telling of their "amazement," the Indian agent went on to explain that "after a little" while this "dazed condition subsided," and after their "faculties again reviv[ed], they maintained a constant flow of inquiries, and began slowly to understand something of the great life beyond the solitudes of their table-lands."[11]

The government representatives also wanted the men to be impressed with the power of the United States military, something they seldom observed on the newly established Hopi Reservation.[12] To accomplish this, government officials brought the Hopis by train to Fort Leavenworth in Kansas to see for themselves the advanced weaponry of the US military.[13] At the fort, the Hopi leaders witnessed American soldiers marching in formation and drill sergeants instructing their cadets to follow their commands. Military officials led the delegation on a walking tour of the fort and demonstrated the destructive power of the army's large canons, small firearms, and the dreaded revolving Hotchkiss gun. The Hopi leaders saw the soldiers' barracks, ate in the fort's mess hall, and visited the stables where the military boarded the cavalry's horses.

But one place at the fort left a lasting impression on the minds of the Hopi delegates. In addition to showing them the barracks and artillery grounds, military officials took the Hopi leaders to the fort's prison, where unruly and disobedient soldiers, including Native warriors from prior Indian wars, remained to serve out their sentences. Hopi tribal historian Leigh J. Kuwanwisiwma once recalled that after they "visited this huge penitentiary," they "realized that this was another part of the white man's way of life, to put people in jail."[14] The message to the Hopis was clear: if you defy the wishes of the US government, you too will be arrested, removed from your home and family, and incarcerated in a federal prison.

While government officials wanted the Hopi leaders to be intimidated by what they saw at Fort Leavenworth, they also took the delegation to certain towns to experience the power and allure of American industry. One of these towns was Terre Haute in west-central Indiana. Having served as the town's chief of police prior to becoming an Indian agent in the Southwest, Vandever was very familiar with the city's industries and its residents.[15] Staying at the Boston House, also known as the Sullivan Hotel, the Hopi chiefs toured the town with Vandever and Keam, attracting attention from the townspeople wherever they went.[16] Unaccustomed to seeing Indian people in their city, especially Native leaders, the residents of Terre Haute took great interest in the Hopi delegation, and some even followed the chiefs around as they toured the town. In his history of Vigo County, Henry C. Bradsby observed that in the early 1890s, Terre Haute had become a major center for American industries, manufacturing electric lights, pianos, clothes, and many other products.[17] Here, government officials took the Hopi delegates to see the town's "car shops, [the] hub and spoke factory," the Vigo County Courthouse, and the Rose Orphan Home. In his report to the Commissioner of Indian Affairs, Vandever noted that the Hopi leaders appeared "keenly interested" in the "industries of the city and in the rural pursuits upon the farms." He also observed that the Hopi delegates seemed "charmed with the kindness and hospitality they received at every hand," and that they "left Terre Haute with extreme reluctance."

The Hopis' keen interest in the "rural pursuits upon the farms" is significant for several reasons. Back on their mesas, the Hopi chiefs belonged to an agricultural society where they farmed lands belonging to one of several Hopi clans. Often referred to as the "master dry farmers of the world," the Hopi farmers cultivated small corn, bean, and melon fields.[18] In the early 1900s, Special Enumerator E. S. Clark highlighted the agricultural practices of the Hopi in the US government's Eleventh Census and compared the dry climate found on the Hopi mesas with other damp and humid regions of the United States. "To those of us living in this arid belt," Clark remarked, "who grow nothing except by irrigation and with the idea that nothing can be grown here . . . without it, the success of Indians in agriculture is a wonderful revelation." But unlike Indiana, or other parts of the Midwest where it rains large amounts each year, Hopi lands are situated in an arid climate. Receiving less than ten inches per year on average, Hopi farmers relied on their ceremonies and prayers for rain to make their crops grow. Hopi "farms," Clark concludes, "many of them being miles away from the villages they inhabit, located in valleys totally devoid of water," require them to carry "all their products, fuel, and water on the backs of their men, women, children, and burros these long distances up the steep sides of their several mesas."[19] And the Hopi chiefs also realized that unlike the farms in Indiana, healthy and bountiful crops back home required clan runners to run with happy hearts, to be in harmony with the natural world around them, and to run swiftly so as to entice the rain clouds to follow them back to their fields.

After their brief visit in Terre Haute, the Hopi delegation headed east to Washington, DC, where they planned to meet with Commissioner of Indian Affairs Thomas J. Morgan. When they arrived in the city, Indian Agent Vandever checked them into the Tremont Hotel, also known as the Tremont House, on Indiana Avenue and Second Street. After the chiefs had a night to rest from their journey, Vandever led the group on a tour of the nation's capital, where they saw the White House, the Washington Monument, and the Library of Congress.[20] Similar to the reception they received in Indiana and elsewhere, the Hopi chiefs fascinated and intrigued the city's residents and other visitors. "No delegation of Indians in Washington of recent years," wrote a reporter for the *Washington Post*, "has attracted the attention which is now bestowed upon the Moqui chiefs."[21]

Describing one of the chiefs named Shimo, the *Post* observed that he was "seventy years old, but still bright-eyed and active." The newspaper noted that Shimo wore "eagle feathers in his long black hair," and that he had on a flannel shirt that was accented by "several yards of beads" around his neck. In addition to wearing beads, Shimo wore a "pair of immense silver rings in his ears," with enough metal in each ring to "make a silver dollar." All five chiefs wore a "sombrero," and one wore a "pair of buckskin trousers, with leather fringe down the legs, and a thick [woolen] shirt" with openings that revealed the "wide expanses of [his] copper colored skin."[22] Furthermore, whenever the chiefs "appeared outside" on the hotel's front veranda, "crowd[s] of children" and others gathered to see them. And so, when they desired to smoke cigarettes or talk among each other, the chiefs gathered in the hotel's backyard, away from curious onlookers.

During their stay in Washington, the Hopi chiefs, along with Indian

Agent Vandever and Thomas Keam, attended an opera at the Albaugh Opera House called *Amorita*.[23] Performed by the Lamont Opera Company and written by Alfons Czibulka, *Amorita* was a romance comedy that took place in fifteenth-century Florence, Italy.[24] By the summer of 1890, the opera had delighted audiences in cities throughout the eastern half of the United States, including Cincinnati, Philadelphia, Pittsburg, and New York. Occupying two of the boxes in the balcony, the Hopi chiefs watched the opera with great amusement. "The Indians enjoyed the performance very much in a quiet way," described the *Washington Sunday Herald*, "until the appearance of the two little 'coons' in the second act, when they became so much excited that they attracted the attention of the whole audience."[25] When the opera had finished, a local military surgeon invited the chiefs to his house on the "West End" for a reception. Here the chiefs ate ice-cream for the first time, and they each gave a short speech in the Hopi language, which Keam translated into English. "After they had fed [on ice-cream,]" the *Herald* noted, "they expressed their appreciation of the kindness that they had received" and remarked that "when they returned home they would tell all their people" about their experience.[26] At the end of the gathering, the hostess presented the chiefs with gifts of "bright-colored silk handkerchiefs," after which Keam and Vandever accompanied the men back to the hotel.[27]

Prior to 1890, the US government routinely used the Tremont Hotel to lodge Indian leaders who came to Washington, DC.[28] In the summer of 1875, Spotted Tail, Red Cloud, and other Sioux leaders stayed at the Tremont Hotel as part of their visit to the nation's capital to meet with President Ulysses S. Grant.[29] They made the more than fifteen-hundred-mile trip to speak with the president about their complaints involving Indian Agent J. J. Seville of the Red Cloud Agency, and to argue with him and other officials about the US government's attempts to obtain their sacred Black Hills.[30] Nearly five years later, in April 1880, a group of Crow chiefs from Montana Territory traveled to Washington and stayed at the Tremont House to express concerns to Secretary of the Interior Carl Schurz about "white miners" who had "encroached upon" their lands on the "south side of the Yellowstone river."[31]

While most newspaper accounts at this time reported on Indian leaders who lodged at the hotel, US government officials also used the hotel to quarter Indian children on route to boarding schools. For example, in the early 1880s, the *Washington Post* noted that "seventeen little Indians from

Sitting Bull's band" had "arrived at the Tremont House" for a brief visit before heading to a predominately black boarding school called Hampton Institute in Hampton, Virginia.[32] Accompanied by Lieutenant Le Roy Brown of the US Army, the children toured the "beauty of the city" and "wonders of civilization" before continuing on to the school.[33]

In addition to introducing the Hopi leaders to military forts and modern cities, government officials wanted the leaders to see and appreciate the education and industrial programs at off-reservation Indian boarding schools. One of these schools was the Carlisle Indian Industrial School in Pennsylvania, which at the time was the largest and most prominent school in the government's off-reservation Indian boarding school system.[34] Founded by Captain Richard Henry Pratt at an old unused military barrack, Carlisle existed to transform reservation Indians into modern American citizens,[35] a goal perhaps best reflected in Pratt's motto for the school: "Into civilization and citizenship."[36] At Carlisle, officials introduced the Hopi delegates to the school's academic and industrial programs. Superintendent Pratt wanted the Hopis to witness happy and content Indian students going about their school routine.[37] He wanted them to imagine Hopi children alongside these Indian students learning about American history, arithmetic, and language arts in the school's classrooms. And he wanted them to imagine Hopi children being trained in the school's blacksmith and carpentry shops, or in the domestic programs offered for girls. He also showed them various aspects of Carlisle's growing athletic program, and perhaps even envisioned Hopi youth running with other Indian athletes on the school's not yet established track and cross-country teams.[38] Pratt believed that Hopi children belonged at the school, and his predecessors would soon go to great lengths to enroll them.

Although the Hopis had made this journey to voice their concern to Commissioner Morgan regarding problems they had with their neighbors the Navajos, government officials had also intended for the Hopis to be intimidated and impressed by what they saw on their trip. And they also hoped that those impressions would result in their compliance with US government mandates. "They witnessed cities," Daniel Honahnie from the village of Orayvi once recalled, "transportation systems, overwhelming numbers of non-Indians and a huge variety of food and clothing, which influenced the delegation members to recognize what the future held for their children."[39] When the Hopi delegates returned home, they told people in their villages about what they had witnessed. They spoke of the advanced arsenal of the US military, the "acres and acres of corn" growing in Indiana and in other parts of the Midwest, and the wonders of modern cities.[40] They also reported back on the large number of white people they saw, and compared it to the relatively small Hopi population living on the reservation.[41] And perhaps most importantly, they recalled their impressions about Carlisle, and argued among each other whether they should send their children to the Indian school.

Some of these conversations took place in their underground ceremonial chambers called kivas, where they debated about the meaning of Hopi prophecy and how to respond to the encroachment of American society on their land and culture. Other conversations occurred in their village plazas, on their corn and melon fields, or within the rock-and-mud walls of their homes. Children, caught in the middle of the drama, sensed tensions between their parents and other village members and wondered how these debates would dictate their futures. Hopi leaders, including chiefs on both sides of the issue, reminded the people of teachings of the ancient ones and attempted to situate their dilemma within a larger Hopi context. One Hopi chief from Orayvi named Loloma, who had been part of the delegation to Washington, saw benefits in sending their children to Indian schools.

Hopi oral history recalls that when Loloma returned from his trip, he called a meeting in one of the kivas at Orayvi and expressed his desire for them as their village leader. Speaking to them as a father addresses his children, Loloma told those who gathered in the kiva that the white man's "way of life" was there to "stay," and that they "must accept that." Confident that his people could "find a way to survive" the encroachment of American values and ways into Hopi society, the chief provided them with a path forward. "Learn the Whiteman's tongue," he instructed them, "Learn how he thinks," and "learn his ways so that we can survive [as a people]."[42] Other Hopi leaders, however, understood the imposition of American ways to be an attack on their sovereignty, which led only to the eventual erosion of the Hopi way of life.[43] No consensus existed among the people regarding the school issue or any other issue, resulting in divisions of all kinds throughout Hopi country.

During the 1890s, government officials routinely hosted visits from Indian chiefs at the Carlisle Indian Industrial School. Often in route or having just returned from meetings with high-ranking officials in Washington, DC, the chiefs came to Carlisle to check on the welfare of children from their communities. In February 1891, forty-two Sioux chiefs from the Dakotas, some of whom had previously attended the school, came to Carlisle. When they arrived at the school, Superintendent Pratt, along with a number of teachers, met and escorted them to the school gymnasium for a large assembly. Pratt began the gathering by welcoming the chiefs to Carlisle and expressing his hope that they would return home with a favorable report of the school. After Pratt's opening remarks, students "gave an interesting programme of exercises" that pleased many in attendance. Then a Sioux student named Chauncey Yellow Robe delivered an address entitled the "Indian Messiah," which was followed by speeches from four of the Sioux chiefs: Hollow Horn Bear of the Rosebud Agency, John Grass, Little No Heart, and American Horse. The latter chief spoke for an hour and took advantage of the opportunity to talk directly to those children from his community. While American Horse "praised" the education that the students received at Carlisle, he urged the Sioux children to "use it in detecting the frauds by the whites." He reminded them that all lands collectively known as the United States once "belonged to the Indians," and he exposed the government's failure to appoint Sioux individuals to agency positions so that they could make positive changes for their people. Not wanting the chief's criticisms to go unchallenged, however, Pratt spoke next and acknowledged the government's shortcomings, but argued that Indian people at Carlisle had "improved" and had collectively earned thousands of dollars from their labors.[44]

At off-reservation Indian boarding schools such as Carlisle, officials required students to work on and off campus to earn money, gain experience, and to meet the labor needs of the larger non-Native community through the school's Outing Program. Five years after the Sioux delegation visited Carlisle, the New York Tribune observed that immediately after the school year had concluded, officials at Carlisle sent many male and female students to work on farms throughout Pennsylvania. "The advantages to the Indian boys and girls of being thus surrounded with the influences of a Christian home are great," the New York Tribune noted, as they are able to "learn how white people live, and at the same time they are able to earn a little money for themselves."[45] But while government officials used the Outing Program to further assimilate students into a civilized American society and to raise needed funds for the school, Native people had reasons of their own for laboring at the school and beyond. In his book on Indian labor at Sherman Institute, historian Kevin Whalen observed that as "Native people used outing programs in Southern California to earn money and acquire new skills and perspectives, they became part of a broader story in which American Indians integrated new ways of working into their cultures in order to carry on into the twentieth century."[46]

While Pratt believed that Indian students needed a strong work ethic to "carry on into the twentieth century," obstacles existed on Indian reservations that he and other school administrators had to overcome. Similar to the Sioux visit to Carlisle in 1891, Pratt also wanted the Hopi delegation to return to Hopi with a favorable opinion of the school. He wanted them to speak well of the school with other Hopis back home and to convince them of the great benefits of Hopi attendance at Carlisle. But when some of the chiefs returned home, their opinion of the school and the so-called white man's world in general did not always sit well with members of their community. For example, not long after Chief Loloma and the other chiefs returned to the Hopi mesas, people at Orayvi grew suspicious of Loloma and challenged his willingness to adapt certain aspects of American values and culture. In an article in the *Boston Daily Globe*, a newspaper writer noted that Loloma "obtained his progressive ideas from a visit to Washington," and that he wanted to "introduce some of the ways of the white people in his own tribe." Upon returning to Orayvi, Loloma "commenced to relate to his fellow-citizens the wonders he had seen. He described the immense numbers of people, the railroads and gigantic buildings, but he could not convince his companions that he was telling the truth." In response, some people at Orayvi concluded that he was "crazy," "confine[d] him in a hole,"[47] and kept him there for "some time" before he was "finally released."[48] When government officials at Hopi heard of Loloma's capture and imprisonment, they informed Commissioner Morgan, who then sent "troops," including Lieutenant L. M. Brett, to the reservation to help settle the disputes surrounding the "vexed school question."[49]

The US government's use of the railroad to exploit tensions on the reservation and to broaden Hopi understandings of the outside world did not stop after the Hopi delegation returned to the mesas. Four years later, in November 1894, a new group of Hopi runners refused to accept US government policies, including the forced removal of Hopi children to government-run schools. While the leaders openly resisted the federal government mandates, they also created problems among members of the Hopi and non-Hopi community. Hopi tribal historian Kuwanwisiwma recalled that beginning in the 1870s, Hopis at Munqapi allowed a group of Mormons to farm small fields near their village. However, by the 1880s, the Mormons "slowly began to take over farming areas, creating friction with local Hopi farmers." Escalated by Mormon attempts to control additional Hopi lands by applying for "formal land permits" from the US government, the situation intensified by the early 1890s when "Hopis had lost valuable arable land to the Mormons." In spring 1894, Chief Loloma "hosted a meeting with all his advisors and families" from Munqapi and declared that they had "every right to take back their traditional farmlands" from the Mormons.

In response to Loloma's instructions, the Hopi farmers at Munqapi planted corn, beans, and melons in their traditional fields before the Mormons had a chance to plant. Angered by their actions and determination to reclaim their fields, the Mormons argued with the Hopi farmers and quickly sought the help of US government officials and troops at Fort Wingate and Fort Defiance.[50] In his report to the Commissioner of Indian Affairs, Captain Constant Williams, Acting Indian Agent at Fort Defiance, noted that "the troubles at Oraibi resulted from the disposition on the part of the hostiles to drive the friendlies from the fields at Moencopie and in the spring, threatened to do the same thing at Oraibi." Consequently, officials arrested nineteen of the "ringleaders" and transported the Hopi men by foot while soldiers rode horses to Fort Wingate in New Mexico. Recalling their trip from Orayvi to Fort Wingate, George H. Guy of the *Los Angeles Times* remarked: "The Moquis can run better than they can do anything else, and think nothing of a journey of a hundred miles at a jog-trot. Whenever the horses trotted, [the Hopi prisoners] kept up with them with the greatest ease, for miles."[51] When the Hopi runners arrived at Fort Wingate, officials put them on trial for six weeks before sentencing the "worst of the offenders" to a federal military fort and prison on Alcatraz Island in the San Francisco Bay. Separated from their families and village communities, they remained on the island from January 1895 to September of the same year.[52]

While the US government, and Hopi oral history accounts, attribute the Hopi resistance at Munqapi to disagreements over land rights and the Mormons, American newspapers blamed Hopi refusal to send their children to government schools as the reason for the tensions and their ultimate arrests. With a headline that read "A Batch of Apaches," the *San Fran-*

Hopi corn, melon, and bean fields at the village of Munqapi. Photograph by author.

cisco Chronicle described the Hopi "ringleaders" as "murderous-looking" and noted that the "hostiles held a council of war and decreed that going to school was not compatible with the dignity of the tribe."[53] When the defiant Hopi leaders "commanded" that the "friendly Indians keep their children away from school" and then proceeded to host a dance to affirm their identity as Hopi people, US government troops "swooped down upon them and gathered them in."

After government officials sentenced some of the Hopi leaders and runners to prison, Lieutenant D. L. Brainard of the Second Cavalry and a "strong guard" of troops transported the prisoners to Gallup, where they accompanied them on a train for California. When the train left the mountain community of Flagstaff in north-central Arizona, one of the Hopi prisoners named Kochiuentiva "wrapped a blanket around his head as if composing himself for a nap." Pretending to sleep, Kochiuentiva rammed his head "through a window" and jumped out of the railroad car and into the "darkness" while the train sped along at thirty miles per hour. Having been notified of the prisoner's escape, the train conductor immediately applied the brakes and reversed the train for nearly a mile before stopping at the location where the Hopi leader jumped. Lieutenant Brainard then instructed his troops to scatter in "all directions along the rail" to search for the prisoner. When the soldiers discovered the Hopi leader "some distance along the track," they found him "lying down on a heap of rocks" injured and unconscious.[54] Once he awoke, soldiers handcuffed him and brought him back to the rail car, where they chained him to his seat for the remainder of the journey. His "head was cut," a writer for the *San Francisco Chronicle* reported, and "his body was badly bruised, but he uttered no complaint for the duration of the trip to California."[55]

When the leaders and runners arrived on Alcatraz Island, federal officials assigned an armed guard to watch over them and to ensure compliance. Similar to nearly every other US military prison at the time, officials at Alcatraz required prisoners to work and to contribute something useful to the prison and even the surrounding community. Less than a year before the Hopi runners entered Alcatraz, a sergeant at Alcatraz named Duffy remarked that the prison's commandant required every able-bodied prisoner to work. The prisoners routinely "repaired roads on the island," labored in carpentry and metal work, and daily policed the island and its buildings to keep them "tidy."[56] Officials at Alcatraz also required the Hopi leaders to work. They shoveled coal, dug gravel, cleaned harnesses, and split wood.[57] "A visitor landing from [Fort] McDowell on a fine day," a reporter for the *Pittsburgh Daily Post* observed, "can see" the nineteen Hopi men "in the sun slowly accomplishing their tasks," paying no attention to attempts by the visitors to get them to "gesture." Dividing themselves into "little groups, with a listless, mechanical steadiness," some of the Hopi leaders worked together on a cross-saw to cut through piles of logs to be used for one of many structures on the island. Another group of Hopis, situated on a "high bank overlooking the bay," drove "huge spikes into piles," while the "click of their uneven strokes was all the noise that broke the silence." "They never looked up from their task," the writer for the *Post* went on to observe; instead they "hammered away with the unskillful regularity of inexperienced but dogged men."[58]

While the Hopi men labored on the island they spent hours with each other talking, remembering, and longing for the familiar. Singing the katsina songs of their people as they worked, the Hopis thought about home. They thought about their families, wives, and children. And they remembered the various dances and other ceremonies taking place at their villages. They compared the small confines of the island to the vast openness of their mesas; the walking paths of the fort to the running

Working on Alcatraz Island, *by Neil Logan.*

trails connecting their villages. Nearly twenty acres large, and with only a portion of the acreage accessible to prisoners, Alcatraz Island was not suitable for long-distance running. Even if prison officials allowed the men to run on the island, they would have limited their running to a small courtyard area near the prison's citadel. The men arrived at Fort Alcatraz as leaders, runners, and prisoners of the US government, but while they remained on the island they also demonstrated to all that they were extremely hard workers.

While working on the island, the Hopi men also observed the hustle and bustle of life in San Francisco. Less than two miles from the mainland, they could listen to the sounds of trains arriving and leaving the city and hear the horns of large cargo and passenger ships entering and departing the bay. In the early morning hours the prisoners likely saw Italian and Chinese crews on fishing boats casting their nets.[59] At night, the Hopi leaders could see the twinkling lights of San Francisco and that of Oakland, and perhaps they even witnessed firework displays when the people celebrated the Fourth of July. For most observers on the mainland, the fireworks represented freedom, but to those imprisoned on the island, the displays gave the prisoners little reason to celebrate. As a reporter for the *San Francisco Chronicle* once remarked: the ultimate punishment for the prisoners came not as a result of "severe" discipline on the island but at the sight of the "city's lights across the waters. The sounds of revelry on the passing steamers and all the freedom which honest comrades were enjoying are known to be beyond the reach though within the sight and hearing of the gray clad criminal at the island post."[60]

While the Hopi leaders and runners daily witnessed life in San Francisco from a distance, they also had at least one opportunity to experience the city in person.[61] Nearly one month after the Hopis arrived on Alcatraz Island, prison officials transported the prisoners on the steamboat *McDowel* for a day-long trip on the mainland. Accompanied by a "lieutenant and two privates" of the US military, fifteen of the nineteen Hopi prisoners toured the city. Causing a "spectacle" among the city's residents, the Hopi leaders visited a number of locations in San Francisco, including the "corridors and departments of the new City Hall."[62] And they also beheld the building's nearly completed dome, which city architects intended to resemble the US Capitol dome in Washington, DC.[63] While government officials wanted the tour of City Hall to "inspire the Indians with a due appreciation of the greatness of the white man and his institutions," they also wanted the Hopi prisoners to be "impressed with the advantages of civilization." To help accomplish this on their tour, city officials provided each prisoner with a cigar, which they "puffed with apparent satisfaction."[64] Their time in San Francisco concluded at the ocean beach where the city's mayor, Adolph Sutro, hosted a "bountiful luncheon." Lieutenant Treat recalled that "what they were unable to get into their stomachs they carried away inside their shirts."[65]

Although government officials sent the Hopi men to Alcatraz to be removed from the influences of their people, they also brought them to the Pacific Ocean, a body of water that had and continues to have special meaning in Hopi religious culture. In an article in the *Los Angeles Times* that described a Hopi chief who visited the Pacific in 1928, the author noted that "Hopis believe that the ocean is the 'mother of all rain'" and mentioned that the chief had come to the Pacific because it was the "duty of every chief of the villages to make a pilgrimage," often by running, to the "western coast" and to offer a "prayer for rain on the ocean shore."[66] According to Hopi belief, the ocean is a giver of life. It is the "mother of all rain," and when Hopi leaders ventured to the Pacific to offer prayers and ceremonies, it ensured that water from the ocean evaporated, formed clouds, and brought much-needed rain to water their fields—hundreds of miles away in northeastern Arizona. For the Hopi leaders imprisoned on Alcatraz, their immediate access to the "mother of all rain" provided opportunities for them to offer similar prayers, which would in turn further the tradition of Hopi pilgrimages to the Pacific Ocean.[67]

The Hopi imprisonment on Alcatraz was not the first time the US government had sent Indian people, including leaders, to the Island. In May 1873, government officials sent a Hualapai (Wallapi) chief from Arizona named Quiwhatanava to prison at Alcatraz for two years. He had been accused of murder in Arizona, but rather than hanging him for his supposed crime, officials decided to send him to Alcatraz to be "initiated into the sublime mysteries of civilization" so that "on his release he might let his tribe know the power of the white people."[68] Less than a year later, government officials imprisoned a Paiute (Piute) chief from the Pyramid Lake Reservation in California named Natchez for "denouncing the remarkable ways of Indian agents in general and the Piute agent in particular."[69] And from 1889 to 1892, government officials sent chief Skolaskin of the Colville Indian Reservation in Washington State to Alcatraz for "subverting reservation discipline."[70] Officials only released him from prison after concluding that he no longer had the ability in his old age to negatively influence his people. His old age, however, did not stop him from continuing to criticize the US government after his release.[71]

By the early 1900s, government officials rarely sent problematic Hopi leaders to federal prisons such as Alcatraz with the hope that they would return and inform their people about modern advancements and changes in American society. At this time, many Hopis knew that the world beyond the mesas had changed, and would continue to change. Even without the testimonies of the Hopi chiefs, Christian missionaries on the reservation had been telling Hopis about these changes for years. Mennonite missionaries such as Heinrich R. Voth shared the Gospel message of salvation with Hopis while simultaneously desecrating Hopi religious culture and championing the supposed superiority of white American society.[72] Voth made few, if any, Mennonite converts, but he labored tirelessly in collecting Hopi religious items, drawing sacred shrines, and depositing his collection in American museums, most notably the Field Museum in Chicago.[73] Tourists and other visitors also brought photographs of the outside world and told the people about life in modern towns and cities. And some Hopis had left their ancestral lands and ventured throughout the United States. They traveled south to Phoenix, west to Los Angeles, east to Albuquerque, and north to towns in Utah, Colorado, and beyond.[74]

Government officials at the reservation's only boarding school in Keams Canyon also worked hard to broaden Hopi children's understanding of life beyond their mesas. Established in 1887 near a trading post and the region's Indian agency headquarters, the boarding school existed to provide Hopi youth with a Western education that was somewhat removed from the influences of their families and village communities.[75] White teachers at the Keams Canyon school, and at various Hopi Day Schools, told their students about life in the outside world. They shared stories about the towns and cities of their childhood and the many places they had lived and worked before coming to the Hopi mesas. They instructed them on important landmarks in American society such as the Statue of Liberty and the White House, and they described tall buildings that seemed to touch the heavens over Chicago and New York City. The stories, and the pictures that accompanied the lessons, surely captivated the minds of Hopi children, and perhaps they thought that they too might have an opportunity to experience what they read about in books or heard from their teachers.

Prior to their attendance at government schools, Hopi children had been taught at an early age about the oral narratives of their people. In the early 1890s, Indian Agent Julian Scott observed that Hopis taught their children stories of "giants, giantesses, hobgoblins, fairies, and all kinds of spirits, which they believe once lived and inhabited the earth in time long since gone by." "Every cliff and mesa," Scott explained, "every mountain and canon, has some story attached to it," which the people "treasure[d] with care."[76] Children listened intently to these stories and committed them to memory to ensure that the information and lessons embedded in the orations would continue from "generation to generation." Community members also taught the children that their people were once great travelers; runners who used their fleetness of foot to transport themselves to places far beyond Hopi ancestral lands and back. They learned about how their people had originated in a series of three underworlds. And they recalled the ancient migration stories of their people, when Hopi clans eventually emerged from these underworlds and migrated in all four cardinal directions and returned to form the foundation of their society.[77]

Before attending the Keams Canyon boarding school in the late 1890s, Hopi artist and writer Edmund Nequatewa from the village of Songòopavi had learned about the founding of his village, not from a Western archeological perspective but according to Hopi oral history. Community members, including his village elders, had also taught him about the origin and migrations of his clan, Qalwungwa (Kala-wungwa), or the Sun Forehead Clan. They shared with him stories about how his clan had come from the ancient Hopi settlement of Homol'ovi and explained that when they migrated to Songòopavi, the people gave the clan the responsibility to protect Hopi villages from outside forces.[78] Some clans also ventured to present-day California, Colorado, or New Mexico, while others, such as the Parrot Clan, traveled south, often running, deep into central Mexico. All Hopi clans experienced hardships on their migrations, but they also learned from their experiences, and they took this knowledge with them when they eventually migrated back to their Hopi ancestral lands.

Near the turn of the twentieth century, Hopi children and young adults also participated in the second wave of Hopi migration when the US government began sending them by train to federal off-reservation Indian boarding schools such as Haskell Institute in Lawrence, Kansas, the Phoenix Indian School, and Sherman Institute. Government officials created these and other schools to destroy American Indian cultures and languages and to train Native students in industrial trades. Part of the government's efforts to assimilate Native people into mainstream American society, off-reservation schools served as battlegrounds for the minds and affections of Native people. While teachers and other officials at the schools instructed Indian children and young adults in traditional academic disciplines such as history, geography, and language arts, they primarily emphasized industrial training so students could fill the labor needs of the surrounding areas, including Indian reservations. In this regard, government officials wanted Native students at Indian schools to look, behave, and think less like Indigenous people, and more like white Protestant Americans. Or as historian David Wallace Adams once observed: "The [Indian] boarding school, whether on or off the reservation, was the institutional manifestation of the government's determination to completely restructure the Indians' minds and personalities."[79]

But the US government's attempt to "restructure" the minds of Hopi people did not go unchallenged by members of the Hopi community. In September 1906, the Hopi had endured an internal division at Orayvi over the encroachment of American ways on Hopi culture, the US government's insistence that Hopi children attend Western schools, and disagreements surrounding the interpretation of Hopi prophecy.[80] Two factions emerged whom federal officials and Christian missionaries referred to as "hostiles" and "friendlies," based on their association with the federal government.[81] While all Hopis at this time valued education, many did not want the US government to impose its Western or American education on the people, especially at the expense of traditional Hopi teachings. In the months leading to September, tensions at Orayvi increased between those who saw benefits in sending their children to Indian schools, and those who refused to accept or obey US government mandates.[82] The tensions resulted in a major division at Orayvi, where nearly half the residents left the village to eventually form a new village called Ho'atvela. Known as the Orayvi Split, the event served as a turning point in Hopi history, and it reenergized the government's efforts to remove Hopi children and problematic Hopi leaders to schools far beyond the Hopi mesas.[83]

One of these leaders was Tawaquaptewa from Orayvi. Serving as chief, or Kikmongwi, of the village, during the Orayvi Split, Tawaquaptewa attempted to work with US government officials and Christian missionaries regarding the school issue. Among the so-called friendly faction, Tawaquaptewa followed in the footsteps of his predecessor Loloma and encouraged the people to send their children to school, including the Oraibi Day School and Keams Canyon boarding school. But shortly after the split, the relationship between Tawaquaptewa and US government officials crumbled when the chief "evicted" more than two hundred people belonging to the "hostile" faction from the village. In response, government officials rebuked Tawaquaptewa for his actions and accused him of violating American laws that prohibit one from evicting another person without proper notice. As tribal historian Kuwanwisiwma once observed, government officials quickly seized upon this opportunity to force Tawaquaptewa to choose between going to prison for his crime or agreeing to serve out his punishment at an Indian school. Not wanting to go to prison, Tawaquaptewa requested to be sent west by train to Sherman Institute with nearly seventy "friendly" children and young adults from Orayvi.[84] In November 1906, Tawaquaptewa and his "Hopi followers" arrived in the "land of oranges," a term Hopis used to describe the region surrounding Riverside, California, and remained at the school for nearly three years before returning home.

Tawaquaptewa's compliance with government officials and the removal of certain Hopi families from the village did not lessen tensions between the "friendlies" and "hostiles" on the reservation. Just prior to Tawaquaptewa's departure to Sherman, a group of evicted "hostiles" from Orayvi went to other villages to gain a "following" to incite a rebellion, and to recapture the "pueblo."[85] Some of the Hopis from these villages returned to Orayvi with the "hostiles" and engaged in "serious fights" with the "friendlies," but none of the conflicts resulted in deaths. When military officers at Fort Wingate heard of this plan, and of the worsening situation in Hopiland, they sent First Lieutenant John H. Lewis and "two troops of cavalry" to Orayvi to prevent "open warfare" between the groups.[86] Seeing that the "hostiles" had "besieged the pueblo," Lieutenant Lewis and his men arrested 115 of the problematic Hopis and transported them more than a hundred miles east to Fort Defiance near the Arizona and New Mexico border. "[Lieutenant Lewis] was unable to bring about peace among the factions," a reporter for the Associated Press remarked, and so the "Indians will be held at Fort Defiance until order has been restored."[87]

One of the men that Lieutenant Lewis arrested was thirty-four-year-old Louis Tewanima from the village of Songòopavi on Second Mesa,[88] who at the time was numbered among the "hostile" sympathizers at Orayvi.[89] Months before the split, government officials saw Tewanima and the other "hostiles" on Second Mesa as obstacles in their attempt to force Hopi children to attend Indian schools.[90] To them, Tewanima and the other resisting Hopis threatened efforts to civilize and subdue the people on the reservation. The Hopi from Songòopavi had also shown leadership qualities, but officials despised him and all Hopis who went against their mandates. And so, two months after the Hopi leaders arrived at Fort Defiance, government officials transported Tewanima and ten other Hopi prisoners—including Tawa Ventawa (Tawaventewa), Wallace Houma, Glenn Josytewa, and Washington Talayamptewa (Talayamtewa, Talyumptewa)—forty-six miles east to Fort Wingate. Years before, government officials had taken nineteen Hopi prisoners to the fort before sending them by rail to Alcatraz Island. Twelve years later, Hopis found themselves at the same outpost, waiting as powerful men in Washington contemplated their fate. Once there, military officials, in consultation with the Office of Indian Affairs and Carlisle school superintendent William A. Mercer, made the decision to send Tewanima and the other Hopi men by rail to Carlisle. Under

Eleven Hopi "prisoners" as they entered the Carlisle Indian Industrial School. Louis Tewanima sits in the front row, second from the left, 1907. Todd Photo Archives, 12-27-01 (DR 2-45). Photograph courtesy of the Cumberland County Historical Society.

the care and watchful eye of Lieutenant Lewis, who accompanied them on their trip, they went to the Indian school in Pennsylvania to learn English and appreciate the supposed superiority of American ways.[91]

When Tewanima and the other Hopis arrived at the school, one newspaper writer described them as "crude specimens. Long hair hung down their backs, they were garbed in discarded khaki uniforms and blue army coats, and none of them could speak a word of English." The writer also noted that Tewanina and his tribesman spoke in a "garbled language," wanted nothing to do with any of the other students," and kept to themselves during the initial weeks of their arrival. Newspaper accounts of the men reflect the paternalistic and racist belief of the day that Native people needed a Western education to redeem them from their supposed state of savagery. And some white Americans and so-called progressives and reformers believed that this transformation best occurred not at a federal prison but at an off-reservation Indian boarding school. However, while newspapers described the Hopis as uncivilized and savage-like, one official at Carlisle provided a different description of their Hopi students. The school's athletic director, Glenn "Pop" Warner, described the men as

Eleven Hopi students after attending the Carlisle Indian Industrial School for one year. Louis Tewanima stands in the back row, far left, exact date unknown. Todd Photo Archives, 12-27-02 (DR 2-46). Photograph courtesy of the Cumberland County Historical Society.

"studious," quick at learning the English language, and extremely popular with the other students. And although he noted that all of them were excellent long-distance runners, there was one among the group, Louis Tewanima, who clearly stood out from all the rest.[92]

Tewanima arrived at the Indian school as a "prisoner of war" and ambassador for his people. And he followed in the footsteps of those earlier Hopi travelers who boarded trains in Arizona for destinations on the East and West Coasts. But he also came to the school as an exceptionally talented runner. And when Lieutenant Lewis and his men arrested him at Orayvi and transported him to the army's military forts, they could not have foreseen the significance of their capture or these events. To them, Tewanima was one of several Hopis on the reservation who had caused trouble for the government. They did not realize, however, that their prisoner would use his incarceration and mandatory enrollment at Carlisle to "turn the power" and create a new reality for himself and his people in the twentieth century.[93] And they did not realize that in a relatively short period of time, Tewanima would prove to be among the top runners in the nation, representing all Americans, including those who had arrested him, in the world's most prestigious athletic event.

CHAPTER THREE

Hopi Olympian

On July 11, 1908, two days before King Edward VII officially opened the Olympic Games in London, a crowd of people gathered to watch Hopi runner Louis Tewanima practice at the Brighton Football Club running track in East Sussex. A member of the US Olympic team, Tewanima had won numerous events in North America, and his reputation as a distance runner had spread to England, where people anxiously waited to see him compete in the Olympic marathon. A reporter from the *New York Times* noted that the "long distance champion" received considerable attention from the British, who could not "understand how an apparently fragile creature" could "aspire to marathon honors." At 5 feet 4¼ inches tall and 115 pounds, Tewanima's short stature and thin physique did not match the profile of other successful runners with longer legs and torsos. News of Tewanima even attracted the attention of a British humorist who wrote that the runner had been "trained on chutney and rice." While not based on fact, the idea became popular with the British public, who consequently gave Tewanima the nickname "Chutney Rice."[1]

On the day of the race, fifty-five runners from sixteen nations gathered near the starting line at Windsor Castle, 700 yards from a statue of Queen Victoria. The marathon wound through the streets of London for 26 miles and 385 yards, ending at White City Stadium. The *Times* of London observed that the "glorious hot July afternoon, with hardly a breath of wind, [was] ideal for a bathe or a game of cricket perhaps, but terrible for a feat of endurance."[2] At 2:30 in the afternoon, officials arranged the runners into "four rows," and the Princess of Wales, Mary of Teck, began the event by signaling for a "pistol to be fired." During the first mile, Tewanima remained with the last group of runners while William Clarke of the United Kingdom and Arthur Burn of Canada set the lead pace. At the twelve-mile mark, Tewanima ran alongside Canada's George Goulding and Gustaf Törnros of Sweden.

Accompanied by a young American trainer named Neil McCarthy, who rode a bicycle beside him for the remainder of the race, the Hopi runner kept a steady pace while McCarthy urged him to hasten to the finish line.[3] Twenty miles into the marathon, the gap between Tewanima and the front-runners had increased, although some of the athletes in the lead pack showed signs of severe fatigue.[4] Heat exhaustion forced Tom Longboat of the Six Nations Reserve in Canada to quit the race as he approached mile marker twenty-one. With Longboat out, Tewanima entered the Olympic stadium to a "roar" of "cheering" to complete the marathon in ninth place.[5] Philip J. Deloria once argued that Native people have regularly "created new Indian worlds, fusing diverse cultures, or fitting themselves into the interstices between core Native tradition and new practices introduced from the American periphery." Tewanima's participation in the Olympics and other running events points to a moment in history when a select number of Hopis used running to enter national and international contexts far beyond their homelands in present-day northeastern Arizona. These events signaled a transition in Hopi society when men navigated between the "interstices" of their religious beliefs about footraces and American ideologies of sport.

Although some writers, including Norm Frauenheim, might consider this a "clash of the ancient and modern," Tewanima's story represents one runner's ability to redefine Hopi running in the twentieth century and shows how he maneuvered within American and European perceptions of Natives and sport. It tells of a time when white Americans situated Indigenous people on the fringes of US society but embraced them when they brought honors to the country by representing the nation in athletic competitions at home and abroad. Furthermore, Tewanima's involvement in marathons and Olympic races demonstrates the ways Americans used his success to advance the ideals of US nationalism as he simultaneously continued the long tradition of running among his people. But while Tewanima created a "new Indian" world of Hopi running in the early 1900s, he "did so within the constraints of American rules, regulations, expectations, and power."[6]

For more than thirty years, the literature on Indigenous runners of the Southwest has increased with contributions from various scholars.[7] However, apart from Peter Nabokov's *Indian Running*, which includes lengthy discussions on Tewanima and other Hopi runners, the majority of the literature on Tewanima is found in larger narratives on Natives and sports, most notably Joseph B. Oxendine's *American Indian Sport Heritage* and John Bloom's *To Show What an Indian Can Do*. Although popular audiences read Tewanima's story in newspaper articles, magazines, and books, these publications tended to focus on his participation in the 1912 Olympic Games in Stockholm, Sweden, and many of them perpetuate a romantic portrayal of Tewanima by retelling accounts of him running after rabbits as a young man and running to Winslow, Arizona, "just to see the trains [go by]." Contrary to one contemporary writer who noted that Tewanima was "almost totally forgotten," scholars have remained intrigued by his accomplishments, although they are often overshadowed by accounts of his Carlisle teammate, Sac and Fox athlete Jim Thorpe. While references to Tewanima grace the pages of many articles and books, further studies are needed, particularly ones that interpret his accomplishments within the contexts of Hopi and American sport culture.[8]

When Tewanima competed in the 1908 Olympics, people in American society closely associated sport with US nationalism and the notion that athletic victories established the United States as an emerging world power. American reformers such as A. G. Spalding, Price Collier, and Theodore Roosevelt believed that sports fostered national unity and a "republican civilization" and demonstrated US political and economic dominance over other nations. Furthermore, Mark Dyreson once observed that prior to World War I, Progressives believed that sports created "social reform," encouraged the sharing of "communal values" among Americans, and increased the "public good." Still other American thinkers argued that US athletes won national and international competitions because they were American, not merely as a result of their physical abilities.[9] While the concepts of American identity, democracy, and communal values dominated conversations about US sports in the early 1900s, not every athlete who competed on the Olympic team embodied these ideals.

Less than two years before the London Games, Tewanima appeared to be an unlikely candidate to represent the country. Although Hopis had reportedly received American citizenship under the Treaty of Guadalupe Hidalgo in 1848, certain rights did not apply to them or other Indigenous people.[10] As a second-class citizen, Tewanima ran for a country that considered him and his people to be wards of the US government. These wards, government officials believed, needed the civilizing influences of a Western education, especially if they were to become full American citizens. Therefore, under the direction of Jewish school superintendent Moses Friedman, who succeeded William A. Mercer in 1907, Carlisle encouraged Native students to look, behave, and think like white Protestant Americans, not as Indigenous people.[11] When Tewanima entered Carlisle, the school's established athletic program included football and track teams.[12] Athletic teams increased the visibility of Indian schools and taught athletes the Western concepts of competition and fair play. Sports historian Gerald R. Gems noted that at Carlisle, "sport instilled discipline" utilizing "teamwork, a strong work ethic, and perhaps most importantly, deference to authority in the form of a coach or game official that might ready one for a compliant workforce."[13]

One of the most significant authority figures Tewanima encountered at Carlisle was athletic director Glenn "Pop" Warner. Previously, Warner had successfully coached football and track at various colleges including the University of Georgia and Cornell. Tewanima told Warner that he could run well, and he even demonstrated his talent to the coach.[14] A report in the Des Moines Register observed that in the summer of 1907, Warner initially allowed Tewanima to run a two-mile event. But as he increased this distance over time, the Register explained, "Warner discovered Tewanima's unusual ability as a long-distance runner."[15] It did not take long for Tewanima to attract the attention of his peers on the track team with his ability to run long distances. In the Indian Helper, the Carlisle school's official newspaper, a reporter noted that Tewanima had never run in a marathon or trained in distance running before he entered Carlisle.[16] Yet he originated from a people who understood running as an integral part of their social and religious culture.

In Hopi culture, fields belong to one of several matrilineal-based clans. Hopis of the Tuwangyam, or Sand Clan, sent runners to distant lands to entice rain clouds to follow them back to the mesas. In the late 1890s, ethnologist Alexander M. Stephen recorded that when a Sand Clan chief named Si'mo ran, he did so "swiftly, that the clouds may come swiftly, that his prayers may be quickly answered."[17] Sand Clan runners had the responsibility of running far beyond Hopi ancestral lands. As a member of the Piqösngyam (Bear Strap Clan), Tewanima learned the centrality of rain in Hopi running from older male clan members.[18] They reminded him of their responsibility to run great distances for the benefit of the clan and for all Hopi people. And similar to Jemez Pueblo runner Steve Gachupin of New Mexico, who won six consecutive Pikes Peak Marathons in Colorado during the 1960s and early 1970s, Tewanima ran to "honor" his village and to continue its long tradition of distance running.[19]

While Tewanima used running to bring honor to his people, government officials believed that his participation in the Olympics also brought honors to the nation. Shortly after the Olympic team, including Tuscarora athlete Frank Mount Pleasant, returned to the United States from London, President Theodore Roosevelt hosted a special reception for them at his home in Sagamore Hill, on the shore of Oyster Bay, New York.[20] As members of the team approached Roosevelt's residence, Olympic Committee secretary James E. Sullivan assembled the athletes into two lines, and Tewanima and his teammates marched in formation while whistling the song "A Hot Time in the Old Town." When the athletes reached the front porch, Roosevelt stood by the door to congratulate each person and shake his hand. As Tewanima greeted the president, Roosevelt told him that he was extremely "glad" that a "real original American Indian competed for America and represented the country abroad."[21]

In contrast to Tewanima's white teammates, whose families had immigrated to the United States, his people were among the first caretakers of North America. For Roosevelt, Tewanima looked like an American Indian; he still spoke fluent Hopi, and had only recently been fully exposed to the civilizing influences of American society. And for Roosevelt, Tewanima gave hope to all Americans that even a "savage" and "hostile" Indian, a "prisoner of war," could be changed for the good if introduced to a Western education and American sport. Although Tewanima did not win a medal in the marathon, his participation in the Olympics symbolically demonstrated to the nation the possibility of a new role for Native people in American society. No longer resisting the US government on the reservation, Tewanima now represented the United States, and few things could have been more "American" than an "original" American who brought honors to his country.

Tewanima earned the privilege to emblematize the nation, his school, and his people by outrunning top competitors at national and international events. One such event was a ten-mile race that took place at the Pastime Athletic Club's games in New York City's Madison Square Garden on January 25, 1909. Some of the best distance runners in the nation participated, including James J. Lee, George J. Obermeyer, and Tewanima's 1908 Olympic teammate Mike Ryan. During the first five miles, Lee had a commanding lead over the forty-five other runners. As Tewanima gradually shortened the distance between him and Lee, Coach Warner instructed him from the sidelines, pointing Lee out to Tewanima as the person to catch.[22] Using a common race strategy among runners, Tewanima held back from making any push for the lead until the seven-mile mark. At this point, Coach Warner yelled out to him, saying, "He's gaining! Come on you, Lewis."[23] Eight miles into the race, Lee tried to "get up on even terms with the flying little Indian" but was unable to stay with Tewanima for more than a "half lap." At mile marker nine, the Hopi runner continued to hold the lead position, with Lee following shortly behind. A *New York Times* reporter noted, "When the warning at the beginning of the last half mile was given[,] Tewanima started a sprint that completely finished Lee, the Indian winning in commanding style in 54:27⁴/₅."[24] One newspaper writer remarked that when the Hopi runner snuck passed Lee, a "roar went up" among the four thousand spectators, and the "Indian responded" by making a dash to the end.[25]

A month after his victory in New York City, Tewanima won the Young Men's Gymnastic Club twenty-mile marathon in New Orleans with a time of 2 hours, 10 minutes, 53 seconds. At the Indian school in Phoenix, officials included the news of Tewanima's New Orleans victory in the weekly school newspaper, the *Native American*, and proudly noted that Tewanima had shown his "heels to the fastest distance runners in the country."[26] Off-reservation Indian boarding schools regularly included news about the accomplishments of Native athletes in their newspapers. Superintendents wanted students to look to Tewanima and other successful Native athletes as role models. Their accomplishments in American sports demonstrated the positive outcomes that one might expect from hard work and perseverance. Shortly after the division at Orayvi in 1906, government officials sent children from the so-called hostile Hopi families to the Phoenix Indian School. Many of these students knew about Tewanima and kept track of his running progress in the school's newspaper. At times, school officials at Carlisle even informed Hopi students personally about the runner's successes. For example, in September 1908, not long after Tewanima returned from the London Olympics, Superintendent Friedman enthusiastically shared news of his accomplishments with other Hopis at the school. "I suppose you know," wrote Friedman to Washington Talayamptewa, who was away from school on an outing, "that Lewis Tewani went across the Atlantic Ocean to England this sum-

"It's No Wonder Tewanina Can Run," Globe and Commercial Advertiser (New York City), March 13, 1909, in "Tewanima, Louis," file 3766, box 79, Carlisle School Files, Records of the Carlisle Indian Industrial School, Carlisle, PA, Records of the Bureau of Indian Affairs, 1793–1989, Record Group 75, National Archives and Records Administration, Washington, DC.

mer" and "made a great name for himself as a runner and you boys have reason to be very proud of him."[27]

Although Talayamptewa, who also earned a reputation as an accomplished runner while at Carlisle, and the other Hopi students understood that Tewanima's desire and ability to run stemmed from his culture, sports writers of the day provided readers with their own reasons why he won so many events. In an article titled "It's No Wonder Tewanina Can Run," an illustrator for the Globe and Commercial Advertiser depicted a Hopi man running away from a Spanish vaquero on horseback shooting bullets at him. The caption reads, "They always had plenty of training." A second illustration describes a more commonly held explanation. In the late nineteenth and early twentieth centuries, reporters frequently wrote about how Hopis traveled up and down their mesas, oftentimes to care for their fields. In this illustration, a Hopi father stands high on a mesa edge with a tomahawk raised in the air. He yells to his son who is running down the mesa, "If you don't hurry to the store an' get that bread I'll bounce this hammer off your bean."[28]

A third illustration connects Tewanima's success to Hopi religious culture, particularly the Hopi Snake Dance. At this time, the ceremonies associated with the dance fascinated newspaper reporters and many white Americans. The dance attracted tourists from across the nation, including former president Theodore Roosevelt, who traveled to the village of Walpi on First Mesa in August 1913 to witness the religious ceremony.[29] Part of the ceremony involved a messenger runner who took prayer feathers to shrines beyond the mesas. Building upon this American fascination with the Hopi ceremonies, a newspaper illustrator depicted a warrior-like runner departing a village with a snake in his hand. As the snake cries out for its mother, one of the snakes back at the village exclaims, "Save Me Child!"

The illustrations provide a telling commentary on colonial explanations for Tewanima's success. The newspaper portrayed the Hopi as a peaceful and cowardly people who never cared to fight. According to the illustrator, the Hopis preferred to run away when pursued by forces of colonialism, which provided them with practice in running and the endurance needed to win American marathons. Moreover, the bizarre depiction of Hopi religious culture, contrasted with the picture of Tewanima standing in modern running attire, speaks to the transforming powers of sport and the triumph of Western civilization over Indigenous cultures. In his examination of Māori masculinity and sport, Ngāti Pūkenga scholar Brendan Hokowhitu once observed that "Māori sportsmen, in particular, were the greatest trophies of colonization because they signified assimilation and the success of British imperialism."[30] Similarly, Americans considered Tewanima to be their trophy of colonization. His accomplishments in US marathons reflected the presumed "success" of American democracy, which allowed him to be a civilized, and therefore colonized, member of US society.

In spite of what the newspapers printed, Tewanima's ability to compete in American races could more accurately be traced to his way of life. One of his most remarkable races took place in September 1910, when he won the "George W. Bogar seven-mile handicap Marathon" in Harrisburg, Pennsylvania. Defeating fifteen of the top runners in the state, Tewanima won in front of ten thousand people and completed the course in 38 minutes and 10 and ⅖ seconds. But just two months later, when he attempted to defend the "10-Mile Champion" title that he earned by winning the Pastime Athletic Club race in January 1909, Tewanima came in third place to Win Bailey and George Obermeyer of the National Athletic Club in the ten-mile Amateur Athletic Union championship at Celtic Park in New York.

Undeterred by his loss, Tewanima responded by entering and winning additional races throughout the Northeast, including the New York Modified Marathon of twelve miles on May 6, 1911. He defeated nearly one thousand runners and won in 1 hour, 9 minutes, 16 seconds. On November 30 of the same year, Tewanima outdistanced twenty-two runners to win his third consecutive Thanksgiving Day Berwick Marathon in Pennsylvania of 9 miles, 386 yards. One *Washington Star* reporter noted, "The Indian may be fading from the map—he may have reached the sunset of existence as a nation—but as a member of the sportive colony his rank was Number One in 1911 at almost every start. Tewanima, an Indian, won the [*New York Evening*] Mail's [sic] big marathon and proved himself to be the best long-distance runner in America."[31]

In the early 1910s, many white Americans considered Tewanima and other Native Americans to be part of a vanishing race who belonged to the fringes of society. At this time, Native people struggled to retain portions of their ancestral lands and confronted the imposition of US government policies on their Indigenous cultures. On the Hopi Reservation, government officials separated children from their parents and village communities at Indian boarding schools. While the situation for Indigenous people was grim, in the sporting scene, select Native runners—including Tom Longboat, Penobscot runner Andrew Sockalexis, and Tewanima—availed themselves of opportunities that did not exist in their reservation communities. Furthermore, Tewanima brought attention to the Hopi people, and he encouraged non-Hopis to understand and judge him on his ability to run, not on the racist "ideologies" emphasized in American and European newspapers.[32]

Within a few months after the Berwick Marathon, the symbiotic relationship Americans saw between sport and US nationalism had increased, especially as the country's athletes prepared for the 1912 Olympic Games in Stockholm. Since the United States dominated several events at the 1904 and 1908 Games, Americans believed that the nation would secure additional honors in Stockholm, but not without fierce competition from athletes in England, France, Finland, and Canada. "The victories of American athletes in past Olympic games," wrote a reporter for the *Morning Oregonian*, "have been so consistent that every other competing country is making special arrangements to break the chain of triumphs." To further the country's Olympic "supremacy" and to "maintain" its high standing, the American Olympic Committee (AOC) held regional tryouts at Marshall Field in Chicago, Stanford University in California, and Harvard University in Massachusetts to select the majority of the athletes to represent and defend America's honor abroad.[33]

Tewanima's remarkable achievements in US marathons made him a strong candidate to compete in the 1912 Olympics. At Carlisle, students watched with much interest as Tewanima intensified his training. In his examination of Jim Thorpe, Jack Newcombe noted that "Warner had Tewanima pounding methodically around the board track" and made him run "long stretches" on "Carlisle walks and roads." Although Talayamptewa was also training for the Olympic team as a miler, Carlisle students looked primarily to Thorpe and Tewanima with great confidence that both athletes would win medals in Stockholm. One reporter wrote, "Probably none of the Americans will go abroad more fully equipped than the little Hopi redskin." Even high-ranking members of the AOC such as James E. Sullivan, who boasted that the "great Indian" Tewanima would "win the Marathon," held this sentiment.[34]

Prior to the Boston Marathon in April 1912, an event that determined the final US distance runners for the Olympics, newspapers published a partial list of athletes who had already qualified for the team, including Clarence DeMar, Mike Ryan, Sockalexis, and Tewanima.[35] On June 14, 1912, Tewanima and a group of 150 US athletes set sail from New York City on the Red Star Line steamship *Finland*. Before the team's departure, the AOC had the ship transformed into a "veritable floating gymnasium," including a 100-yard cork track on the "upper deck" for the sprinters and distance runners, so that the athletes could train en route to Stockholm.[36] Although US running victories qualified Tewanima to be on the team, his past accomplishments did not guarantee him an opportunity to compete for a medal. To determine the finalist for the 10,000-meter event, officials hosted three qualifying heats on the day before the race. The top five runners in each heat earned a spot in the final. In the second qualifying heat, Tewanima finished in second place behind Leonard Richardson of South Africa.[37]

On July 8, 1912, Tewanima took his place alongside ten other runners in the Stockholm Olympic Stadium in front of thousands of spectators. When the race began, people "showered" Tewanima with "cheers as he glided around the track." But by the second lap, Hannes Kolehmainen of Finland secured the lead and never gave up this position for the duration of the race. By lap six, Kolehmainen pulled a complete lap ahead of Tewanima and defeated him by 20 seconds with a time of 31 minutes, 20.8 seconds.[38] Tewanima came in second place, "300 yards behind Kolehmainen," to win the silver medal, and Albin Stenroos of Finland won bronze. Reflecting on the 1912 Games, Sullivan noted that Tewanima "gave a remarkable exhibition of grit and persistency" and that with "Kolehmainen out of the way, he was superior to all other long distance runners."[39]

When news of the Indian athletes reached the United States, citizens of Carlisle sprang into action to raise money for a city-wide celebration. A day before the Olympics officially ended, residents of Carlisle had already raised $552.50, and a city newspaper urged people, including owners of local businesses, to contribute even more.[40] While residents did their part to prepare for the homecoming, the Carlisle Town Council called a special meeting to approve $50 for the grand homecoming, make arrangements for the celebration parade, and pass a series of resolutions, which read in part: "Whereas, By their achievements Thorpe, Tewanima and Warner have not only acquired great personal renown, but have added to the splendid reputation of the great school in which they are being trained and educated, as well as spread abroad the fame of the town of Carlisle . . ." (Appendix C). Nowhere in the resolutions did the Town Council mention how the Indian athletes brought honors to the nation. Instead, the council emphasized how they represented the school and the honors they brought to the town by taking its name to a world stage. Furthermore, the resolutions did not only focus on Tewanima's and Thorpe's accomplishments, but rightfully credited Coach Warner for providing the Indian athletes with "wisdom and counsel" and the training needed for them to compete at the highest levels.[41]

Tewanima's and Thorpe's achievements in the 1912 Olympics also unleashed a flurry of excitement among the students, teachers, and officials at Carlisle. With the headline "Carlisle Honors Her Olympic Victors on the Return from Stockholm," the Carlisle Arrow noted that Tewanima, Thorpe, and Coach Warner arrived in the city by train at 12:30 p.m. on August 16, 1912. Shortly thereafter, officials drove the men by carriage to the Cumberland Valley Station, "where a committee of prominent citizens received them and congratulated them on their great achievements." Later that day, seven thousand people gathered on the Herman Bosler Biddle Athletic Field, on the campus of Dickinson College, to participate in a celebratory ceremony. Superintendent Friedman delivered the second speech. He began by noting that "all America" was "proud" of the two runners' achievements in Stockholm.[42]

Friedman referred to the men as "real Americans" whose "forefathers were on the reception committee which welcomed" to this "glorious New World the famed first settlers who arrived here on the Mayflower." Friedman said that Tewanima had come to Carlisle as a "prisoner of war." He talked at length on how he and the other Hopis on the reservation had given the US government "much trouble" and had opposed "progress" and "education." He referred to them as "pagans" who had disregarded "American civilization" prior to their enrollment at the school.[43] At no point in Friedman's public remarks did he praise the runner for his athletic achievements or inform his audience that Tewanima had come from a people of great runners. Not wanting to showcase Tewanima's culture, Friedman attempted to demonstrate how the civilizing influences of Carlisle had created Olympic athletes, which in turn brought recognition and honor to the school.

While the Indian school at Carlisle celebrated Tewanima's silver medal, other Americans voiced their disappointment in his performance. Since he had dominated middle-distance events in the United States prior to the 1912 Olympics, many Americans assumed that he would defeat the competition, including the "little Finn phenom" Kolehmainen. A writer for the *Washington Post* noted that Tewanima's loss was a "slap" at American pride. The writer argued that the "first wallop . . . came when the cable brought" the people of the United States the "news that a diminutive little Finlander . . . had trimmed Tewanima, [Louis] Scott and [William] Kramer" in the 10,000-meter race. Although Tewanima established an American record in the event that stood until Oglala Lakota runner Billy Mills won the same event at the 1964 Olympic Games in Tokyo, his rank as a world-class runner had diminished. Even Mike Murphy, the US Olympic coach for the 1908 Olympics, once claimed that Tewanima was one of the best runners in the world, but he could not deny the significance of Kolehmainen's Olympic victories. This "Finn," Murphy remarked, "is the greatest runner I have ever seen, and greater than I ever expected to see."[44]

While newspapers in the United States lamented Tewanima's loss, sports writers abroad reflected on the United Kingdom's overall poor performance and provided reasons why Americans excelled in Stockholm. "The great factors in the success of the United States athletics," British sport authority Charles Otway of the *London Sporting Life* observed, "as in nearly every other thing our American cousins have taken up, is their capacity for organization, their gift of spreading enthusiasm."[45] Noting that in the United States, organized sport began in the elementary schools and continued in the "high schools, preparatory schools, colleges, and universities," Otway argued that competition generated and encouraged within school athletics was the "secret of it all." "Then American schoolboys performances are better," Otway concluded, "mainly because of increased competition. . . . School races against school; college against college, and in every district there are interscholastic and intercollegiate championships." For athletes at Carlisle, however, who on occasion competed against other off-reservation Indian boarding schools, they also more often played colleges and universities known for their excellent athletic programs. And Indian runners such as Tewanima, who raced against their peers at Carlisle and elsewhere, also regularly competed against top runners in various city, regional, and national cross-country meets.

A month after the Olympic Games, Tewanima prepared to leave for his home in Arizona. In September 1912, one newspaper columnist noted that he planned to "give up athletics for good" to farm and "settle down to domestic life." Shortly before he migrated back to the reservation, he took several of his running medals and gave them as parting gifts to his peers at the school, including girls who used them to fashion "buckles on their shoes." Tewanima had no use for his running medals and trophies on the reservation.[46] Even early in his running career at Carlisle, he placed little emphasis or importance on his awards. For example, immediately after he won the race in Madison Square Garden, he forgot to pick up his trophy, a "three-foot Mercury on a handsome base." As he sat on the floor of his dressing room, race officials handed the Hopi runner his award, but Tewanima gestured to Warner that he had no use for it.[47]

Philip J. Deloria once observed that while sports involved various layers of meaning for Native athletes, "it was not the stuff of life and death." Tewanima and other Hopi runners seldom ran in any marathons after their terms at Indian boarding schools expired.[48] The schools and various athletic clubs had provided Hopis with opportunities to run in city, regional, and international running events beyond the mesas. When Tewanima ran for Carlisle, the school paid his entry fees, transportation costs, and a host of other related expenses. Once runners returned to their homelands, their formal association with their schools ended. Although Tewanima had reached celebrity status beyond his village, he knew that many runners back home had the ability to outrun him and other Hopis who competed at Indian boarding schools. Newspaper reporters had often remarked that the runner from Songòopavi was the best runner in the nation. But it is doubtful that Tewanima agreed with these flattering statements.

Not long after Tewanima returned home from the Olympics, Friedman wrote to him and inquired how he and the other returned students were "getting along." "I want to get some news from you," he wrote. "I am writing to ask you if you will not take the time and write me a long letter, giving me the names and addresses of the various boys and their occupations, and any other information which you have concerning them." In his letter, which was similar to letters he sent to other returned students, Friedman did not mention Tewanima's past running achievements or how he had brought prestige to the school. Instead, he focused on determining whether Tewanima and the other former "savages" and "sun worshippers" had applied their skills and so-called civilization on the reservation. An unpopular superintendent among students at Carlisle, Friedman wanted information about their current status and told Tewanima that if he did not know the answers to his questions, that he should ask his "friends" on the reservation.[49] Although Friedman never fully attributed Tewanima's running success to the centrality of running in Hopi society, Tewanima's desire to join Carlisle's track team and his participation in marathons was deeply rooted in who he was as a Hopi runner for the Bear Strap Clan.

When Tewanima returned home, he quickly settled back to life on the mesas. He had left for Carlisle a farmer and sheep herder, and upon arriving back at his village, he returned to these occupations and Hopi lifestyle. Apart from running against other Hopis on the mesas, Tewanima only left the reservation once to compete in a footrace after he returned home from Carlisle. In the late 1960s, LeRoy Berman of the *Albuquerque Journal* remarked that in 1924, Tewanima won "his last race" in Gallup, New Mexico.[50] While in his early fifties, the Hopi runner likely competed in a race that was part of the Inter-Tribal Indian Ceremonial, an annual event in Gallup that attracted many Indian people from across the nation. Held over a three-day period beginning September 10, the events surrounding the ceremonial highlighted Indian crafts, culture, and "competitive games and sports."[51] Had Tewanima indeed competed in a race during the ceremonial, he would have done so against a group of talented Indian runners, all of whom probably had aspirations to outrun the former Olympic medal winner.

Forty-two years after winning the silver medal in Stockholm, Tewanima had one last opportunity to travel to lands far beyond his village of Songòopavi and to revisit an American city he first experienced in his younger days.[52] In October 1954, the Helms Athletic Foundation out of Los Angeles invited Tewanima to New York City to honor and recognize him on the foundation's "all-time U.S. track and field team." The last time that he made a trip to the East Coast, he did so by train, but over the years the way people traveled long distances had changed. Accompanied by a newscaster named Bill Close of KOOL-TV in Phoenix, Tewanima departed the state capital in an airplane for New York. Having never before traveled by air, the Hopi runner seemed to enjoy his flight immensely. Edwin McDowell of the *Arizona Republic* noted that while Close was suffering from "prolonged air sickness," Tewanima "was sitting back contently smoking a large cigar."[53] Not long after he arrived at the airport, a newspaper reporter asked him how he felt about "this new honor" bestowed upon him by the foundation. "I feel very good," Tewanima responded, "It makes me happy to know that people remember me. I am humbly proud to know that I can bring honor to the Hopi people."[54]

Years before, the Hopi runner had made a name for himself in New York by winning the ten-mile race at Madison Square Garden. Now in his eighties, Tewanima had returned an aged man, anxious to greet old friends and see how the city had changed. Newspaper writer Ray Silvius recalled that "one of the first persons to greet Tewanima" in New York was Simon P. Gillis, a champion hammer thrower who competed on the 1908 and 1912 US Olympic teams.[55] They easily "recognized each other," and after greeting his friend Tewanima smiled and said: "I am so glad to see him. It has been such a long time."[56] In addition to visiting with past teammates, the Hopi runner had a chance to once again experience the sights and sounds of the city. Wearing clothes of traditional Hopi style, including a white shirt, dark velvet jacket, a headband, and silver and turquoise jewelry, Tewanima toured New York with Close and attracted attention wherever he went.[57] They "walked to the top of the Statue of Liberty" and "surveyed the Manhattan skyline from atop the Empire State Building." Close re-called that when Tewanima looked out over the City, the old Hopi run-ner jokingly remarked: "Not enough land for sheep."[58] At the turn of the century, Hopi children attending day schools had learned about American society. They received lessons on the nation's famous landmarks and me-morials and listened to stories about buildings so tall that they appeared to touch the sky. Few of these children would actually ever witness the New York skyline. But Tewanima did. His remarkable ability to run long distances gave him opportunities that simply did not exist for the vast ma-jority of people on the mesas.

While in New York, Tewanima had a captive audience of reporters and other admirers who followed him and asked him many questions. Hal Boyle of the Associated Press noted that when Tewanima was asked about the significance of running in Hopi culture, the old man responded by saying: "It is part of our religion. The body is our temple, and we must keep it well." When a reporter asked him about the "recipe for living long and staying healthy," Tewanima answered and said: "Eat good . . . keep sheep . . . keep garden . . . " Although reporters gathered quotes and other anecdotes to share with their audiences, Tewanima also had a message for the American people. Prior to his trip, Hopis back home ap-pointed Tewanima as their representative, and they provided him with a community message to deliver while in New York. It read: "We shall not be ashamed of ourselves as being who we are, but to stand firm on our own foundation, to walk along together as brothers and sisters, holding fast to our identity to receive grand and glory at the end."[59] Tewanima had come from a proud people, a rich culture, and a community who sought to look beyond past injustices to ensure a better future for all humanity. Following Tewanima's comments, a newspaper reporter remarked that "Tewanima's people would have been proud to see this man of humble worldly means showing the assemblage in the Waldorf he was truly an all-time Olympic great."[60]

When the foundation recognized Tewanima by placing him on their "all-time U.S. track and field team," other organizations soon bestowed similar honors on him.[61] In 1957, three years after Tewanima returned from New York City, the Arizona Sports Hall of Fame inducted Tew-anima as its first member at the Phoenix Press-Box Association ban-quet. Honored alongside baseball player and Athlete of the Year Don Lee, Coach of the Year Dan Devine, and Professional of the Year Jimmy

Piftukas, or Imitator Clowns, by *Marshall Lomakema (of Songòopavi), watercolor, 11 × 14.5 in., created before 1966, reprinted in Byron S. Harvey III, Ritual in Pueblo Art: Hopi Life in Hopi Painting (New York: Museum of the American Indian, 1970), 49–50, figure 115. Image courtesy of the National Museum of the American Indian.*

Bryan, Tewanima addressed the crowd of more than eight hundred people with gratitude and a brief story from his youth. He told his audience that when he was younger, he "occasionally ran to Winslow, a 120-mile round-trip, just to watch the trains go by," and often ran down rabbits for the "fun of it."[62] This was not the only time, however, that Tewanima publicly talked about running down an animal. While in New York, the Hopi runner also told people that when he was young, he could easily run down a rabbit "in a few minutes," an antelope in a "half day," and it took no time at all for him to "catch" a horse, an animal that quickly tires.[63]

Tewanima's description is similar to the running practices of other Native people. In the early 1900s, a Nez Percé Indian named Caleb Carter recalled that prior to the Nez Percé War in the 1870s, a seventy-year-old member of their community named Lawyer ran after a black bear for over sixty miles. "He might have succeeded in catching" the bear, Carter remarked, "but it grew too dark for the chase, so he calmly trotted back home."[64] Furthermore, at this time, American newspapers routinely published stories of Indians running down animals for sport or for hunting purposes. Such stories intrigued and entertained readers and contributed to their exotic understandings of Indians. Describing in great detail how Apache runners pursue a deer on foot, a writer for the *Los Angeles Herald* remarked: "If a deer is young, an Apache hunter will run it down within a distance of sixty miles, but they have been known to prolong a chase for one hundred miles."[65] And some newspapers reported on Indian youth who took these cultural practices with them to off-reservation Indian boarding schools such as Haskell Institute in Kansas. "The small Indian boys out at Haskell," the *Ottawa Daily Republic* observed, "are having great sport these days in chasing rabbits and capturing game for delicacies at meal time."[66]

Hopis on the reservation did not need the Olympics or American-sponsored marathons to affirm their identities as long-distance runners. While Friedman failed to acknowledge Tewanima's culture, Hopi people never forgot the Hopi runner's accomplishments and demonstrated their respect and honor to him in his old age. This was evidenced, possibly during the early 1960s, when Hopi clowns at Songòopavi performed a skit that highlighted his achievements. In the skit, which Tewanima attended, one of the clowns dressed up as a Carlisle cross-country coach, with "CC" written on his shirt. Another clown represented a cross-country runner from Carlisle, and a third clown remained in typical Hopi clown attire. Confident that he could beat the Olympian, the younger runner challenged Tewanima to a footrace and invited him onstage. As Tewanima took his place alongside the clown who represented the runner from Carlisle, people laughed and hollered as the skit played out in the village square. After Tewanima "won," the clowns showed their respect to the elder Hopi by asking him to display his running trophies for everyone to see. While anthropologist and art collector Byron S. Harvey III once argued that the skit showed the "high values which the Hopi place upon racing and physical fitness," it also demonstrates the continuity of Hopi running and the people's belief that each clan possesses great runners.[67] When Tewanima returned to the Hopi Reservation as a celebrated Olympic runner, the village elders reminded him of those beliefs. But when Tewanima was an old man, the people used him and his many running victories to teach a younger generation of Hopi runners, especially those who competed at

Indian boarding schools, that they came from a long tradition of great runners.

In the years that followed the skit at Songòopavi, the old Hopi runner spent the remaining months of his life on the reservation. He watched over his sheep, gardened, cared for his peach trees, and remained deeply committed to his religious responsibilities as an elder in the Hopi Antelope Society. On the evening of January 18, 1969, Tewanima participated in one of the society's ceremonies in a kiva at Songòopavi. When he finished for the night, he left the kiva by himself and began walking back to his house. At some point, Tewanima looked out over the mesa and mistook a light coming from another village, perhaps Supawlavi, to be one from his own village. He walked toward the light until he reached the mesa edge and then fell seventy feet to his death. Concerned for his well-being, his family and other village members searched for him and found his body the next morning. That same day, the people buried him according to Hopi custom.[68] While the Associated Press spread news of Tewanima's death across the nation, the incident proved especially sad for those in his community and home state. "The Arizona Senate yesterday stood for a moment of silent tribune," a reporter for the *Arizona Republic* remarked, "after passing a legislation regretting the death of Louis Tewanima, first person named to the Arizona Sports Hall of Fame."[69]

While government officials had sent Tewanima by train to Carlisle as a "prisoner of war," he came to the Indian school as an ambassador for his people.[70] Contrary to a reporter who portrayed a romantic image of Tewanima "roaming the forests" of his homeland before coming to school, he arrived at Carlisle as a Hopi runner for the Bear Strap Clan, and he continued the tradition of running far beyond Hopi ancestral lands. Sport historian John Bloom once noted that while a "tradition like running" at an Indian school "might be seen as a debasement" that fragmented a "cultural form from the contexts in which it was originally meaningful," it also provided Indigenous athletes with a "resource from the past" that gave them a lens to comprehend their "present circumstances."[71] Tewanima used this opportunity to create a privileged experience for himself at the Indian school. His success in marathons and other events gave him notoriety that extended well beyond his school community, and his involvement in national and international marathons expanded his understanding of the world in the early twentieth century. Similar to the practices of Hopi Sand Clan runners who brought blessings to their vil-

Runners at the start of the Thirty-Seventh Annual Louis Tewanima Footrace on Second Mesa, Songòopavi, Arizona, 2010. Photograph by author.

lages in the form of rain, Tewanima brought honors to his community and provided the people with a running legacy that continues today.

Five years after Tewanima's death, the Hopi Athletic Association and members of his family began hosting the annual Louis Tewanima Footrace of 6.2 miles at the village of Kiiqòtsmovi (Kykotsmovi) to honor him as a great long-distance runner.[72] The race, now starting at Songòopavi, attracts runners from around the world and testifies to the importance of running in Hopi society and the understanding that runners are best honored when their village hosts a race. But the race does more than honor Louis Tewanima. It celebrates the continuity of running and reemphasizes the cultural reasons for running in Hopi society. While Tewanima spent his marathon career competing in events far beyond his ancestral lands, the annual footrace calls Hopis to return to the running trails of their people. It reminds Hopi runners, particularly those who aspire to marathon honors off the reservation, of their responsibility to their villages, and it demonstrates the ways Hopis used Tewanima's accomplishments to affirm old Hopi running practices and introduce new ones in the twentieth century.

Although the annual race at Songòopavi focuses on the life and running accomplishments of Tewanima, he was not the only Hopi worth remembering who excelled in American races in the early 1900s. At the same time that Tewanima made a name for himself at Carlisle and on the eastern seaboard, other lesser-known Hopis ran for Indian schools out West. They also arrived at these schools as representatives of their people and used skills first developed back home to excel in distance running. While government officials and sport writers often saw Tewanima as a representative of the nation, officials at the Phoenix Indian School in Arizona, for example, wanted Hopis and other Indian runners to represent the school and to showcase the school's city or region as places of business, leisure, and athletics. And while American fascination with Indian runners increased prior to 1909, newspapers focused much of their coverage on individuals and events in the East. However, as more Indian schools developed track and cross-country programs in places such as Arizona, Colorado, and California, other Hopis emerged on the American running scene out West and continued the long tradition of tribal racing among their people.

CHAPTER FOUR

A Tribe of Racers

On a hot summer day in July 1909, a young Hopi runner named Harry McLean left the Phoenix Indian School in Arizona and traveled west to Southern California.[1] He departed with his trainer, John E. Lewis, and two other Indian runners, Manuel Parsisk and Chaff Ponsol, to compete in the Pacific Athletic Association Marathon in Los Angeles.[2] Sponsored by the Benevolent and Protective Order of Elks, the marathon of eighteen miles[3] attracted amateurs and the "cream of the athletic-world," including G. B. Haggart, Otto Boeddiker, and William Garvin.[4] While most of the top runners ran for various American athletic clubs, including the Olympic Club, Swedish-American Athletic Club, and the Los Angeles Athletic Club, McLean and his teammates ran for their off-reservation Indian boarding school. Competing for a "handsome loving cup, and six gold, silver and bronze medals," the Indian runners had trained for this event on the streets and dirt paths of Phoenix and in the blazing heat of the Arizona desert. When asked by a reporter for the *Arizona Republican* about the race, track coach Lewis confidently predicted that McLean would "take the marathon, and finish in better condition than many of the runners [would] be in at the end of the third mile."[5] Lewis also remarked that he had never "seen a runner in better condition than Harry McLean," and that if he did not "make the whole west sit up straight and take notice" of him, it is "because something is the matter the last minute." "He has been making time that is remarkable," Coach Lewis concluded.[6]

Prior to the marathon in Los Angeles, McLean attracted the attention of newspaper reporters in Arizona, who kept their readers informed about the Hopi runner and his preparation for the upcoming event. One writer for the *Arizona Republican* remarked that in the previous month, McLean ran a mile in six minutes and fourteen seconds. And later that night he completed a ten-mile race in fifty-five minutes. "This is remarkable work," wrote the reporter, especially when one takes into "consideration that he had nothing to pace him or to keep up his enthusiasm."[7] Ten days after his back-to-back races, the same newspaper offered additional observations on the runners from the Phoenix Indian School, including the young Hopi runner. "McLean is in the pink of condition,"[8] wrote a reporter for the *Arizona Republican*, "his body a network of muscles trained to the minute and devoid of nerves." At this time, most newspapers focused on Hopi runners and their "short stature" or small physique, and they compared the runners to much taller white runners with "longer legs and torsos." But here, McLean's height held little to no significance on how he performed as a runner. Instead, the writer centered his commentary on the Hopi runner's muscles and nerves and other internal parts, and he attempted to give the readers less obvious reasons why McLean did so well in long-distance competitions. "Someone called him the Indian without lungs," the reporter noted, "and it almost seems so, for after tearing off five, ten or [thirty] miles at a 6 minute and 25 second clip he returned to his quarters, not even panting."[9]

While McLean's success required his muscles, nerves, and lungs to operate at efficient and optimal levels, it also depended on his ability to read and control his body. McLean's uncles and elders back home taught him how to maintain his pace to go the distance. And when he arrived at the Phoenix Indian School, McLean received further instruction in this from the school's cross-country coach, John E. Lewis.[10] Prior to the race in Los Angeles, a reporter for the *Arizona Republican* remarked that "Trainer Lewis will not allow his Marathon runner to go the limit, or reach his reserve force, but is holding him back for the event." Lewis knew the limits of McLean's running. He knew the impulse of young runners to exert too much energy too quickly, and he realized that running a smart race was just as important as running a fast one. But Lewis did not want his Hopi runner to only pay attention to his body, he wanted him to be in control of it. "Harry McLean," the writer for the *Arizona Republican* went on to say, "is not only in complete control of his respiratory apparatus at the end of his 13 miles, but can carry on a spirited conversation while reeling off a clip of 6 min. and 24 seconds." Looking ahead to the upcoming race in California, the reporter further remarked that "when the other coast Marathon runners catch the pace set by McLean they will be up against the hardest proposition that has ever been shown on the Los Angeles athletic field. They will realize that there is considerable difference between collegiate running and the kind that the native American turns out."[11]

Before attending the Indian school in Phoenix, McLean and his teammates spent most of their lives in the deserts of Arizona.[12] In summer 1909, however, Hopis such as McLean attended Indian schools on both coasts, and many other places in between. At this time, US government officials sent Hopi students to the Carlisle Indian School in Pennsylvania, the Chilocco School in Oklahoma, and the Albuquerque Indian School in New Mexico. While attending these and other schools, Hopi boys and young men joined track and cross-country teams. However, such opportunities did not exist for Hopis who stayed home. Most Hopi runners who remained on the reservation could not afford the costs associated with training, transportation, or race entrance fees. In this regard, McLean and other Hopi runners who competed at off-reservation Indian boarding schools represented a small and privileged group of young Hopi athletes in the early twentieth century. Schools and city athletic clubs backed them financially to outfit them with athletic uniforms and shoes and a host of other related expenses.[13] Even Coach Lewis routinely sacrificed his own money to send Hopi and other Indian runners from the Phoenix school to compete in Los Angeles or elsewhere. Lewis realized that much was at stake when his Indian runners ran in American marathons, and he knew that regardless of how they performed in California, they needed to take ownership of it. "We have everything to gain, and nothing to lose," Lewis exclaimed just prior to the Los Angeles race, "and what we bring back will be ours, and ours alone and we won't be ashamed of it either, whether it is stiff muscles, or the loving cup and medals."[14]

What Coach Lewis and his team brought back to Phoenix was a major victory when McLean outpaced his competition on the streets of Los Angeles. Throughout the entire marathon, McLean "ran at a clip of" 6 minutes and 45 seconds, a pace that proved too fast for the other runners. When the Hopi runner entered the Ascot Park grandstand, ten thousand people cheered as he crossed the finish line in 2 hours and 4 minutes, two miles ahead of second-place competitor Otto Boeddiker. The *Arizona Republican* noted that upon crossing the finishing line, McLean was "Panting, dripping with perspiration, yet smiling in his own Indian way." The writer noted that the "Phoenix Redskin, tore by the Ascot grand stand . . . two miles ahead of his closest rival mid roaring, yelling mass of ten thousand Elks and members of the Los Angeles Athletic Club."[15] After noting McLean's quick and consistent pace, the writer went on to remark that "Such advanced training of a Marathon runner without even a pacer, has never been known in the west and only in the east, where an indoor track of about eight laps to the mile is accessible."[16]

Hailed as the "champion Marathon runner of the Pacific coast," McLean continued his winning streak just two days later, on July 14, 1909, when he competed in the annual Pacific Athletic Association (PAA) track and field competition's two-mile run at Ascot Park. During the first mile of the race, William Garvin of the San Francisco Olympic Club took the lead and opened a "gap of seventy five yards on McLean." However, in the second mile, McLean "began to gain on the Olympian" as the "enthusiastic spectators in deafening applause cheered the little runner from Arizona." With only a half mile to go, McLean picked up his pace and passed Garvin to win the race in 9 minutes and 54 seconds.[17] The reporter explained that at the two-mile race in Los Angeles, McLean "met the fastest goods that could be gathered anywhere on the coast, and defeated [E. A.] Hunger, the crack long distance runner of Cornell." While Hunger had an established running reputation in the East, he faced serious competition from McLean in the West. The Hopi runner "ran circles around him," wrote the *Arizona Republican*, "and loafed home, to the steel tape."[18] A writer for the *San Francisco Chronicle* also noted that "while all of the performances were meritorious, the large crowd of spectators who crowded the grandstand were loud in the applause for the Indian runner, who with apparently no effort, defeated Garvin, heretofore considered the best two-miler on the Coast." Although "McLean appeared confident of winning the two-mile race from the San Francisco boy," the reporter concluded, "it was not considered a reasonable aspiration in view of his having run a Marathon race on Monday, in which he defeated a field of eleven starters decisively."[19]

Nearly two weeks after McLean returned from Los Angeles, Walter W. Christie, trainer for the Olympic Club at Berkeley and for the University of Southern California, wrote the editors of the *Arizona Republican* a letter praising the Hopi runner. "I am writing you concerning Harry McLean," Christie noted, "the Indian distance runner of your place." Christie explained that he had witnessed McLean win both races in Los Angeles, "beating William Garvin of the Olympic club" of San Francisco. Recalling the Hopi runner's strong performance in California, Christie urged the editors to convince Coach Lewis and the Phoenix Indian School to enter

McLean in the Amateur Athletic Union (AAU). Championship in Seattle in August of the same year. "He can, in my mind, win the five mile easily," Christine remarked, and "it would reflect great credit on the state of Arizona, [and] on the hustling Phoenix itself." Christie knew that it would be expensive for the school to send Lewis and McLean to Seattle for the meet. And so he wanted the editors to help garner support for this effort from individuals in Phoenix who saw this as an opportunity to showcase the city before a large American audience. "Just think what an ad it would be—forever in the books—," Christie argued, "his name on all the programs, east and west—the free advertising east gratis, 'Harry McLean, five mile champion of the United States, etc., of Phoenix, Arizona.'"[20]

McLean's performance in the Los Angeles races caused older members of the Phoenix community to recall other great Indian runners from the area. In an article entitled "An Old Time Runner of the Maricopas," a writer for the *Arizona Republican* noted that McLean's victories reminded the "old timers" of Phoenix about a local Indian runner named "Slim Jim" of the Maricopa people in the southern Arizona Territory. More than twenty years before, Slim Jim had been "employed to run between Phoenix and [Fort Whipple] at Prescott to carry dispatches." Covering a total distance of 122 miles over mountains and canyons, Slim Jim ran "between sun and sun" and returned to Phoenix "on the following day." The "old timers" recalled that Slim Jim "always left Phoenix on a swinging trot and he always arrived at the fort on the same kind of a trot. People who now and then encountered him on the way said that he was always in the same gait. He never seemed the worse for one of these jaunts and it used to be a wonder how far he could run. Not long ago he was in town and Joe Bush asked him if he would not like to get into a Marathon. He replied, 'No run 'em now; too many cigareets.'"[21]

While McLean's victories in the Pacific Athletic Association Marathon and the two-mile event furthered competitive Hopi running in the West, it also helped establish McLean as a world-class runner. In response to his performance in Los Angeles, reporters of the *Arizona Republican* provided both details of McLean's accomplishments and directed readers to the running legacy of his people. McLean is a "typical Arizona Indian, a Hopi," a reporter noted, known "throughout Indiandom as the tribe of racers." While McLean came from a "tribe of racers," his identity as a Hopi person, coupled with his ability to run long distances and compete at the level of other Indian and white athletes, was anything but "typical."

Considered a "Territory" in 1909,[22] Arizona encompassed the ancestral lands of more than twenty tribes. Although all Southwest Indian tribes had traditions of distance running, not every Native people group was known as a "tribe of racers." For those Indians in Arizona who came from noted running communities such as Zuni, Navajo, or Hualapai, relatively few runners from these tribes went on to compete in major national or international running events. And fewer still won major races, whether in Arizona or elsewhere.[23]

Although McLean's win in Los Angeles demonstrated his ability to compete against the top runners in the nation, it also enhanced the reputation of Phoenix as an ideal city for athletics. "The athletic world outside," said Coach Lewis, has the "mistaken idea into its head that Phoenix is home of the sick, sufferers of tuberculosis, a locality where anything but athletics can be made a go." Responding to the notion that the climate in Phoenix was too hot to properly train runners, and that such high temperatures caused athletes to "lose all desire to compete," Lewis argued that there was no "better city" for "year around training," and noted that Phoenix had "better air," and superior "natural facilities" that contributed to the development of "top notch athletes." Comparing athletes to horses whose handlers also trained them in the heat of Phoenix, Lewis explained that both men and horses had the "advantage" over their "rivals," and did far better when racing against competition from cooler climates.[24] "I want the Phoenix people to see Harry in action," exclaimed Lewis, "to see what a real product of this locality can do."[25] Lewis saw in McLean an opportunity to start changing the city's reputation and even its economic fortunes.

In the early 1900s, few Americans considered the warm and dry climate of Phoenix to be suitable for serious athletic training, especially long-distance running.[26] Part of this stemmed from how outsiders perceived the town, especially in regard to its connection between health and Native peoples. In his work on the Phoenix Indian School, historian Robert Trennert, Jr., observed that by November 1907, tuberculosis had become a serious problem at the school, and one that was intensified by the East Farm Sanitarium located just outside the school grounds. "Of particular concern" to officials, notes Trennert, was that the "school was surrounded by private lands being used as tuberculosis camps." And due to its "dry climate, Phoenix had become a haven for health seekers, especially those afflicted with respiratory ills."[27] By summer 1909, the same summer that McLean returned victorious from Los Angeles, the Department of Indian

Affairs increased the number of Indian students it sent with tuberculosis to the sanitariums in Phoenix. Whether or not Coach Lewis wanted to admit it, Phoenix had indeed become the "home of the sick," and this reputation hindered his attempts to portray Phoenix as an ideal location for athletics.[28]

Coaches and trainers often wanted high-profile athletic events to bolster the reputation of their home cities. Shortly after McLean won the Elks' marathon in Los Angeles, Coach Lewis remarked that his victory promoted the city of Phoenix in a way that others had not. "Harry McLean is not only a good runner," Lewis noted, his victory became an "advertisement" for the town of Phoenix "that will be hard to beat." Explaining to an Arizona newspaper that McLean had done "more than anything else to advertise the city at the recent" marathon, Lewis further commented that the Hopi runner's name had been "read in every paper by sports [enthusiasts] from all over the country as well as capitalists, and businessmen."[29] In this regard, McLean's victory not only promoted the school but had the potential to encourage the arrival of new commerce and businesses in the city of Phoenix. "This is one of the reasons" why Phoenix should promote the upcoming race in August, Lewis said, for at "that time I will place Harry in a five mile event, to run his five in better time than two men can run a relay of two and one-half miles each."[30]

In the early 1900s, businesses in Phoenix sought to attract people from across the state to move to the city. With an advertising headline that read, "Phoenix Is the Best Town in America," the city's Davidson's Cash Bargain Store urged outsiders to consider moving to the desert location. Describing how the city had grown from a "few adobe houses in a barren waste to a city of 12,000 inhabitants," the advertisement noted that Phoenix now had "fine schools and churches, electric lights and street cars, in the midst of a valley made rich and verdant by irrigation." "To the newcomer," the ad concluded, "we want you to say, you have made no mistake in coming to Phoenix, whether for health or for business reasons."[31]

That same summer—July 1909—and less than a week after Coach Lewis urged city officials to see the economic benefits of running competitions, the city of Phoenix organized the two-mile Lewis Benefit Meet at the state's Territorial Fair Grounds. Wearing a white running suit and a race bib with the letters "B.P.O.E." (Benevolent and Protective Order of Elks)[32] and the number "335" written "across his chest," McLean was "met with cheers" as he approached the start line to begin the race. But right before the start, a race official gave the runners "vague instructions," which he followed with a "faltering ringing of the warning bell" to commence the two-mile event. Although McLean "lost a fraction of a second in getting down to business," he quickly found his "invincible stride" and completed the first mile in "5 minutes and 38 seconds." As he rounded the corner of the track to begin his second mile and lap, he quickly caught up with the two lead pace setters, Indian runners Boswick and John Curley. "For the first half mile of the last lap," the Hopi runner pressured them to increase their pace in an attempt to tire them out. The strategy worked. With a quarter of a mile remaining in the race, "things changed, and a pace that killed Boswick, headed by McLean brought forth every ounce of go in Curley to play." Less than a hundred meters from the finish, the Hopi runner sprinted to the end. At this point Harry's wife, Mrs. McLean, whom he had married less than a year earlier, wearing a "dainty white silk gown," joined others in rising from her seat to witness her husband narrowly defeat Curley with an elapsed time of 10 minutes, 47 and ¾ seconds. "To see this wonderful Indian run alone, seems nothing less than marvelous," a reporter for the *Los Angeles Times* observed, "but when side by side with another [Indian runner] there is as much difference as between night and day."[33]

While McLean dominated several running events in the West, his winning streak did not last for very long. In August 1909, McLean lost a three-mile race in San Francisco to Joseph E. Ballard of the Boston Athletic Association.[34] In an interview after the race with a reporter for the *Arizona Republican*, McLean commented: "They tell me that for once a good Indian is not a dead Indian . . . I tried to run my best and I haven't a thing to regret."[35] Two months later when he competed in the Marathon Derby in Seattle on October 17, 1909, McLean ran against some of the best runners in the nation, but stopped running at the twenty-two-mile mark and collapsed from exhaustion. Race officials and other spectators rushed to his aid. Seeing that McLean was not able to walk on his own, Coach Lewis and others from the Indian school carried him off the field to the surprise and disappointment of his supporters. Frenchman Henry St. Yves went on to win the marathon in 2 hours, 40 minutes, and 50 and ¾ seconds. A writer for the *Arizona Republican* observed that McLean began to "lose steam" fifteen miles into the race.[36]

His failure to finish the race drew sharp criticism from sport enthusiasts and newspaper reporters, who saw McLean's poor performance as proof that white runners were ultimately superior to their Native counterparts. McLean's "failure," wrote one reporter for the *Arizona Republican*, provides "further evidence in support of the assertion often made by experts in athletics, that the Indian is not the white man's equal in certain forms of physical stamina."[37] While the reporter acknowledged that Native runners had accomplished notable achievements running on or near their reservations as Indian messengers, he argued that a fundamental difference existed between white and Indian runners. "What, then, is the Indian's failure in such competitions as the race at Seattle?," asked the reporter. "The explanation, we surmise, will be found in the failure of the Indian to measure up to the white man's standard in will power."

In the early 1900s, newspapers often published articles that reflected sentiments about Indians that white people held in American society. According to these sentiments, which were usually based on a romanticized understanding of the past, Native people had lost the battle. Their land and dignity had been taken away from them, and forces of colonialism had suppressed their culture.[38] Therefore, as a defeated people, they no longer had the willpower to carry on.[39] But newspaper writers and other Americans also believed that in sport competitions, Indians could reclaim the pride that they had lost. On the track field, or on city streets and pathways, Indian runners such as McLean could demonstrate to American society, and to themselves, that Native people had some fight still left in them. However, when Indians failed in these competitions and lost to white athletes, newspaper commentators used it as an opportunity to highlight the supposed racial superiority of white Americans and the demise of Indians. When an Indian competes in sports, "All his moral fortitude is put to the test," a writer for the *Arizona Republican* observed. "But when there is a supreme call upon a man's vitality plus his will power, the white race alone seems able to produce consistent winners."[40]

The newspaper writer's claim that the "white race alone" produced "consistent winners" is misleading. Since the vast majority of athletes competing in America at this time were white, it stands to reason that white runners also won a number of marathons and other running events. In the early 1900s, relatively few Indians or other so-called minority runners from marginalized communities competed in official American races. Furthermore, at the same time the newspaper writer made his claim about Indian runners, Hopi runner Louis Tewanima dominated running competitions on the East Coast. Just one month before, a writer for the *In-*

dianapolis Star remarked that Tewanima had become famous across America "because of his remarkable long-distance running." And as a result of his consistent winning, those in America's running community highly anticipated that the Hopi runner would become one of the top distance runners in the nation. "Mike Murphy the famous Pennsylvania trainer," the writer for the Star observed, "has picked Tewanima as one of the greatest of prospective American runners, saying that he will unquestionably make the country's best ten-miler, if properly trained."[41]

While some sports writers interpreted McLean's performance as a loss in willpower, other athletes still considered the Hopi runner to be a strong competitor and worthy of their challenge. In March 1910, a Danish "champion long distance runner" named William Stanley announced that "he would like to challenge Harry McLean, the fleet-footed Indian discovered by Coach John Lewis, to a race for any distance up to twenty miles." Willing to travel to Phoenix to race against the Hopi runner, Stanley was eager to "talk business" with any individual who would "undertake the management of the event." While this was the first time Stanley had openly challenged McLean, both runners competed against each other in the Seattle Marathon five months before, and both quit the race at the twenty-four mile mark. Although Stanley claimed that he quit "because he was sick and was ordered from the track" by his physician, he had since won twelve races and was eager to compete in Phoenix.[42]

The thought of McLean and Stanley racing against each other in Phoenix remained with Coach Lewis in the weeks and months that followed. Six months after Stanley's challenge, Lewis told a reporter for the Arizona Republican that Stanley and other distance runners wanted to come to Phoenix to race against McLean at the upcoming city fair events. Lewis remarked to the reporter that "if he can do nothing better he hopes to get Stanley here" to run "against McLean" in a race of no "more than fifteen miles."[43] Lewis knew the importance of attracting top athletes from across the nation to his regional event. Having accomplished runners registered for the race increased public interest in the race, encouraged other top runners to participate, and provided his runners with a chance to bring notoriety to themselves and their school. But Lewis also realized that attracting top runners and arousing public interest in his small regional race was not an easy task. At this time, reports of upcoming congressional, senate, and state elections dominated the news and occupied people's attention, and Lewis questioned people's interest in competitive running or any sporting activities. "While this political discussion is going on," Lewis lamented to an *Arizona Republican* reporter in reference to various nationwide congressional races, it "is pretty hard to interest any one in any thing else."[44]

Stanley and McLean, however, never had an opportunity to race against each other in Phoenix or any city. After McLean's loss in Seattle in October 1909, the Hopi runner returned to his residence in Sacaton, Arizona, and remained there indefinitely. In 1910 and 1911, American newspapers did not report any races that McLean competed in in the Southwest or elsewhere. In September 1912, the *Arizona Republican* noted that city officials in Phoenix planned a modified marathon of fifteen miles at the annual fair, and that McLean was scheduled to participate. The newspaper writer, however, did not mention whether the Hopi runner was still associated with the Indian school in Phoenix.[45] When McLean returned to Sacaton in fall 1909, he readapted to life back on the Pima Indian Reservation, a place where he had been relocated to as a child by Mary McLean, a white Christian missionary who adopted him.[46] At the time McLean was in his mid-twenties, and he likely chose to obtain agricultural work in Sacaton instead of running for the school. Furthermore, after losing so badly in Seattle, McLean may have decided to quit running competitively so that he could move on in life as a young adult. Whatever the circumstances are that surrounded the abrupt end to his short running career, McLean's willingness to compete in American races came at an important time for his school, his tribe, and the city of Phoenix. And even years after McLean ran his last recorded marathon, newspaper writers still remembered him and his remarkable accomplishments.[47]

While Harry McLean was making a name for himself out West, another Hopi runner named Saul Halyve (Halaivi) from the village of Musangnuvi began attracting attention for his ability to run as a member of the cross-country team at Teller Institute (originally the Grand Junction Indian School), an off-reservation Indian boarding school in Grand Junction, Colorado.[48] Named after Senator Henry M. Teller of Colorado, who served as the secretary of the interior during the early 1880s, Teller Institute opened its doors in 1886 to reclaim the "offspring of the savage American Indians." By 1893, government officials enrolled 102 Indian pupils at the school ranging in age from six to twenty-one years of age, including students from the Navajo, Ute, Mojave, Yuma, Tonto, and Coyotero Apache communities. Similar to the industrial education students received at other off-reservation Indian boarding schools, the boys at Teller Institute received instruction in farming, carpentry, saddle making, and blacksmithing, and some of the advanced students honed skills in "architectural drawing." Female students, however, learned domestic science, including "sewing, cutting, fitting, cooking, housekeeping," and "everything" that school officials believed a civilized woman should be well-versed in as "useful" members of society.[49]

Unlike the Phoenix Indian School, few Hopi students enrolled at the Indian school in Grand Junction during the early 1900s. Originally, the majority of students came from the Ute Reservation in Utah, but by the beginning of the twentieth century, students from the Apache communities of Arizona and New Mexico accounted for the largest tribal representation at the school. In addition to Saul Halyve, fellow Hopi student Don Atokuku attended Teller Institute, and both individuals competed with each other in a number of running events, including the *Daily Sentinel* Modified Marathon of ten miles on May 29, 1909, in Grand Junction.[50] In his article "Saul Halyve, Forgotten Hopi Marathon Champion," historian Ben Fogelberg noted that prior to the race, Halyve was unknown to the running community in Colorado. Other local runners, including white athletes Rex Barber, Paul Burgess, and J. G. Carothers, captured the media's attention and gave little regard to Halyve or his teammates. Fogelberg remarked that the *Sentinel*, the main Colorado newspaper that covered the event, "mentioned the Hopi boy as a 'surprise' entrant and possible contender, but few outside the Indian school had ever heard of him." However, as Fogelberg, noted, "One hour, four minutes later, Saul Halyve was well on his way to becoming a city hero and world-class distance runner."[51]

On the same day that Halyve won the *Daily Sentinel* Modified Marathon, Halyve and Don Atokuku took a train to Denver, Colorado, to compete in the Rocky Mountain Amateur Union Marathon that was ultimately postponed until the first week in June 1909. Fogelberg remarked that Halyve won the 26.2-mile event in commanding style with a time of three hours, one minute, and fifty-three seconds, finishing "more than a mile ahead" of American Olympian and bronze medal winner Joe Forshaw.[52] After Halyve won that marathon, Halyve, Atokuku, and Superintendent of Teller Institute Charles E. Burton boarded a train and headed back to Grand Junction.[53] Listening to the sound of the engine and feeling the vibrations of clanking metal, Halyve contemplated his victory and his new standing as an American distance runner. But when the "train pulled into

the station every engine in the yards blew a long blase [sic] of welcome."
With a "blare of a brass band" playing in the background, hundreds of the
town's citizens and students from Halyve's school met the Hopi runner at
the station to cheer and congratulate him for his outstanding victory. "He
had gone to Denver an obscure Indian boy," a writer for the *Reading Times*
observed, and "returned to find himself suddenly famous."[54]

In addition to providing details about Halyve's sensational homecoming, the newspaper writer recalled a "conversation" that his friend
had with the Hopi runner following the race. After his victory in Denver,
Halyve apparently remarked to the reporter's friend that he came from
the village of Musangnuvi on Second Mesa, Arizona, and that even as a
child, he and others from the village had competed in footraces. "When
we ran to the spring," Halyve explained, "we always followed our leader
who wore a bell tied to his belt." He noted that he had older brothers with
"reputations as good runners," and he discussed the differences between
running back home on the mesas and doing so in modern towns and
streets. When asked about the race, Halyve recalled that one of the other
runners from behind had accidently kicked him, "but then after that" he
"went ahead and never let any one near" him. At the fifteen-mile mark, the
Hopi runner had become dizzy, but he regained his strength by thinking
about his school, the superintendent, and the "boys at home." And "so I
just set my teeth and kept running," he explained, and although "I was
awfully tired, I kept on until at the finish." Halyve then supposedly went
on to tell the writer's friend that "This is my fourth public race and I am
becoming accustomed to the yelling which bothered me at first, and to the
other runners who rather frightened me."[55]

While patrons of the *Reading Times* likely found this conversation interesting, and perhaps even amusing, its credibility is suspect. The writer
never mentioned the name of his friend, or the context of the conversation.
Furthermore, the vast majority of Hopi runners at this time were quiet and
reserved and rarely if ever talked much about themselves or their accomplishments. In preparing for their stories, newspaper reporters seemed
hard pressed to secure comments from Hopi runners, and when they did,
they usually uttered only a few words to appease their interviewers. Finally, the writer seemed more concerned with providing readers with an
intriguing story rather than an accurate one. He gave readers what they
wanted; a highly sensationalized account that resonated with their own
preconceived notions of Native people.

In the weeks that followed the Rocky Mountain Amateur Union Marathon, Halyve continued his winning streak by securing his "second consecutive marathon victory" in the "championship of the Rocky Mountain region" race on June 20, 1909.[56] Competing on a one-mile track, Halyve defeated his competition, including Joe Erxleben of the Missouri Athletic Club, in 3 hours and 15 minutes.[57] Realizing his remarkable ability as a long-distance runner, people in Colorado urged Halyve to "represent the United States in the International Marathon to be run over the historic course at Athens, Greece, in 1910." They even submitted Halyve's application to James Sullivan of the Amateur Athletic Union for a "position on the team," but the Hopi runner never competed in this event.[58] His win in this race also caused people in the running community, including Forshaw, to speculate on Halyve's chances of competing in the 1912 Olympic Games in Stockholm, Sweden.[59] With this in mind, Fogelberg noted that the Daily Sentinel wanted to send the Hopi runner to "big track meets across the country to get him noticed" by a larger American sport audience. However, Halyve insisted on running his meets out West and preferred to compete in Colorado. As Fogelberg observed, "Race organizers were only happy to oblige" the Hopi runner's request and responded by hosting a ten-mile race in Grand Junction on July 19 of the same year. But unlike the two previous races that Halyve competed in, the race in Grand Junction took place on a track at the local fairgrounds, and only a handful of athletes ran in the event. In spite of having difficulty breathing due to smudge pots race organizers used to light the evening race track, Halyve won the event in commanding style in 52 minutes and 25 seconds, just "thirteen seconds" off from the ten-mile world record.[60] The next month, Halyve ran and also won his final marathon, defeating Danish runner William Stanley, who had earlier challenged Harry McLean in a twenty-mile race on August 26.

By early 1911, life for Halyve changed. In March of the same year, he married a Hopi woman, Josie Sekonginenia. Married by Protestant minister Reverend G. S. Smith of Grand Junction, Halyve and his bride had attended Teller Institute together and likely participated in Christian services at Reverend Smith's church.[61] But as Halyve began a new chapter in his life with Josie, the couple left the Indian school and Halyve ended his career as a long-distance runner. After March 1911, when he left Teller Institute, Halyve did not compete in American running competitions. As a student at the Indian school, he had opportunities to run for the school's cross-country team. The school had paid for his race entrance fees and provided transportation to meets throughout Colorado and beyond. When he left the school, he left behind these opportunities and resources. Life back on the Hopi Reservation required Halyve to focus on obtaining work and providing for his wife and family. His days of running at Teller Institute had come to an end.

While abruptly stopping his career in early 1911, Halyve's accomplishments as a distance runner were never entirely forgotten.[62] Less than two years later a former student at the Carlisle Indian Industrial School named Amy G. Adams wrote a short essay entitled "The Hopi Indian Runner" for the school's newspaper, the *Carlisle Arrow*. In her article, Adams explained that Hopis at different Indian schools across the United States had made names for themselves "on the long distance race track." She described the accomplishments of Louis Tewanima, including his performance in the 1908 Olympics and upcoming participation in the 1912 Olympic Games in Stockholm, Sweden. And she mentioned Tewanima's West Coast Hopi rival, Philip Zeyouma, who had recently won the *Los Angeles Times* Modified Marathon of twelve miles. While highlighting the careers of Tewanima and Zeyouma, she spent the majority of her commentary on Halyve of Teller Institute. "In all races he came out first and generally finished with a nice sprint," Adams remarked, "which all his competitors were unable to do." "He won many prizes," she concluded, "much to the surprise of the big runners that ran with him."[63]

Adams also commented at length about the many Hopi runners on the reservation who never ran for an Indian school and therefore did not receive attention from the greater white American population. While Tewanima, Halyve, and Zeyouma made names for themselves beyond the reservation as great long-distance runners, Adams argued that the reservation was "full of them," which was correct. "There are some who are faster than any of the above mentioned ones," she explained, "but they have never had the chance to show themselves to outside people." But even these runners, she noted, are not as great as runners of the past. "In former years" the Hopi seemed "to have been in much better condition" and better "prepared for running." "Of late years," Adams remarked, "many of them became owners of ponies, and their running on foot up and down the mesas" had been "practically been done away with." Describing the Hopi runner as "naturally small" and "quiet" and unassuming, the writer observed that they excel in their abilities to go the distance. "He is not swift," Adams remarked, "but his endurance, and the longer the distance of the race, the better he likes it, for he knows he will win." "Were they to compete in the big races," she concludes, "the list of names of the world's championship runners would be different now and forever."[64]

Four years after Adams wrote her commentary in the *Carlisle Arrow*, sports writer Albert F. Warden of the *Salt Lake Tribune* published an editorial on the rising popularity of marathons in the United States He also wrote on the accomplishments of past runners in the American West and recalled Halyve's victory in the Denver marathon in 1909. He explained that American runner Joe Forshaw had competed in the race, and that a runner named Sidney Hatch had been expected to win the event. But the "altitude was too high for the veteran and he was compelled to give way" to Halyve, the "crack Indian runner of Grand Junction." Describing Halyve as a "has-been," and a "midget, tipping the scale of 105 pounds," Warden went on to explain that the Hopi runner was "classed among the world's best" and "perhaps the greatest runner ever produced in the west at the regulation distance."[65] Warden's comments reflect the sentiments of Fogelberg, who concluded: "Saul Halyve never went to the Olympic Games and never stood next to an Indian brother at a medal ceremony. His name is not in the record books. But he remains one of Colorado's greatest marathon champions."[66]

While Halyve's short career as a marathoner caused him to receive considerable attention in American newspapers, other Hopi runners in the Southwest began seeing their names mentioned by sports writers. In February 1914, officials of the Phoenix Indian School and the Phoenix High School hosted a track and cross-country meet that started and ended at the city's Eastlake Park.[67] While the relay races included runners from both schools, the five-mile cross-country event only consisted of runners from the Phoenix Indian School, including Hopi runners Dennis Quimayousle, Don Atakuku, Herman Ashee, and Guy Maktima. Johnny Brown (Pima) and Patacio Hahkee (Zuni) also competed in the running event. Competing for a sweater that local businessman Vic Hanny donated for the first place prize, the athletes ran through the streets of Phoenix, attracting many spectators.[68] "The race through the center of the city was attended with much interest on all sides," wrote a reporter for the *Arizona Republican*, with many spectators having "come to town and out of the stores to witness the passing of the Indian runners." In addition to the spectators, a "band composed" of Indian and white students from the two schools "was on hand to encourage the Braves as they passed." After winding their way through the streets of Phoenix, the runners made a dash for Eastlake Park, where Hopi runner Quimayousle won the race in 31 minutes and 31 and ⅔ seconds. The other Hopi runners took second, third, and fourth places.[69]

The following year, in November 1915, Hopi runner Howard Talayamptewa, from the village of Paaqavi, broke the state record for the mile, with a time of 4 minutes and 42 and ½ seconds.[70] A relative of Washington Talayumptewa who had competed with Louis Tewanima at the Carlisle Indian Industrial School, Howard was especially good at running shorter distances. Referring to Howard as the "Little brown-skinned chap" who won the event "despite the handicap of his heavy Hopi name," a writer for the *Arizona Republican* noted that the runner from the Phoenix Indian School "beat the state record so bad that it was painful." After Howard's first-place finish in the one-mile race, officials "presented [him] with a certificate by the timers, declaring his victory." However, since the race did not take place "in a track meet, authorized by the state athletic board, its result" could only "stand as an unofficial record for" for future "milers." Charles Swiggett of the Phoenix High School had previously held this record with a time of 4 minutes and 46 seconds.[71] Building on the momentum created by Howard's victory, Howard and his fellow Hopi runners Herman Ashee, Mark Chimeme, and Ernest Wungnema went on to win the two-mile team event in the same meet.[72]

Five years later, in November 1920, Phoenix Indian School disciplinarian and cross-country coach Jacob Duran entered nine of his top runners to compete in the annual Gardner Modified Marathon of ten miles.[73] Mack Gardner, a local businessman, founded the event the year before to promote Phoenix and his jewelry business on Central Avenue. He donated a solid gold medal with a "beautiful steel blue diamond set in the center" for the first-place prize. Displaying the medal in the window of his Gardner Jewelry store in the weeks leading to the race, Gardner hoped that the prize would attract the best runners in Arizona. Phoenix businessman Vic Hanney offered a "Stetson hat" for the second-place winner, and Gardner also gave a "trophy to the runner-up."[74] The athletes included Zuni runners Gordon Coola and Leon Hallian, Papago runners Havier Jose, Juan Patricio, and Jose Pablo, and Hopi runners James F. Lewis, Max Polingyowma, Louis Kooyouhoma, and Loyde Tenakhonynewa.[75] On the day of the race, a writer for the *Arizona Republican* noted that the marathon brought "out fifteen of the leading athletes of the Salt River valley, each one eager to be hailed as the southwest champion and wear the diamond studded medal that goes to the victor."[76] At ten o'clock in the morning, the runners assembled at the starting line in front of Gardner's business to begin the ten-mile race. Running first down Central and then Bethany Home Road, the runners ran entirely on pavement as they made the final stretch to the finish. The year before, Gordon Coola had won the marathon,[77] and many considered him a favorite for the event. But on this occasion, Hopi runner Max Polingyowma won the race and rekindled the rivalry between these two great Indian runners from the Southwest.[78]

A year after Polingyowma won the Gardner Marathon, American sports writers continued highlighting the accomplishments of Hopi runners and the long legacy of running among the people. In an article describing the running abilities of Indian runners, including Deerfoot, Tom Longboat, and the Seri Indians of Tiburon Island in Mexico, Robert Edgren of the Bell Syndicate also praised the Hopi runners and informed his readers that a "marathon" was nothing new for the Hopi. Noting that the "Hopi Indians have had a marathon of their own, for centuries," Edgren explained that their races began high on top of the mesas. They ran "across the desert" at full speed, he remarked, to a return point ten miles in the distance. In the Hopi marathons "There is no measuring" the course or "timing" the runners, Edgren wrote, and the "young men of the tribe" understand the race to have "religious significance" and "train" accordingly. "If the Olympic commissioners want to find an Olympic Marathon runner who can beat the world it might be a good scheme to look the Indian reservation over."[79]

In the same month that Edgren praised the Hopi runners and suggested that the Olympic commissioners look over the reservation for potential competitors, he also highlighted the running talents of other Indigenous runners from Mexico. With a story headline that read, "Mexican Youths May Be World's Best Athletes," Edgren remarked that "Mexico could turn out a great team of long distance runners" in the upcoming 1924 Olympic Games in Paris, France. "Some of the Yaqui Indians," he noted, "are the greatest runners in the world, trained from youth to cover distances over rough country that would kill a horse, and to take the trail of a deer and

Hopi runners who came to Phoenix for Memorial Day celebrations on May 30, 1923.
From left: Arthur Pohequaptewa, Herbert Honanie, Phoenix School Disciplinarian
Jacob Duran, Myron Poliquaptewa, and Nicholas Qömawunu. Photo courtesy of Willard
Sakiestewa, Sr.

run it down." Providing a brief history of how Yaqui ancestors of long ago,
including the Aztecs and the Incas, relied on their abilities to run long distances during and for battles, Edgren concluded: "When the descendents
of runners like these begin competing in the Olympic Games we're likely
to have some new marathon records."[80]

While Edgren remarked on the Olympic prospects of the Yaqui Indians,
a group of Hopi runners began attracting the attention of race promoters,
newspaper writers, and even officials at off-reservation Indian boarding
schools. In May 1923, Coach Duran invited four Hopi "Marathon runners" to Phoenix to witness the city's Memorial Day activities. The runners
included Arthur Pohequaptewa, Herbert Honanie, Myron Pohequaptewa,
and Nicholas Qömawunu (Quomawahu) of Orayvi. Organized by the Al-
lied Association of Service Organizations and the American Legion, the
"elaborate program" largely consisted of a parade, speeches from veterans, and an afternoon picnic that the American Legion hosted for all past
or current military personnel. City officials such as Secretary Smithey of

the Merchants' and Manufacturers' Association asked stores and other shops to honor the dead by not conducting business unless absolutely necessary.[81] Even the town's post office had to take the day off, and Postmaster S. J. Michelson instructed that his employees "spend most of the day picnicking at Joyland park."[82]

The day began at 9:30 in the morning with a "monster parade" that included veterans, automobiles, military organizations and other societies, and various bands, including cadets and members of the Phoenix Indian School band. Led by Coach Duran, the band, which held a prominent role throughout the procession, started the day's events by playing the "Star Spangled Banner." After veterans of past wars gave speeches, the band played the song "There'll Be a Hot Time in the Old Town Tonight," and the audience closed the first part of the ceremony by singing "America" and listening to "Taps" being played on the trumpet.[83] When the playing of "Taps" had finished, members of the Indian school band began marching, and Indian veterans of prior wars walked behind them in formation according to rank. A writer for the *Arizona Republican* observed that these "representatives of the first race wore their cadet uniforms as proudly as any daring Anglo Saxon lad ever did when sallying forth in the defense of home and country."[84]

Although Duran invited the Hopi runners to Phoenix and likely paid for their transportation expenses, he did not enter them in a race. At this time in American society, Memorial Day tended to be a somber day of remembering those who sacrificed their lives in past wars. And some people still held on to long-standing beliefs that hosting athletic competitions on Memorial Day did not reflect the seriousness of the occasion. For example, more than thirty years before, a writer in the *Los Angeles Herald* argued that the "practice of making Memorial day a day of athletic sport and picnics is foreign to the purpose for which it was set apart, and such desecration of a day that ought to be sacred to the memory of our patriotic dead, is deserving of censure."[85] In the early 1920s, however, city organizers more regularly included sporting events as part of their Memorial Day festivities. While it is unclear why city officials did not host athletic events on Memorial Day in Phoenix in 1923, one possible reason may have more to do with the weather then people's sentiments about the day itself. With highs in the low nineties, city organizers may have concluded that the temperature was simply not conducive or safe for outdoor long-distance competitions.[86]

Hopi runners who competed in American races throughout the Southwest had indeed come from a "tribe of racers." When Harry McLean and Saul Halyve competed for their respective schools, they also ran for their tribe in northeastern Arizona. Their ability to run long distances, a skill first honed on their mesas, allowed them to travel and experience life in cities such as Seattle, Phoenix, Los Angeles and in various towns in Colorado and beyond. Although they ran for their own reasons, which included a desire to represent their village communities, school superintendents and sport trainers wanted their Hopi runners to showcase their schools, and city officials wanted to use their success to rebrand their cities as places of business, athletics, and leisure. However, with Louis Tewanima dominating races on the East Coast, and Harry McLean and Saul Halyve winning events out West, interest in the "tribe of racers" increased across America. A year after Halyve ran his last race for Teller Institute, and while Tewanima was wrapping up his career at Carlisle, a new wave of young Hopi runners began competing at Sherman Institute in southern California. And they too left their villages for a school far from home and took with them knowledge of running that allowed them to compete for Sherman, their tribe, and a nation that closely associated sport with US nationalism.

CHAPTER FIVE

Land of Oranges

On the afternoon of April 20, 1912, fifteen thousand people lined the streets of Los Angeles to witness 151 contestants compete in the *Los Angeles Times* Modified Marathon. Officials of the *Times* hosted the marathon to secure a Western candidate for the 1912 Olympic Games in Stockholm, Sweden, and news of the event attracted runners from across California, Arizona, and throughout the nation.[1] Two Hopi runners, Guy Maktima and Philip Zeyouma, stood beside the many athletes who gathered near the starting line and waited for the sound of the pistol to begin the race.[2] The Hopis ran for the newly established cross-country team of Sherman Institute in Riverside, California. When the race commenced, Howard W. Angus, a reporter for the *Los Angeles Times*, noted that Zeyouma wore "moccasins" that Hopi women had made for him on the reservation and a shirt that depicted the legendary "winged" (flying) snake of the Hopi.[3] At first the Hopi runners "received no attention" from the other athletes, who "kept their eyes on the many famous" runners in the group.[4] During the initial two miles of the race, the Hopis positioned themselves near the front of the pack, but refrained from making a sudden advance for the lead. At the halfway point, the Hopi runners increased their pace and shortened the gap between them and the other frontrunners.[5]

When word spread among the thousands of spectators that the "little Hopis" had broken away from the lead group, people rushed to the finish line and waited for the runners to make their final approach. One reporter recalled that "every eye was turned down the course at which the leader would first appear," and when Zeyouma turned that final corner and headed toward the finish line, a roar of "cheers announced his coming."[6] As the crowd cheered, Zeyouma remained focused and ran with his head down, "oblivious" to the spectators and "heedless of their advice."[7] Not far behind him, a competitor from the San Francisco Olympic Club bent "every effort" on catching the Hopi runner, but Zeyouma "raised his head and sprinted the remaining two blocks to where a white tape stretched across the street to mark the finish." Not only did he win the event in 1 hour, 12 minutes, and 8 seconds, he established a "new world's record for cross country running for twelve miles."[8] Having defeated his competition by two hundred feet, Zeyouma "acted as though he was used to winning Marathons," and waited at the finish line with a big smile.[9] Although Zeyouma gave the impression that he was "used to winning" marathons, he had never competed in one prior to the *Los Angeles Times* Modified Marathon in 1912. Newspaper reporters considered Zeyouma and Maktima to be the least experienced marathon runners in the race. Zeyouma had been on the school's cross-country team for only four months. He was unknown to the long-distance running community in California, and he competed for a school that had not yet established a winning reputation for its cross-country program. And yet, he was Hopi and since his childhood he and his tribesman Maktima had learned to run the Hopi way on the mesas of northern Arizona.

In the early 1900s, individual cross-country teams at off-reservation Indian boarding schools seldom raced against each other. Although schools such as Carlisle paid the expense for its football team to play colleges, universities, and other Indian schools, Native runners at boarding schools typically competed in city and regional marathons. The first major running event for the Sherman cross-country team was the modified marathon of twelve miles that the *Los Angeles Times* hosted in 1912. Realizing that a victory at the marathon would heighten the status of the school's new track team, Joseph Shoulder, athletic director of Sherman Institute, informed Hopi runners Guy Maktima and Philip Zeyouma about the event and had accompanied them to Los Angeles so they could register for the race.[10] Prior to 1912, few Hopi runners apart from Harry McLean had raced in Southern California, and when the athletic editors for the *Times* saw the athletes, they teased the Hopis about their small stature and wondered how men who were so short could compete against the much taller runners. In true Hopi fashion, Zeyouma took the editors' comments in "good humor" and "confined his amusement to a broad smile."[11] Rather than responding to the editors with words, Zeyouma wanted them to judge him on his ability to run, and not on his height.

In the early twentieth century, relatively few white Americans in Southern California had seen a Native person compete in a sporting event. By 1912, however, Indians at other boarding schools had developed reputations as remarkable athletes, and newspaper reporters realized that a story on the Hopi runners from Sherman Institute would capture the attention of their readers. With this in mind, Owen R. Bird, a reporter for the *Los Angeles Times*, followed Zeyouma on an automobile tour of the course on the day before the race. He noted that the "little Hopi Indian" had come to Los Angeles for the "first time in his life" and that he "saw his first street car and had his first automobile ride."[12] Bird observed that Zeyouma "did not say much," but that he carefully noted every turn and stretch of the course. When Bird asked Zeyouma why he had taken "so much notice of the curves," the Hopi runner replied that he "wanted to remember where to go" on the day of the race.[13]

The concrete and brick streets that formed the marathon course did not resemble the dirt-and-rock trails that Hopis used on the reservation. Usually no more than three feet wide, the Hopi clan trails went up and down the mesa's edge, and back and forth between small canyons and crevices. Similar to the way Zeyouma took "notice" of the course in Los Angeles, Hopi runners on the reservation carefully studied the trails for obstacles, as well as sudden dips and turns, and meditated on different aspects of the trail. Aware of the seriousness of each footrace, Hopi runners felt the burden of the entire community to run with "good hearts," as running brought rain and provided life to the Hopi villages.[14] Although Zeyouma realized that he would not be running primarily for his clan or village, he knew that a victory in the *Los Angeles Times* Modified Marathon would bring recognition and honor to his school community.

Shortly after Zeyouma won the *Los Angeles Times* Modified Marathon, school officials at Sherman honored the Hopi runner with a special ceremony in the school's auditorium. In addition to seven hundred Indian students, reporters from Southern California attended the service.[15] At the front of the auditorium, Zeyouma calmly sat with Superintendent Frank M. Conser and Bird. When Bird presented the trophy cup to Zeyouma, the Hopi runner told his classmates that while he was "proud of the cup," he was "more proud" of the "honors" he won for Sherman by "winning the race."[16] When Zeyouma finished speaking to the audience, his classmates "let loose their school yell," which people heard a mile and a half away. Following Zeyouma's speech, Superintendent Conser told the entire school that Zeyouma won the race "not because of a few days' training, but because of the fact that he [had] been a runner all of his lifetime" and that Zeyouma's people "were the greatest runners in the world."[17]

In the Sherman Bulletin, the student-written newspaper of Sherman Institute, the pupils at the school wrote that as a result of Zeyouma's win, "Sherman was on the lips of thousands in every part of California" and commented that the "praise of the little Indian was sung from one end of the state to the other."[18] Proud of their Hopi schoolmate, the students at Sherman looked at Zeyouma as a victorious example of one of their own.[19] They had sent Zeyouma to the marathon to represent the school and demonstrate their rightful place in the running community of Southern California. Zeyouma's peers had great confidence in his ability as a runner and noted that with "Tewanima from Carlisle guarding the Atlantic Coast and Zeyouma from Sherman Institute guarding the Pacific, America's laurels would be in safe hands" for the 1912 Olympic Games.[20]

But less than a week after the school honored Zeyouma for his win, other Indian runners at Sherman anxiously waited for a chance to run against their teammate. This opportunity came on May 14, when Sherman hosted its annual Commencement Day exercises on the school grounds. As part of the festivities, school officials organized field events, including a two-mile race between runners at the school. Having just defeated several top runners in the nation, Zeyouma confidently entered the race alongside his teammates, but the result was not what he or his classmates expected. Instead of seeing Zeyouma run first across the finish line, students at Sherman witnessed Albert Ray, a Pima runner from southern Arizona, win the race in 10 minutes and 15 seconds. The celebrated Hopi runner came in third, some 35 yards behind Ray. With a headline that read "PHILIP ZEYOUMA EASILY BEATEN," the Los Angeles Times noted that the "defeat of the Hopi was a great surprise to the whole school."[21] However, while surprised at Zeyouma's loss, they did not lose confidence in him or his ability to represent the school in future meets.[22] Nor did they allow his performance at the commencement to diminish what he had accomplished in Los Angeles.

The success of Native athletes in large American cities had a tremendous effect on their peers at Indian schools. Their victories in sporting events, particularly the contests in which Indians defeated white athletes, filled the pupils with pride and motivated them to support the school's athletic program. In July 1913, a reporter for the Los Angeles Times recalled that Zeyouma's victory in the 1912 *Los Angeles Times* Modified Marathon "aroused the students of the institution to such a pitch of enthusiasm that they called a mass meeting and perfected a student organization."[23] Known as the Sherman Institute Athletic Association, the organization consisted of nearly every pupil who could afford the fifty-cent membership fee, which the students used to send the track team to "various interscholastic meets held in Southern California."[24] Furthermore, Zeyouma's sensational finish created a tremendous excitement at other off-reservation Indian boarding schools.

When news of the Los Angeles marathon reached Moses Friedman, superintendent of the Carlisle Indian Industrial School, Friedman told Conser that he would be "particularly glad to see" Zeyouma join Tewanima at the Olympics, as the United States could not be "represented by too many" of the Hopi athletes. He also remarked to Conser that since Zeyouma was Tewanima's "fellow tribesman . . . it would be company for him to have Philip along."[25] In addition to the excitement expressed by Superintendent Friedman, students at both schools eagerly anticipated the Hopi showdown, and gloried in the thought that one of their runners would win an Olympic medal. However, in spite of their enthusiasm, students at Sherman Institute did not send their top runner to the Olympic Games. Although the American Olympic Committee was supposed to choose Zeyouma to be on the team, Zeyouma most likely declined the committee's invitation to compete, and instead returned home to help his parents and other family members for the summer with other Hopis from his school.[26] In August 1945, Donald H. Biery, superintendent of Sherman Institute, described in a memo that although Zeyouma had been "selected to go to the Olympic games at Stockholm," he "did not go because of his father's objections."[27]

The complex relationship between Hopi parents and their children did not simplify when Hopi pupils left their villages for government schools. In the 1940s, Wayne Dennis, a psychologist who conducted research on Hopi children, once commented that the Hopi child on the reservation "owes obedience to his mother and father, to his mother's brothers, and to some extent to his father's brothers who are called 'fathers.'"[28] Similarly, Hopi fathers had an important influence on the lives of their children who attended Indian boarding schools.[29] During the twentieth century, Hopi fathers encouraged their sons or daughters to remain at Sherman Institute to receive a "good education" or instructed them to return home for different reasons.[30] While school officials attempted to weaken the influence of Hopi parents on their children, especially with parents who criticized school policies, Hopi pupils seldom went against the counsel of their fathers.

Although Zeyouma's father's exact objections remain unknown, his disapproval may have stemmed from a tragedy that happened to his family two years earlier. In the summer of 1910, Zeyouma's father had lost a son and grandchild from an influenza epidemic that swept across the Hopi Reservation. Perhaps worried about his son's safety, Zeyouma's father insisted that he return home. In addition to worrying about his son's well-being, Zeyouma's father may not have seen the value of allowing his son to compete for a nation that had not yet granted his people full US citizenship.[31] For example, the Bill of Rights did not apply to the Hopi people until the federal government passed the Indian Citizenship Act in 1924, but this did not prevent the American Olympic Committee from choosing "second-class" citizens—first Americans—to represent the United States.[32]

Rather than conform to the expectations of an entire nation, however, Zeyouma relinquished his opportunity to compete in the Olympic Games and honored his father according to the Hopi way. Consequently, his decision to remain behind directly affected his Hopi rival, Tewanima, who no longer had the challenge of racing against one of the top distance runners in the nation. Taking advantage of Zeyouma's absence, Tewanima went on to represent the Hopi people, his school, and the United States in the 1912 Olympic Games in Sweden and won a silver medal in the 10,000-meter event.[33]

The rivalry between the two Hopi runners, however, did not cease when Tewanima migrated back to the Hopi mesas as an Olympian. In September 1912, shortly before the new school year had begun, Zeyouma and Tewanima challenged each other to a race at the village of Songòopavi on Second Mesa.[34] On the day of the race, Hopis from the surrounding communities gathered around the starting line in the village plaza and anxiously watched as the two runners made their mark for the twelve-mile course. Zeyouma proudly wore his "Sherman colors," while Tewanima "appeared in his Carlisle track suit."[35] By wearing their running uniforms, the Hopi athletes saw the event as a race between the two schools and identified themselves according to their school affiliation. However, such a display of school loyalty did not go unchallenged by the other Hopi runners in the crowd.

Showdown on Second Mesa, *by Neil Logan.*

Seconds before the race began, some of the older Hopi men remarked that the "boys did not look like [Hopi] runners" at all, and teased Zeyouma and Tewanima for wearing their running outfits and said that they could "beat them easily." A *New York Times* reporter noted that when Tewanima heard the men's insults, Tewanima replied, "If you don't like our looks get in, and show what you can do."[36] The men promptly accepted his challenge and entered the race with no shoes or track suits, and wore "merely discarded" clothes. Six miles into the race, the older men proved too much for the young runners and Zeyouma and Tewanima quit and left the "race to the barefooted runners in the lead." Coach Shoulder recalled that the winner was about fifty years old, and he looked like he was "dying of consumption" (tuberculosis).[37]

The outcome of the race provides a telling commentary on running in Hopi culture, as well as the relationship between older and younger runners. While the younger runners migrated to off-reservation Indian boarding schools, the vast majority of the Hopi people, including older men who were known for the ability to run long distances, remained at home. Consequently, some of the best long-distance runners in US history received little or no attention by those outside of the Hopi community. Although newspaper reporters seemed surprised that men in their fifties had the ability to defeat the younger athletes, the people knew that other Hopis could easily outrun the Hopi Olympian and the track star from Sherman Institute. Furthermore, in Hopi culture, elders and uncles taught the boys of the village to run according to Hopi traditions, which explains why the older men did not hesitate to turn the situation around on the younger runners by challenging them on the day of the race. Contesting the younger men's decision to become modern Hopi long-distance runners, the older men reminded Zeyouma and Tewanima that Hopi running did not begin, nor was it perfected, at off-reservation Indian boarding schools, but it originated with the people.[38]

Prior to this footrace, people on the reservation, especially those on Second Mesa, knew about Tewanima's victories in American marathons and of his Olympic performances in London and Stockholm. Yet many Hopi runners remained unimpressed with Tewanima's accomplishments. While the older men were among the first to challenge Tewanima to a race after he returned home, it did not take long for younger runners to try to outdistance the Hopi Olympian in other footraces. For example, in October 1913, former Carlisle student Joshua Hermeyesva, brother to Washington Talayamptewa, wrote Superintendent Friedman that his village recently hosted a "foot race" and that Tewanima came in second place to a Hopi "boy."[39]

Not long after the Hopi showdown on Second Mesa, Zeyouma returned to Sherman and rejoined the school's track team in December of the same year. Although his victory in the *Los Angeles Times* Modified Marathon established a Hopi running presence at Sherman, Zeyouma did not win another major marathon in the remaining few years of his career. In the Los Angeles Athletic Club Marathon Road Race held in February 1913, Zeyouma placed second to Albert Ray, who also defeated Zeyouma when he attempted to defend his title at the 1913 *Los Angeles Times* Modified Marathon; Hopi runner Guy Maktima placed second.[40] After the race, a writer named Bert. C. Smith for the *Times* followed Ray, Zeyouma, and Maktima to the dressing room and reported on what he saw. "The Hopi had been hopelessly beaten," he remarked, "His heart was pumping like the exhaust of a motor racing car whose gasoline tank was almost empty." While trainers gave Ray and the other frontrunners rubdowns, Zeyouma "came over to the table" and "looked over the tables sadly." Smith noted that the

Hopi runner "tried not to show his sorrow," but then "gave an excuse" for his performance: "I am sick. Not in condition. Have no chance."[41]

Although newspaper writers expected him to win, Zeyouma did not appear too upset in the days that followed at losing to Ray or coming in behind three of his other teammates. He was, however, disappointed, but for a different reason. Prior to the event, a "manager of the local branch of the Howard Automobile Company" in California had "promised to teach" the Hopi runner the "art of driving" a Buick "30" had he won. At the time, Zeyouma studied auto engineering at Sherman, and there he became enamored with automobiles and planned to open an auto shop of his own. Worse than losing the race, however, Zeyouma hated to "lose the chance of driving a real automobile." Days later, when the company received word of Zeyouma's disappointment, the manager "sent a machine up to Riverside and Philip proudly piloted the Buick '30' around the campus of the Indian school." Newspaper writers, his classmates, and other sport enthusiasts had been fascinated with his ability to run long distances. But on this occasion, the Hopi runner sat in amazement of this relatively new invention of American transportation, telling the *Times* that "some day" he would "own a car of his own" and would return to Sherman and "take all the girls out for a ride."[42]

By the summer of 1914, Zeyouma's term at Sherman Institute had expired. But unlike other Hopis who returned to the reservation after graduating, he remained in the Riverside area to work. Although he was no longer part of the school's cross-country team, Zeyouma still followed the outcomes of regional races and sought ways to run competitively in California. In an article for the *Los Angeles Times*, Howard W. Angus noted that in December of the same year Zeyouma came to see the *Times*'s editors and expressed interest in competing for the Los Angeles Athletic Club (LAAC). "I'm after [Oliver] Millard, the Coast long-distance champion. . . . He's a good runner, but I think I can beat him," Zeyouma told the editors. The Hopi runner further explained that when he and other Indian runners from Sherman ran under the auspices of the LAAC, the club provided them with "clean white baths and white towels and rubbers." Hearing how Zeyouma appreciated what the club offered its athletes, Angus surmised: "Zeyouma has turned white man. He has learned everything the Sherman Indian School has to teach him."[43]

Contrary to what Angus said, the Hopi runner from Musangnuvi had not "turned" into a "white man." Zeyouma wanted to keep racing after graduating, and few if any options existed for him apart from joining a city athletic club. He had also read news about running in the *Times* and other papers, and he knew that he still had the ability to run competitively in American races. Although he liked certain privileges associated with running for the LAAC, and he had received a so-called white man's education, Zeyouma's identity remained deeply rooted in his Hopi community. Surely, Zeyouma had changed as a result of his time at Sherman, and he had learned to run according to American rules and customs, but he had not forgotten or abandoned his Hopi culture. For it was only two years before the meeting with the *Times*'s editors, that people back home had schooled Zeyouma on distance running and reminded him of his place in Hopi society.

In the years following Zeyouma's stint at Sherman, Hopi runners encountered intense competition from their Indian peers. Other athletes, such as Navajo runner Peter Begay and Ray, dominated running events at the school and often outran their Hopi rivals. Although Hopi runner Roscoe Poleytewa won the six-mile *Riverside Enterprise* Thanksgiving Race in 1913, Ray won far more prestigious events such as the *Times* Modified Marathon and the Sierra Madre Mount Wilson Climb Marathon in the same year.[44] For much of the late 1910s, few Hopis emerged at Sherman as top distance runners. In addition to Ray, Sherman runner William "Willie" Azul, a Pima who also hailed from Sacaton, Arizona, kept the Hopis and others at bay by winning the Sawtelle Modified Marathon (1915), the Ocean Park Marathon (1919), and the Sherman Indian 10 Mile Race (1920).[45] In the event hosted by Sherman, Azul outran two Hopi runners, Homer Yoyweidwa and Matthew Conywamama, to win in 59 minutes and 58 seconds.[46]

Although non-Hopi Indian runners such as Ray, Azul, and Begay dominated distance running throughout most of the late 1910s, this changed during the 1920s as a new wave of Hopi talent began arriving at the Indian school in Riverside. At this time, Hopi and other Indian runners at Sherman competed in a US society with a heightened interest in and fascination with individual physical accomplishments. Geoff Williams, a freelance journalist, remarked that each "decade [had] a cultural touchstone," and during the "Roaring Twenties, endurance competitions ruled."[47] And as competitive Hopi runners arrived at the school, the number of marathons and other long-distance races that organizations hosted increased throughout the nation. Athletic clubs on both coasts also sent their best runners to compete in marathons such as the Auto City Marathon in Detroit and the Laurel-to-Baltimore Marathon in Maryland, and Indian runners from off-reservation boarding schools eagerly participated in the marathon frenzy.[48]

While non-Indian organizations often hosted these marathons, sport trainers at Indian schools also wanted their athletes to participate in the frenzy to showcase the school and to give them experience competing against elite runners. In April 1925, Coach Bert Jameison, an Indian athletic trainer at Sherman who graduated from Haskell Institute in 1912, entered eight athletes to compete against Finnish runner Paavo Nurmi in a special three-mile "Indian" race in Los Angeles. Considered to be one of the world's greatest distance runners, Nurmi won gold and silver medals in prior Olympics, and news of the race between him and the Indian runners created excitement in the sporting community. "Paavo Nurmi," a newspaper writer remarked, "was ready today to meet in a three mile event, eight of the fleetest Hopi Indians ever to stray off the reservation."[49] While not all eight entrants from Sherman hailed from Hopi, those who did included Bruce Ahtuhu, Amos Hoyowesva, and Thomas Humphrey.[50] Standing before forty-five thousand people in the Los Angeles Memorial Coliseum, Nurmi and the runners from Sherman took their mark to begin the race.[51] At the sound of a gunshot, the runners leaped from the starting line with Humphrey taking the lead. Following behind in fourth place, Nurmi completed the first lap, raised his right hand to look at his "stop watch," and began increasing his pace. At this point, as Nurmi "slid past his plucky Indian rival," the "phantom Finn" took the lead position and slowly increased the gap between him and his competition. Unwilling to let Humphrey get close to him during the remaining laps, Nurmi won the race in commanding style, "three-quarters of a lap" ahead of the Hopi runner, with a time of 4 minutes and 34 seconds. After the race, Braven Dyer of the *Los Angeles Times* remarked that "Humphrey gave a gritty exhibition and for a youngster of 19 years ran a marvelous race, being but 45 seconds behind the Great Finn."[52]

At the time of the event, Humphrey was still a relatively inexperienced runner. Although he had come from a community of running, he had few if any opportunities to compete in a major American race before April 1925. As a twenty-seven-year-old, Nurmi arrived at the coliseum an Olympic champion, a winner of hundreds of races in Europe and the United States and a seasoned athlete with thousands of fans.[53] And he drew on his experience in other races to execute a winning strategy against the runners from Sherman. He examined the clay track minutes before the race, he held back from making an immediate push for the lead, and he closely kept track of his time by glancing at his watch. Humphrey, on the other hand, had less competitive experience. But the opportunity for Humphrey and his teammates to run against Nurmi and to learn from him, especially in a shorter race, was perhaps worth more to the runners than a victory. "Nurmi's victory did not dim the glory of the Indian lads," wrote a reporter for the Associated Press, "who for generations have been trained in a different style, that of a 'dog trot,' which they could maintain for hours at a stretch, while the Finn represented the contrast of more recently accepted training methods."[54]

In the years that followed, runners at Sherman had other opportunities to compete in highly publicized meets. One such meet was the International Indian Marathon in eastern Kansas on April 21, 1928. Two Hopi runners, Franklin Suhu from Ho'atvela and Harry Chaca from Polacca,[55] represented Sherman Institute, while nine of the other eleven contestants ran for Haskell Institute. Part of the Sixth Annual Kansas Relays, the marathon included runners from the Southwest, the Midwest, and Canada. When the thirteen runners began the 26 mile and 385 yard course from Topeka to Lawrence, they battled a "chilly north wind" as they made their way on the hardened asphalt of "U.S. Highway No. 40."[56] Providing a brief account of the marathon, a writer for the Associated Press noted that "after the first half of the run," a Winnebago named Harold Buchanan took the lead and won the race in 3 hours, 4 minutes, and 56 seconds. Chaca finished in second place, just two minutes behind the frontrunner. "Chacca, who only weighs 125 pounds," the reporter remarked, "was the smallest of the 13 runners who started."[57]

When Chaca competed in Kansas, he had yet to make a name for himself as a top distance runner. However, this changed more than a year later when the Southern Pacific Amateur Athletic Union (AAU) held a special run in Los Angeles to time him at a distance of six miles. Hosting the event at the Los Angeles Memorial Coliseum on May 4, 1929, the AAU organized the timing to determine if Chaca had the ability to set a new world's record. At the time, English runner Alfred Shrubb held the record with a time of 29 minutes and 59.8 seconds, a feat he accomplished in 1904. As Chaca ran in the coliseum, three officials from the AAU timed him, with one of them paying close attention to the number of laps the Hopi runner had completed. To the astonishment of some, Chaca finished the six miles in 29 minutes and 44 seconds, setting a new world's record.[58] The Hopi runner had arrived at the Coliseum somewhat unknown, and he left numbered among the top distance runners in the world. However, the excitement surrounding Chaca's accomplishment would not last for long.

Within days of the timed race, powerful individuals in the California running community questioned the AAU's final results. After the event, coaches in the stand complained to AAU official Robert S. Weaver that they had timed Chaca two minutes slower. Even one of the official time-keepers, Sid Foster, later told Weaver that he clocked the Hopi runner finishing the race in 31 minutes and 44 seconds.[59] Others questioned Chaca's accomplishment, including Coach Boyd Comstock of the LAAC. When asked by Braven Dyer of the *Los Angeles Times* to comment on the controversy surrounding Chaca's performance, Comstock replied: "[Shrubb] was a great runner and I can't conceive of Chauca bettering his record." Comstock knew Chaca personally, and he was familiar with the Hopi runner's abilities as a long-distance runner. "Comstock coached Chauca last year and the season before that," Dyer remarked in the *Times*, "and considers the Indian a fine marathon prospect but not a world beater over the six-mile route."[60] Although the controversy slowly diminished, and Chaca ultimately never received credit for breaking the world's record, the situation brought attention to him, and people across the nation wondered what he might accomplish next.

On June 15, 1929, the *Los Angeles Times* hosted the first pre-Olympic marathon, and newspaper reporters immediately focused their attention on the match between the nineteen-year-old Harry Chaca and the forty-year-old Clarence De Mar.[61] Known as the "Melrose Marvel,"[62] De Mar had competed as part of the 1912 and 1924 Olympic teams and had won the Boston Marathon in 1927; many reporters and columnists therefore favored him to win the event.[63] With thousands of spectators in attendance, the marathon started at the Los Angeles City Hall, and the course stretched nearly twenty-seven miles. During the first three miles, Chaca "stayed well back behind the pack," then "gradually moved up among the leaders." Nine miles into the race he ran "easily in fourth place," as Hopi runners Franklin Suhu, Howard Tsemptewa, and De Mar took the lead positions.

At Pico and Robertson streets, "the eleven-mile mark," Chaca "slipped into third place and four blocks farther on he moved right up behind De Mar." The other Hopi runners gradually slipped back "until the race became a two-man battle between" Chaca and the "veteran of all American marathoners." As the race intensified, De Mar "soused himself, both inside and out, with water," while Chaca "took only one or two drinks over the entire route." Five miles from the finish, Chaca wanted to increase his pace, but Coach Bert Jameison urged him to wait just a little longer. Finally, at mile-marker twenty-five on Sunset Boulevard, Chaca "broke away from the celebrated eastern star" and "hit the finish line more than three minutes ahead" of De Mar.[64] An observer of the event recalled that a "huge mob had gathered—a mob that surged and formed into the street" to see and congratulate Chaca as he completed the race.[65]

By the end of 1929, Chaca had achieved celebrity status in the athletic community, and news of his accomplishments had spread to various parts of the world.[66] Six months after Chaca's victory in the pre-Olympic marathon, a report in the *Sherman Bulletin* noted that according to the Los Angeles newspapers, "a Japanese runner by the name of Yoshikiyo Sudsuki announced on November 29, that the main purpose of his trip to America was to run against Harry Chacca, famed Indian runner of Sherman Institute," who at that time ran "under the auspices of the Los Angeles Athletic Club."[67] Sudsuki, representing the Kinjo Commercial School of Tokyo,[68] came to the United States from Japan where he learned that Chaca was one of the "greatest long distance runners in America." Realizing that Chaca was scheduled to run in the Pre-Olympic National Marathon in Vallejo, California, on December 22, 1929, Sudsuki joined the race with the sole purpose of defeating the Hopi runner. Students at the school wrote about the upcoming marathon in the *Sherman Bulletin*. With a headline that read "Jap Athlete Training to Beat Harry Chacca," the student newspaper reported that Chaca appeared to be the "only runner in America" who stood a "chance at beating Sudsuki."[69]

The students' use of the term "Jap" to describe the Japanese athlete likely stemmed from the political and social relationship between Japan and the United States during this period. Gerald R. Gems observed that the "political relations with Japan and the United States deteriorated precipitously" when Congress passed the California Alien Land Law of 1913, which prohibited Asians and other immigrants from owning land.[70] Furthermore, as Eiichiro Azuma has pointed out, the Gentleman's Agreement in 1908 between President Theodore Roosevelt and Japan "put a halt to labor migration across the Pacific," and the National Origins Act of 1924 "prohibited the entry of immigrants from Japan altogether."[71] Now possessing full American citizenship, and aware of the tensions between Americans and Japanese in California, the students at Sherman rallied behind their schoolmate and understood the marathon to be a match between the two nations. In this regard, Chaca represented more than the Hopi people and his school. In this international context, the Hopi runner from Polacca became a representative of the United States, and the marathon became a contest between American nationalism and Japanese imperialism. While American Indians and Japanese immigrants encountered similar experiences during this period, as both Indians and Asians were considered a marginalized minority group in American society, and Japanese and Indian children were required to attend segregated schools,[72] the students at Sherman emphasized Chaca's status as an American runner in their hopes of defeating the runner from Japan.

The pre-Olympic marathon was not the first event in which a Hopi from an Indian school competed for the United States against a Japanese runner. In their examination of Japanese sports history, historians Allen Guttmann and Lee Thompson recall that at the 1912 Olympic Games in Stockholm, Louis Tewanima outran Kanaguri Shizo, a Japanese runner who lost consciousness at the halfway point of the marathon when he stopped for a moment to rest.[73] Guttmann and Thompson point out that Japanese long-distance runners performed poorly in the Olympic Games of 1912, and in the 1920s, and they did not have a reputation of being top competitors in other running venues. At the Pre-Olympic National Marathon in December 1929, Sudsuki had an opportunity to return honor to Japan, reverse US sentiments about Japanese runners, and establish a winning presence in one of America's most revered sporting events. A Japanese win in the marathon would have also helped bolster ethnic pride to the thousands of Japanese living in Southern California during this period.[74] Eriko Yamamoto observed that in the "face of exclusion," many Japanese in California "sought to frame their racial stigma in a positive light," and the "Olympics offered the chance to redefine marginality as a cosmopolitan that could coexist with white culture and contribute to American society."[75]

In the late 1920s, racial hierarchies in the United States situated American Indians on a slightly higher level than Japanese and other Asian people. White Americans considered the Japanese race to be "unassimilable and undesirable in the United States,"[76] while many white people admired American Indian cultures and believed that Indians could be assimilated. The students at Sherman Institute may have been cognizant of these supposed racial differences and wanted to prove to themselves and remind the Southern California community that they were better than the Japanese. Ultimately, Chaca's speed and endurance proved too much for the forty-nine-year-old from Tokyo. The Hopi runner ran at a "killing pace to win" the full marathon in 2 hours, 41 minutes, 25 seconds, a "full second better than the performance of Alpien Stenroos" in the 1924 Olympic Games in Paris.[77] One of the fifty thousand spectators of the marathon recalled that Chaca's "victory" was "all the more noteworthy for his sensational finish. After trailing for twenty-three miles it was at that mark that he applied a final burst of speed that sent him ahead" of Hopi runner Franklin Suhu. "Two minutes behind [Chaca]," Bill Tobitt of the Oakland Tribune observed, "came Franklin Suhu, one of his pace setters, while seven minutes after the leader arrived, Art Myra, Olympic club veteran of San Francisco, rolled over the line for third place."[78] In addition to winning the race, Chaca set a new American marathon record, which immediately confirmed his place as the top runner in the nation.

At this time in history, the political significance of sport had increased, and Americans relished the fact that a representative from the United States had defeated a foreign runner. In his examination of sports in US culture, historian Mark Dyreson noted that in the early twentieth century, "as the United States moved toward becoming a world power of the first rank, American commentators had decided that athletics was a necessary ingredient in the composition of modern states."[79] Strong sentiments of nationalism surrounded American sports, and white spectators enthusiastically cheered for a Native person when he competed against an athlete from other countries, particularly those nations, such as Japan, whose diplomatic relationship with the United States had worsened.

When Jim Thorpe, the Sac and Fox runner from Carlisle, and Louis Tewanima competed in the 1912 Olympic Games in Stockholm, shouts of support resonated among people across the nation. Although many white Americans held to hierarchies of race and class, Natives who competed against white or colored athletes from different countries evoked support from racists and nonracists alike. When Native runners stepped onto the track field and took their mark at the starting line, their brown skin and "uncivilized" heritage momentarily held little significance for white spectators and those in print media.[80] While the "sporting republic," as Dyreson suggests, may have appeared "color blind" when Native runners raced against athletes from other nations, newspaper reporters often used racial stereotypes in their headlines to grab the attention of their white readers. Referring to Indian runners as "Redskinned," calling Harry Chaca the "little brown dynamo," or telling their readers that the "Injuns" had forsaken the "Warpath for the Cinderpath," newspaper reporters utilized racist and unflattering imagery to position Native people in a specific racial hierarchy, and to increase sales among their white audience.[81]

Although Hopi runners were fueled by their accomplishments and the attention they gained in US newspapers, the fame they received at off-reservation Indian boarding schools did not last forever. After their terms at the school had expired, the runners migrated back to their ancestral lands and attempted to reacclimate themselves to reservation life. Harry Chaca returned to his village of Polacca and eventually became the chairman of the Hopi Tribe.[82] Others, however, remained at their villages for a short time and then pursued opportunities beyond the mesas. When Guy Maktima came home to Ho'atvela in 1913, he immediately volunteered in the US Army and served the nation during World War I with the First Arizona Infantry at Fort Huachuca.[83] Maktima's grandson, Nick Brokeshoulder from the same village, recalled that his grandfather was always proud of his running achievements at Sherman Institute.[84]

While he did not compete in a major marathon when he returned to Ho'atvela, Maktima's legacy as a great Hopi runner continued with his family and village community. Unlike Maktima, who sought a life of adventure in the army, Philip Zeyouma married a fellow Sherman student named Christina Campbell after he left the school in 1913 and then moved to Bloomington, California, to work in various trade occupations.[85] In 1927, Zeyouma and his family returned to Arizona and established a trading post at Elden Pueblo outside the mountain community of Flagstaff. Six years later in 1933, Zeyouma moved to the Colorado Indian Reservation near Parker, Arizona. He would eventually work as an electrician for the Bureau of Indian Affairs before passing away in Parker at the age of eighty-seven on February 13, 1969.[86]

Zeyouma also never forgot about his running accomplishments at the school. In the 1940s, Zeyouma asked Superintendent Biery if he could take "some trophy cups he [had] won" back home with him to the reservation.[87] Zeyouma's desire to obtain his trophies may appear as though he went beyond traditional understandings of running in Hopi culture and embraced the value that American society attributed to trophies and medals. However, in Hopi culture, the people have always considered awards

Two of several running trophies that Hopi runner Philip Zeyouma of Musangnuvi won as a member of the Sherman Institute cross-country team, 1912–1914. Photograph by author.

to be an important component of Hopi running. When the Hopi runner won the race between the once-occupied villages of Tikuvi and Payupki, he received belts, bows, and other items for his victory.[88] He gave some of these awards to Spider Grandmother, but he also retained some for himself and his community. Zeyouma may have wanted to keep his trophies for his family and Hopi community, but he was prevented from doing so. Before he died in 1931, Superintendent of Sherman Institute Frank Conser promised to return the cups to Zeyouma. Instead of complying with Zeyouma's request, new Superintendent Biery noted that the "trophies won by Sherman students" were "ordinarily . . . displayed at the school and [were] not given to students." The superintendent further stated that as a result of the "many years" that had passed since Zeyouma won his trophies, he did not wish to give Zeyouma his awards.[89]

For over a hundred years, Zeyouma's trophies have remained at the Sherman Indian Museum in Riverside, California.[90] When Native athletes at Sherman won races and other competitions, school officials immediately claimed ownership of their trophy cups and medals. Although marathon organizers often engraved the pupil's name on the awards, school officials considered the items to be part of the school's property. As visitors came to the school, the display of Indian trophies presented the institution in a positive light and demonstrated to the public that the students at Sherman had the capacity to compete and defeat white athletes at the national and international levels. The polished trophies also impressed the Indian pupils at the school and encouraged them to seek excellence and to value the importance of discipline and hard work.

Many Native athletes, however, disagreed with the school's trophy retention policy. In December 1914, when Zeyouma told the editors of the *Los Angeles Times* that he wanted to run for the Los Angeles Athletic Club, he also shared a grievance with them involving Sherman and his trophies. According to Howard W. Angus, Zeyouma became "sore" at school officials when they insisted on keeping his running trophies.[91] Angus reported that the "Indian school" had "kept all [of] his cups" and that school officials had "filled a whole showcase with them."[92] Zeyouma and other Hopi runners at Sherman Institute seldom reunited with their awards. When they returned to the reservation, the Hopi runners did not arrive with physical proof of their victories.[93] Instead, they told their families about their accomplishments through stories, and relied on their Hopi peers to keep the memory of their running legacies alive.

Superintendents at other off-reservation Indian boarding schools, however, seldom kept individual school trophies from Indian athletes. Barbara Landis, public historian and biographer of the Carlisle school, once remarked that nearly all of the Carlisle trophies housed in the Cumberland County Historical Society (CCHS) collections in Pennsylvania are "team trophies." Landis noted that "since the teams were all pan-tribal, there is not one individual or nation to whom the trophies could be repatriated."[94] The one exception in the CCHS collection is a trophy won by Louis Tewanima in 1910.[95] Although museum curators at Indian schools are often hesitant to relinquish control of objects in their collections, or repatriate items to Indian communities, the individual medals and cups housed at Sherman Institute raise the question of whether the museum should return the trophies to their original owners, especially in light of key legal developments.

In 1990, for example, the US Congress passed the Native American Graves Protection and Repatriation Act (NAGPRA) to require federally funded museums and agencies to repatriate certain cultural or ceremonial objects to Native communities.[96] As a federally funded school with the Bureau of Indian Affairs, one may argue that Sherman Institute, now called Sherman Indian High School, falls within the legal parameters of NAGPRA. However, Indian repatriation cases almost always involve human remains or ceremonial objects, and not individual trophies won by Indian pupils. While sport trophies have great meaning to Indian students and their families, sacred objects, land, and human remains have explicit cultural or ceremonial significance to Indigenous people. Ultimately, the decision to repatriate nonceremonial items from the Sherman Indian Museum rests in the hands of the museum staff and other school officials. Although more than seventy years have passed since Superintendent Biery denied Philip Zeyouma's request for his running trophies, today's museum curator and director, Lorene Sisquoc, makes every effort to provide the public with access to the museum's collection, which includes more than two hundred sports medals and cups that Hopi and non-Hopi athletes have won.

When Philip Zeyouma, Guy Maktima, Harry Chaca, and other Hopis competed and won trophies in US marathons, newspaper reporters, school officials, and other Indian students realized that they had come from a people of great runners. Coach Jameison understood this reality well, and when a reporter asked him about the Hopi runners and the prospect of them competing in the 1932 Olympics, Jameison replied: "[Franklin] Suhu, a Hopi brave, will beat any white man in the world at fifty or 100 miles. . . . This boy will finish five minutes or more in front of any white man at fifty miles. . . . However, let me tell you something. These fellows are nothing compared to their elders back on the reservations. Any one of their grandfathers could beat 'em without drawing a hard breath."[97]

Coach Jameison's remarks came at a time when Americans looked to Hopi and other Indian runners to represent the nation in upcoming Olympics. Even as early as 1925, race promoter Jack Case, who was also the cross-country coach for the Southern Pacific Association of the Amateur Athletic Union, sought Indian runners for the event. "In six years," Case remarked to a reporter, "which is the time we have before the Olympic Games in Los Angeles, we hope to develop a couple of Nurmi's on the Indian reservations in our own backyard."[98] By 1932, it was clear that the Indian in their "own backyard" was Franklin Suhu. "What prospect there is for a native California making the American team rests with Franklin Suhu," a writer for the Associated Press remarked.[99] Although Suhu had won several races during his career at Sherman, including the prestigious

Long Beach Press-Telegram Marathon in spring 1931,[100] he failed to qualify for the Olympic Team at the 1932 *Los Angeles Times* Pre-Olympic Marathon.[101] While he placed second in the event, and rightfully earned a spot on the team, he finished nearly twenty minutes behind the lead runner Whitey Michelsen. Ultimately, Suhu's finishing time of 3 hours, 5 minutes, and 14 seconds likely caused officials with the American Olympic Committee to reconsider whether to enter the Hopi runner in the Olympic Games.

While school officials at Sherman Institute taught Hopi and other Indian students how to play American forms of basketball, football, and baseball, neither Joe Shoulder nor Bert Jameison needed to show the Hopis the essence of long-distance running. For the Hopi athletes at Sherman, the cinder paths of Southern California momentarily replaced the dirt trails on the reservation, and their peers became their community away from home. But they never forgot their connection to the land, and who they were as Hopi people. Furthermore, they used their participation on the school's cross-country team as a venue for broadening their understanding of Hopi running in the twentieth century. They learned to navigate within their tribe and school communities, and among a people who considered their success in marathons to be an important component in the formation of US nationalism.

Although Hopis at Sherman Institute navigated the US cross-country circuit, not every Hopi who competed in America did so as a representative of an off-reservation Indian boarding school. By the 1920s, other Hopis back home had attracted the attention of race promoters, including white individuals on the reservation who recruited Hopis for meets across the country. At this time, race promoters did not have to rely solely on Indian schools to introduce them to exceptional Hopi talent. They could instead work directly with non-Hopis on the reservation to secure runners for American races. These people provided the athletes with race entrance fees, paid for their travel and lodging expenses, and perhaps most importantly, publicized them in American newspapers and other venues. But they also allowed Hopis with no prior school attendance, and no formal training on a cross-country team, to compete in the nation's most prestigious running events. And since they were not associated with a government school, the runners had the freedom and the financial backing to race and train where they wanted. And they did not have to manage school responsibilities or other expectations that Hopi athletes at Indians schools had to contend with.

CHAPTER SIX

Footraces across America

On Sunday, October 10, 1926, officials for the first annual Broad-moor-Cheyenne Mountain Highway Race dispensed white chalk across a dirt road to mark the starting line for the event. With the line established, three Hopi runners named Arthur Pohequaptewa, Ray Honkuku, and Nicholas Qömawunu (Quomawahu) waited to begin the five-mile climb to the top of Cheyenne Mountain near Colorado Springs, Colorado. Standing alongside two Zuni and one Acoma runner from New Mexico, four white competitors from Colorado, and one runner from Switzerland, the Hopis fixed their attention on the ten-thousand-foot summit and contemplated the grueling path before them.[1] For two months prior to the race, the Hopi and Pueblo Indian runners trained together in the high deserts of New Mexico for this moment. They knew each other's running styles, weaknesses, and strengths, and they would soon test their training against some of the best distance runners in the nation.[2]

Before the race, newspapers across the Southwest ran stories to heighten awareness about the great event. While a local newspaper described the race as "one of the most unique sporting events in history" and the "first International marathon" on the mountain, those present knew it was first and foremost a match between the Indian and white runners. Making their final preparations, and waiting for the event to commence, nobody sensed this more than the runners themselves. The tension and excitement filling the air stood in contrast to the cool mountain breeze blowing gently through the ponderosa pines. And as a crowd of spectators looked on, an official standing to the right of the runners raised a gun steadily in the air and fired one round to signal the start of the race. Hearing the "crack of the pistol" and the hollers of the many onlookers, the "six Indian runners" leaped from the starting line and ran with "tireless strides over the steadily rising grades" of the mountain highway.

One newspaper reporter noted that during the race, none of the Indian runners stopped or slowed down, but kept a steady pace that "equaled the speed of an automobile climbing the mountain in second gear." Even marathon officials, "who started out in their cars ahead" of the runners, "found themselves forced to 'step on it'" to "keep the dust" from interfering with the athletes. Wearing "brightly-hued trunks," the Indian runners remained together until just below the summit. At this point all three Hopis broke stride with the Zuni and Acoma runners, which resulted in a "thunderous ovation" from the fifteen hundred spectators lining the route. Sensing the excitement of the crowd, "Little Pohoquapteawa, the smallest of the wiry Indian team," made one last push for the lead and won the race in thirty-five minutes and forty-nine seconds. Six seconds later, Honkuku, the Hopi "distance champion who won national fame at the Gallup and Los Vegas marathon classics," came in second, while Qömawunu, running on an injured ankle, finished third.[3]

Not long after Qömawunu's finish, the Zunis and runner from Acoma reached the summit, but the white runners lagged three to ten minutes behind the "last Indian" to complete the course. Jack Phillipson, a top distance runner in Colorado, was first among the "palefaces" to cross the finish line, while the remaining runners "trotted" or walked to the end. Some of the white runners complained that the weather was "too warm" for a race, but the "Indians, who recently raced in Gallup during their mammoth ceremonial in a temperature of 103 degrees, were only slightly perspiring upon reaching the summit." Having received "skepticism at every hand" when he or others mentioned the "unbelievable exploits" of the Indian athletes, Coach Mike Kirk exclaimed to reporters that America would "soon realize" that Indians from the Southwest are the best runners in the nation, and that "under proper training" could develop into "world champions." "This race," he remarked, "will go far towards attracting the attention" of people out West to the remarkable "athletes living among them."[4]

Kirk's attempt to awaken people's awareness to the exceptional talent of his Indian runners speaks to a larger issue facing Indian athletes and their promoters during this period. In the mid-1920s, few Native athletes had won a major sport competition at the national or international level. Fifteen years had passed since Sac and Fox athlete Jim Thorpe won gold medals in the decathlon and pentathlon in the 1912 Olympic Games in Stockholm, Sweden.[5] And it had been nearly twenty years since Onondaga runner Tom Longboat won the prestigious Boston Marathon in 1907.[6] Although Indians such as Zuni runner Gordon Coola and Pima runner Willie Azul had won various competitions in the West, Americans at this time looked for the next great Indian athlete to rally behind.[7] Five months before the mountain highway race in Colorado, a reporter for the *Baltimore Sun* echoed this sentiment by lamenting that few remarkable Indian athletes remained in American sports. "Where once the annals of sports in this country recorded regularly the triumphs of Indian athletes," the reporter noted, "today there is no outstanding redskin in the whole field."[8]

While the writer for the *Baltimore Sun* concluded that no "outstanding redskin" existed in American athletics, over a thousand people had just witnessed four of them defeat some of the top endurance runners in the nation. Race organizers also appreciated what they had accomplished and honored them at a place and in a way usually reserved only for the elite of white American society. Unlike at the end of other races, where officials conducted the awards ceremony near start or the finish line, organizers for this race hosted the ceremony down the mountain at the Broadmoor Hotel. A "lavish resort that boasted spectacular views" of nearby Pikes Peak, the hotel served tourism needs for local ski runs and various mountain highways, including the Broadmoor Cheyenne Highway.[9] During the 1920s, many celebrities stayed at the hotel, including World Heavyweight Boxing Champion Jack Dempsey, who often trained there.[10] Here race officials hosted a ceremony for the athletes and awarded the Hopi and Pueblo Indian runners with "Silver trophies and medals."[11]

Opportunities for the Indian runners to secure additional "trophies and medals" and fuel Kirk's claims about Southwestern Indian athletes came following the Broadmoor-Cheyenne Mountain Highway Race in Colorado. In May 1927, the Lions Club of Long Beach invited Qömawunu, Pohequaptewa, and the other runners from Acoma and Zuni to compete in the highly regarded New York to Long Beach Marathon. With a headline that read "Four Indians Arrive for Marathon Run," a *New York Times* reporter noted that the runners came to the city to "go on a warpath of 26 miles and 385 yards." Describing the runner's participation as an act of battle between the Indian and white athletes, the reporter elicited interest in the marathon by sensationalizing the Indians as a savage and warlike people. No longer wreaking havoc for the US government or white settlers out West, the Indians had brought the fight to America's largest city, where speed and physical endurance became the weapons that mattered most.

When the runners arrived at the Grand Central Station in New York, Mayor of Long Beach William J. Dalton and Theodore I. Schwartzman, president of the Chamber of Commerce, along with a "delegation" of other esteemed individuals, welcomed the runners and took them to the Hotel Nassau in the nearby city of Long Beach. After the runners had a light meal, they left the hotel and stepped on to the boardwalk for a "limbering-up run after their long [train] ride" from Gallup, New Mexico. Wearing their traditional running attire of "moccasins, a tight and abbreviated pair of running trunks" and wide headbands, the runners ran on the boardwalk for an hour, all the while attracting the attention of tourists and other beachgoers. And to the amusement of the runners, many of these spectators photographed them as they made their way back to the hotel.[12]

Staying in the hotel's "roof garden bungalow," the Indian runners brought more than their traditional ways of running to Long Beach. Hotel staff often heard the runners singing their traditional songs, and they observed the men speaking to each other in their Native languages. At times the staff even heard the runners emitting loud "whoops" and executing a "war dance" according to Indian ways. While the runners practiced certain aspects of their culture with few limitations, other areas proved especially burdensome for them. Far from their homelands and staying in one of the most upscale hotels in America, the runners experienced accommodations to which they were not accustomed. Each morning, hotel staff prepared a large American-style breakfast for their guests, but the runners preferred their traditional foods of corn mush, mutton stew, and jerky.[13] Hearing of their discontent, a reporter for the *New York Times* noted that the four Indian runners "found great inconvenience in eating ham and eggs, waffles, breakfast rolls, coffee and other such foods." Wanting to accommodate the dietary needs of their guests, the hotel staff responded by installing a "coal stove" in their bungalow so that the runners could make and prepare food according to their liking and customs.[14]

From on top of the Hotel Nassau, the Indian runners also had a spectacular view of the city, the coastline, and the vast expanse of the Atlantic Ocean. In their brief history of Long Beach, historians Roberta Fiore, Carole Shahda Geraci, and Dave Roochvarg noted that "high above all, providing a vista encompassing the beach, the ocean horizon, and New York City, was the Nassau's most predominate feature, the Lunetta, its rooftop garden where guests could take afternoon tea or dine and dance under its twinkling lights."[15] Designed in the "Spanish Renaissance style" by architects Lewis R. Kaufman and B. E. Stern, the three-hundred-room hotel and rooftop garden restaurant catered to wealthy patrons who were used to the finer things in life. "Here 1,000 guests could dine on 'cuisine Francaise' or fresh seafood from the Atlantic,'" Bette Wiedman and Linda Martin once remarked, "dance to Neapolitan orchestra in the rooftop garden, and recover their health by taking 'hot or cold sea baths.'"[16]

While their "ocean horizon" view did not resemble the buttes of Zuni or the mesas of Hopi, it was not unrelated to their cultures. For example, in Don Talayesva's autobiography *Sun Chief*, the book's editor Leo Simmons observed that when Talayesva visited the Atlantic Ocean while in New Haven, Connecticut, he recalled the "legendary accounts" of the Hurung Wuhti, or the "Lady of the Eastern Ocean." "When he was taken to the beach," Simmons noted, Talayesva "walked reverently to the water and prayed: 'Our Mother of the Ocean, I have arrived from afar to pray to you. I thank you for all your blessings and I have come to tell you about life among the Hopi.'" Talayesva then asked that Hurung Wuhti "drive off disease" from the Hopi, and to hasten her spirit people to cause the clouds to bring rain to his village of Orayvi. After his prayer, Talayesva "stopped and splashed water four times toward his home, wet his hands, and rubbed them over his heart to make himself 'good and strong.'"[17] Considering that Qömawunu and Pohequaptewa held male society responsibilities back home at Orayvi, the Hopi runners certainly knew the religious significance the Atlantic Ocean held for their people.

With the presence of Hurung Wuhti nearby, Hopi runners Qömawunu and Pohequaptewa joined 133 other runners to race in the New York to Long Beach Marathon on May 15, 1927. The route began in front of the New York Athletic Club building in New York and finished at City Hall in the nearby town of Long Beach.[18] With thousands of spectators lining the route, Qömawunu and Albert (Whitey) Michelsen ran near each other for most of the marathon, lagging just behind Pohequaptewa, who was in the lead. But Pohequaptewa could not maintain his lead for long. Sixteen miles into the race the Hopi runner relinquished his position due to bleeding blisters and other sores on his feet.[19] When Pohequaptewa slowed down, Qömawunu, Michelsen, and "several white runners went by." Seeing that his tribesman had quit the race, Qömawunu picked up his pace and "began to run," passing Michelsen "five miles from the finish line" and running the "rest of the way without slackening the furious pace." Shortly after Qömawunu's win, Robert Edgren of the *Baltimore Sun* attempted to make sense of the Hopi runner's performance. "The great Indian runner was handicapped by many conditions of the race," observed Edgren. "He had never run before except on the desert near his home, the Oraibi pueblo . . . 7,000 feet above sea level, where the air is extremely dry." Edgren explained that back on the Hopi mesas, Qömawunu "ran across the open desert country, on sand or ground made of silt and disintegrated rock washed down from the mountains. He had no experience running on cement or asphalt or brick pavements."[20]

While Edgren considered Qömawunu's experience running on the Hopi mesas to be a handicap when competing against top runners in New York, other newspaper writers argued that the Hopi runner's greatest handicap were the "American shoes" that marathon officials required him to use during the race. In the early 1900s, race officials at times allowed Hopis to run in their traditional moccasins if they desired. Hopi runner Philip Zeyouma of Musangnuvi and Guy Maktima from Ho'atvela ran in moccasins to place first and second, respectively, in the *Los Angeles Times* Modified Marathon in 1912.[21] However, by the late 1920s, race officials at most major running events did not allow Hopis or other Native runners to wear traditional moccasins during competition. When Qömawunu and the other Indian runners ran together on the Long Beach boardwalk shortly after they arrived at the hotel, they did so wearing their tribal footwear. But their deerskin moccasins were not the only things related to Hopi culture that caught the attention of New Yorkers.

In the *New York Times*, sports writer John Kieren noted that not long after the Hopi runners arrived in New York, the city received large amounts of rain, so much rain that team officials for the New York Giants canceled a series of double-header games. Knowing that the Hopis had been training on the boardwalk, team club secretary Edward Aloysius Brannick "took a trip along the south shore of Long Island," saw the Hopi runners, and concluded that the Hopis had caused the rain to fall.[22] "It's those Hopi Indians who caused the downpour," explained Brannick, "They were brought here to race in the marathon from the New York Athletic Club to Long Beach on this coming Sunday. The Lions Club is sponsoring the race and the AAU gave its sanction, but if the Weather Bureau had been consulted maybe those Indians would have been barred. They are amateur runners, but they are professional rain-makers." He went on to explain that the runners had "come from the Arizona desert where rain-making is considered a sacred calling," and as "soon as they saw the sand at Long Beach they thought they were back on the desert and they started their rain-making activities." "It's pernicious," he declared, "that's what it is."[23] But Brannick was right. The Hopis who ran in New York had indeed caused the rain to fall.

Brannick's humorous but astute observation in referring to Hopi runners as "professional rain-makers" provides a telling commentary on Hopi cultural understandings of running. Back on their ancestral lands in northern Arizona, Hopi clan runners ran as a prayer for rain. Long ago, members of the Sand Clan had been instructed to run far beyond Hopi ancestral lands to entice the rain clouds to follow them back to their mesas. The faster the clan runner ran, the quicker the clouds brought much-needed moisture to their arid fields.[24] Brannick's comments also tell something about American understandings of the Hopi in the 1920s and in the decades that preceded it. For years, ethnographers, anthropologists, and other academics had observed and written extensively on the association between Hopi medicine men, including runners, their ceremonies, and rain.[25] Newspaper writers, many of them covering the infamous Hopi Snake Dance, also published thousands of articles on the rituals of the Hopi and their "peculiar" ability to bring forth moisture from the sky.[26] Referring to the Hopi as "drouth breakers," and calling their ceremonies for rain "weird and fantastic," the writers influenced American perception of the Hopi more than any others.[27]

Qömawunu's victory in the New York to Long Beach Marathon made him a highly sought after competitor in other marathons. Within days of winning the event, Qömawunu "received three invitations" to compete in other races, but his trainer Mike Kirk doubted whether he would accept any of them. While running in the marathon, the Hopi runner suffered from "badly blistered feet" and was "able to get around only very painfully." Kirk blamed Qömawunu's foot injuries, and those of Arthur Pohequaptewa, David Lino, and Ross Shack, on the "strange tennis shoes the men had to wear and the unyielding pavements over which they had to travel." Seeing how Qömawunu struggled to walk following the marathon, and how he and the other Indian runners remained in their hotel room due to their injuries, Kirk took Qömawunu and the other men to the town of Long Beach and "made a round of shops" to be "fitted with American shoes of all kinds," especially "athletic footwear."[28]

But the injury from the "strange shoes" was not the only so-called handicap potentially preventing Qömawunu from competing in future marathons. In an article in the *New York Times*, sports writer Bryan Field remarked that after the Long Beach race, "much comment was heard regarding the chances of the Indian joining the next Olympic team." In fact, according to Field, there was an "almost unanimous desire" among those in the American sports community to send the Hopi runner to the Olympic Games in Amsterdam the following year. But Field doubted Qömawunu's participation in the Olympics due to an "unusual circumstance which probably" affected "no other American athlete." "Quanowahu is a priest of the snake dance," Field remarked, "a ritualistic ceremony which is a petition for his tribe for rain." Although Qömawunu had been initiated in the Hopi Snake Society, he did not serve in the society as a "priest" or any kind of leader.[29] Furthermore, the newspaper writer explained that in odd years, the village of Walpi hosted the dances, while in the even years, such as 1928, the ceremony was held at Qömawunu's village of Orayvi.[30] The Hopi runner may have also expressed reluctance to Kirk or others about competing in the Olympic Games, which fell at the same time as the ceremony at Orayvi.[31] Although Field entertained the possibility that a "substitute priest" could be found to take Qömawunu's place, it is unlikely that the Hopi runner would forego his society responsibilities to compete in the Olympic Games, or *any* athletic event.[32]

Qömawunu's supposed priestly association with the Hopi Snake Society, and therefore the Snake Dance, attracted considerable attention from people across the nation. For years, Americans had read about the "world famous" dance and the footraces that accompanied it in newspapers and in other accounts. But for many of them to see the dance or its runners, they had to board trains, travel great distances, and spend money on excursions that most could not afford. However, when Qömawunu and his tribesman Pohequaptewa entered a race, Americans did not have to journey to Hopiland to get a taste of this so-called exotic ceremony. One newspaper writer observed that when the two Hopis ran for the dance back home, they are "clad only in breechcloths and sandals," which is similar to what they wore when they competed in the Long Beach to New York Marathon.[33] For example, with a headline that read, "Indian Snake Dancer Outstrips Big Field in 26-Mile Marathon," an article for the Associated Press observed that "In contrast to their white rivals, the Indians were stripped to the waist, and wore gayly colored bands, about their straight black hair." The Hopi ceremonial runners had competed in New York, and Americans were quite pleased with it, and wanted to see more of them.[34]

Shortly after competing in the New York to Long Beach Marathon, the Hopi runners and their trainer Mike Kirk traveled by train back to Arizona. When they reached Kansas City, Missouri, Kirk told an Associated Press reporter that he challenged the best Tarahumara runners from Mexico to race the Hopi runners who had just competed in New York. The reporter noted that Kirk "believed the Hopis could not be defeated and would post $10,000 for a race with Tarahumara for any distance from a half-mile to twenty-six miles."[35] A few weeks later Kirk furthered his challenge by remarking to a writer for the International News Service that he would "enter the entire team against any picked team of Tarahumarans," explaining that the "Mexican Indians cannot run the 10 miles as fast as the Americans, and neither can they stand the 26-mile pull as well as my men." Recalling how Qömawunu had recently "defeated 212 competitors" running "thru heavy traffic and on pavement," Kirk confidently proclaimed that the "Hopi Indian distance runner from Oribi, Ariz., can outdistance any runner from the famous Tarahumarah tribe of Mexico."[36]

Kirk's proposition to race Hopi and Tarahumara runners against each other was not a new concept among race promoters and newspaper sport columnists. Earlier that year, Damon Runyon of the International Features Service wrote in his newspaper column that while some Tarahumaras had accomplished remarkable feats in races beyond their homelands, their best runners remained back home, untainted by Western society. Quoting a young Mexican sports writer named Alvarez Lamberto Gayou, Runyon remarked that the Tarahumaras competing today are "civilized Indians" and are used to "automobiles and railroad engines," and are "not so good runners as the 'wild' Indians in the mountains" of the Sierra Madre. "It would be interesting," Gayou quotes an individual living with the Tarahumara named Alyuardo, "for an American promoter" to organize a race between the Tarahumara, Zuni, Hopi, and a white runner named Doctor John J. Seiler, also known as "The Flying Yank."[37] Although an American promoter never organized a race between Hopi runners and those of the Tarahumara, Qömawunu soon demonstrated his running prowess in a race that stretched from one end of the nation to the other.

In early March 1928, Charles C. Pyle, a wealthy businessman and sports agent, organized a 3,400-mile footrace from Los Angeles to New York City. Wanting to promote the newly built highway Route 66 and himself, Pyle offered the runners $48,500 in total winnings, and promised to award the first-place runner a handsome sum of $25,000. To raise money for the race, Pyle would charge municipalities to be part of the route, and in true Barnum & Bailey fashion, he envisioned those towns hosting carnivals with animals, acrobats, and "pink lemonade" and "peanut and hot dog stands." "The side-shows and various concessions are expected to inveigle cities along United States highway 66," a reporter for the *Pittsburgh Post-Gazette* observed, "to share in paying for the race which Pyle expects to net him $200,000."[38]

In his history of the Bunion Derby, Charles B. Kastner noted that many of the participants arrived in Los Angeles for their prerace training by locomotive. "They disembarked from trains arriving from snow-bound Midwest farm towns," Kastner observed, "crammed eastern cities, and points far and wide." While the majority of the runners arrived at Los Angeles by rail, Qömawunu and his other trainer and Indian trader Lorenzo Hubbell, Jr., opted for a different mode of transportation. Nearly two weeks before the start of the Bunion Derby, a writer for the *Winslow Daily Mail* reported that Hubbell and his "Indian protege" had made "final preparations" to leave Winslow for Los Angeles by automobile. They are "making the trip by automobile," the writer observed, "to accustom the Indian runner with the road on the first lap of the marathon classic." When asked by the *Mail* about his ability to run long distances, and of his recent victory in the Long Beach marathon in New York "against a field of nationally known runners," Qömawunu simply replied, "I am going to win."[39]

Confident in his prospect of winning the race, Qömawunu and Hubbell left Winslow for the 520-mile journey to Los Angeles. During his road trip to Southern California, the Hopi runner from Orayvi made the gradual incline through the mountains of northern Arizona. To the north, Mount Elden and the snow-capped San Francisco Peaks—or Nuvatukwi'ovi as Hopis call them—stood in the distance. In the past, many Hopis had ventured beyond their mesas to make this journey. Nearly thirty years before, the group of nineteen Hopi prisoners traveled this route by train to their final destination at Alcatraz Island in the San Francisco Bay.[40] And in the early 1900s, hundreds of Hopi children and young adults passed through this region on their way to boarding schools out West, most notably Sherman Institute in Riverside, California.[41] In this regard, Qömawunu had embarked on a journey and route well traveled by Hopis of the past. But whereas they mostly traveled this route by train, he did so in an automobile.

Riding in an automobile allowed Qömawunu to experience the route in way that would have been impossible for him had he taken the train. The Hopi runner and his trainer had the freedom to pull over and study inclines, plan running strategies, and take note of the climate and elevation of certain regions. Similar to when Philip Zeyouma studied the route prior to running in the *Los Angeles Times* Modified Marathon, Qömawunu planned ahead and envisioned crossing this terrain in his mind. As they traveled further west, crossing over the Colorado River and passing through Needles, California, the men had opportunities to talk at length about the vast desert that lay behind and before them. They experienced the dry and warm weather and took special notice of the long stretches of road through the Mojave Desert. And as they approached the dusty town of Barstow and began heading south, they studied the changes in the topography as they made their way through the Cajon Pass and into the San Bernardino area. By the time Qömawunu had reached the city, he knew exactly what lay before him, at least up to the town of Winslow. But he had experienced this route by automobile, and soon he would traverse this path by foot and test the limits of his body and his determination to win.

When Qömawunu arrived in Los Angeles, Hubbell quickly had the Hopi runner begin training with other contestants in preparation for the race. But seven days after Qömawunu left Arizona, a writer for the *Los Angeles Times* reported that the Hopi runner's training runs caused the other athletes to worry about Qömawunu's stamina and endurance. "How to stop Chief Quomawahu," asked the *Times*, "from copping Sunday's twenty-five mile gallop is the problem confronting scores of runners now in training at Ascot Speedway." Concerned that Qömawunu would dominate the race from the start, and likely win, a number of the "best athletes" worked together to figure "out some way to alternate their sprints so as to make the pace too hot for" the Hopi runner. "There is plenty of rivalry all around," observed the *Times*, "and inasmuch as this Sunday's race is the last before the start of the transcontinental journey there are plenty of runners desirous of copping first money."[42]

On the afternoon of March 4, 1928, Qömawunu and 198 other runners gathered in the Legion Ascot Speedway stadium to begin the much-anticipated race across America.[43] With the firing of the starter's revolver, the race commenced and the men left the stadium in groups of twenty-five each, two minutes apart.[44] The first day's leg was an uneventful, and unchallenging, jaunt of sixteen miles to the town of Puente. Qömawunu strolled into the race camp at Puente in fourth place, "traversing" the distance in "one hour and 44 minutes." Finnish runner Willie Kolehmainen, the brother of Hans Kolehmainen, who won the gold medal competing against Louis Tewanima in the 1912 Olympics, was first to arrive in Puente, six minutes ahead of Qömawunu.[45]

Among the top runners to complete the stretch from Los Angeles to Puente, Qömawunu knew that the distance and intensity of the race would only increase. The next day, the runners "braved" the cold and rain to run 34.7 miles, twice the distance they had covered the day before, to the town of Bloomington, a few miles north of Sherman Institute. Kastner noted that many of the runners "made concessions for the weather with tracksuits, while others gave in altogether and wore layers of clothing, raincoats, and wool underwear."[46] To the surprise of some race organizers, Qömawunu arrived in Bloomington in tenth place with a time of 4 hours, 55 minutes, and 20 seconds. Kolehmainen once again took first place, completing the stretch 33 minutes ahead of the Hopi runner. By the second day of the Bunion Derby, sports writers began to question Qömawunu's odds of winning the race, and focused their attention on the young Finnish runner. "It marked the second straight day in which he had led the great field of runners," remarked a reporter for the *Evening News*, and therefore he has "been established as the outstanding favorite to win most of C. C. Pyle's $50,000 prize money."[47]

While newspaper writers doubted Qömawunu's chances of outrunning and outdistancing Kolehmainen, the Hopi runner soon forced them to reconsider their initial conclusions. On the third day of the race, 183 runners made the grueling twenty-mile trek up the Cajon Pass, and then another fifteen miles to the town of Victorville, California. But three miles into the race, Kolehmainen, running alongside his fellow countryman Nestor Erickson, suffered major physical ailments that forced him to slow down considerably. Kolehmainen "self-destructed when he pulled a tendon," Kastner observed, and then he "slowed to a crawl, and began an agonizing nine-and-a-half hour walk to the finish line." With Kolehmainen essentially out of the race, Qömawunu now focused on defeating Erickson. As they made their way through the Cajon Pass, the two runners ran within a short distance of each other, but Qömawunu dug in to keep the lead. Twenty miles into the race, at the summit of the pass, Erickson took advantage of the downhill path toward Barstow and finished the race in first place in a time of 6 hours and 45 minutes, just 5 minutes ahead of

Qömawunu. But while in the three days of running Qömawunu had not won a single race, his "average time for the trip so far" had surpassed all of the other runners. The "Hopi Indian" had now become the leader of the Bunion Derby.[48]

News of Qömawunu's performance ignited a flurry of excitement among American sport writers who saw a highly romanticized and racist connection between Indian runners and the land. "Injun country—that's what they call these desert lands between Cajon Pass Summit and New Mexico," Maxwell Stiles of the *Cincinnati Enquirer* remarked. Describing the Mojave Desert as a place where one "blister[s] beneath an arid sun," Stiles noted that it took "an Injun to make any decent sort of showing in a foot race here—and Injun or a Finn." Suggesting that Qömawunu had an advantage as an "Injun" running through "Injun country," Stiles went on to explain that "with the Injun country stretching out ahead for miles, there is every reason to believe that Quomawahu's weird name will be much in public print for some few days to come."[49]

Although he had taken the lead position, by the time Qömawunu arrived at Barstow on March 7, the Hopi runner was in terrible shape. Sports writers had referred to him as a "son of the desert lands" and had initially expected him to excel in the heat of the Mojave Desert. But near the start of the day's race, Qömawunu "fell victim to cramps," quickly "dropped from the forefront of the pack," and was "forced to slow down to a walking gait."[50] At one point Qömawunu's cramps became so severe that he stopped on the side of the road while his attendants rubbed his legs to relieve his tense muscles.[51] He also suffered from injuries to his feet and ankles, and fourteen miles west of town, the Hopi runner stopped and requested a ride to Barstow in an automobile. But Qömawunu's failure to complete the stretch from Victorville to Barstow did not disqualify him from the race. The next morning, race officials drove Qömawunu to where he left off the previous day and he walked fourteen miles back again to Barstow. Once he reached Barstow, he began the day's race to a small watering outpost thirty-one miles away called Mojave Wells.[52]

While the race up to Barstow required the athletes to run on hardened pavement, the next forty-two-mile stretch from Mojave Wells to Bagdad largely consisted of soft gravel. For many of the runners, including Qömawunu, who had injured their feet or ankles as they pounded along on the hardened surface, the gravel path provided much-needed relief to their aching bodies. The "gravel desert road was a welcome sod for the sore feet" of the Hopi runner, a *Los Angeles Times* writer remarked, and after hitting the "native dirt the Hopi broke from his lagging walk into a run and passed many of the tail-enders."[53] Although Qömawunu seemed to have gained strength and improved his stride once he hit the gravel path east of Bagdad, he struggled to keep even a slow trot for the remaining distance of the day's race. "Nicholas Quamawahu," James Powers of the United Press noted, "Hopi Indian from Arizona, who sprained an ankle two days ago and since has been forced to go slowly, walked today and finished in 76th place." He completed the day's stretch in 11 hours, 56 minutes, and 10 seconds, more than 5 hours behind first-place runner Arthur Newton.[54]

Qömawunu was not the only runner suffering from some kind of physical handicap between Mojave Wells and Bagdad. Covering themselves in grease to protect their skin from the "blazing sun" and wrapping their bodies in tape to secure their injured legs, several of the runners on this stretch began breaking down. The "marathoners," described one writer for the United Press, with their grease and bandages, "presented the weirdest publicity ever collected to forecast the coming circus."[55] Unlike the excitement and pleasure of a coming circus, however, the injured men who traversed the desert brought with them only misery and anguish. At least six runners dropped out of the race before reaching Bagdad, California, a small town in the Mojave Desert that served the Atchison, Topeka and Santa Fe Railway. August Fager, a "Finnish runner" from Ashtabula, Ohio, "retired from the contest with a bad case of sore feet and John Gaughan of Miami, Florida, quit because of exhaustion."

While the majority of the runners who quit the race did so as a result of normal injuries incurred from running in such grueling conditions, one incident involved a reckless automobile driver and a runner from Canada. Ten miles from Bagdad, an "unidentified motorist" traveling in the "opposite direction to the runner" struck Walter Ricketts from Southampton, Ontario, leaving him lying on the side of the road with two fractured ribs. Rather than stopping at the scene of the accident, the driver sped away into the desert. The *Arizona Republican* noted that witnesses said that the car was "travelling at high speed" and "pitching from side to side." Seeing his injuries, and realizing that he was unable to continue the race, some of the witnesses then drove him to the nearest hospital.[56]

The next day, the remaining runners once again braved the heat to embark on the thirty-two-mile stretch from Bagdad to the water stop station at Danby. Arthur Newton arrived in Danby first, making it the "third successive stretch won by the lanky British Marathoner."[57] Fellow British runner Peter Gavuzzi came in second place, while the "negro" runner from Seattle, Washington, Ed Gardner, came in third with a time of 5 hours and 55 minutes. Russell J. Newland of the Associated Press remarked that the "the same distressing conditions that have marked the progress of the runners and walkers for the last three days cropped up today as the long caravan of roadway conquerors descended deeper into the Mojave Desert." Remarking on how the runners suffered through temperatures hovering around "90 degrees," he noted that the "soft dirt or gravel-strewn highway tortured them underfoot, and a scorching sun beat down from the sky above."[58] As the runners slowly arrived in Danby, some doing so in the middle of the night, they knew that in the morning, they would to do it all over again as they made their way to the town of Needles near the California-Arizona border.

Between Danby and Needles, word spread among the Mojave Indians that Qömawunu was still a competitor in the race, and several of them lined the path to cheer for him and demonstrate their support. A report in the New York Times noted that "in groups sprinkled along the route were many Indians of the Mojave Desert out to welcome Nicholas Quamawahu, Hopi Indian entrant, who was an early favorite of the race and winner of the preceding laps. Quamawahu strained an ankle and since then his trainers have held him to a slow gait. He was well back in the ranks."[59] In addition to cheering on their fellow Native runner, the Mojave Indians "paid tribute" to the Hopi runner by "sending a 12-piece Indian brass band to escort him over the last two miles" of the race. "Traveling in a huge red truck," James Powers observed, the "musicians led a parade of machines" and "played its loudest pieces" while the "other tribesmen offered their best war whoops." Hearing the music and loud cheers for him, Qömawunu "responded" by breaking "into a fast sprint, his first running since he injured his ankle several days ago to finish the heat."[60]

When the Hopi runner and other competitors departed Needles for the twenty-mile stretch to the old mining community of Oatman in Arizona, they left behind the state of California and the dreaded Mojave Desert. For Qömawunu, it also meant that he entered his home state of Arizona. Historian Charles Kastner observed that race organizers had hired a group of Indians, most likely Mojave Indians, to help ferry the runners, and their trainers, across the Colorado River to Arizona in "open canoes."[61] When the Indians took Qömawunu across to Arizona, people who gathered near the bank of the river showed their enthusiasm for him by cheering and embracing him as one of their own. The "picturesque Hopi Indian runner," James Powers, observed, "was accorded a rousing welcome as he entered Arizona, his native State."[62]

Encouraged by the support he received near the California-Arizona border, reality soon set in for Qömawunu as he struggled on the mountainous path to the town of Oatman. Plagued by a sprained ankle, the Hopi runner finished the leg of the race in thirty-fourth place. Other runners, however, fared far worse. By the time the runners reached Arizona, the race became a "survival for the fittest." Many runners began "dropping by the wayside" out of exhaustion and waited on the side of the road to be picked up by an "ambulance squad."[63] The next day, on the 28.8-mile route to the town of Kingman, the runners felt no relief for their tired muscles, sunburnt skin, and mental fatigue. Qömawunu's condition also worsened. Although Qömawunu and his trainer Hubbell had expressed confidence to newspaper writers that the Hopi runner's ankle injury would improve, Qömawunu's chances of completing the Bunion Derby lessened with each passing mile. The "Hopi Indian from Oraibi, Ariz.," a writer for the Los Angeles Times observed, "was forced out of the running when an ankle he sprained in the first week of the race began to swell."[64]

The next morning, only 127 of the original 199 runners remained in the race.[65] Since Qömawunu failed to complete the previous day's leg, race officials allowed Hubbell to drive him back nearly halfway to Oatman to the spot where the Hopi runner had quit. At this point, Qömawunu then proceeded to cover the remaining thirteen miles to Kingman, a railroad town nearly three hundred miles east of Los Angeles. Once he reached Kingman, the Hopi runner began the fifty-two-mile stretch to Peach Springs on the Hualapai Indian Reservation. The route between the Colorado River and Peach Springs was brutal and claimed the inner wills and hopes of runners who, out of pure exhaustion and fatigue, could not go any further in the race. "You have no idea how fatiguing this sort of thing is until you attempt it," runner Lloyd Johnson of Santa Ana, California, remarked after he quit the race. "You just have to keep on, keep on, keep on and then when you get to the control point you are so tired that you drop off to sleep and when you awaken it is time to start running again and keep on and on and on." With "blisters all over the bottom of his feet," and with a determination to train for the next transcontinental footrace, Johnson left Kingman by train to resume his work at Raitt's Dairy in Santa Ana.[66]

The following day, Qömawunu, or "Nimble Nick" as "some of the newspaper boys affectionately dubbed him,"[67] joined the remaining athletes to run 38.8 miles to Seligman. Running against severe "chilling" winds, and a constant gradual incline, the runners slowed their pace, and many of them even stopped to "seek the soup kitchen for hot refreshments."[68] But the hot soup and refreshments did nothing to soothe the extreme pain in Qömawunu's ankle. Throughout the day's stretch, race physicians closely monitored Qömawunu's declining condition. They observed him struggle to run, and saw how he favored one ankle over the other. And at this point, even the "stoic" Indian could not hide the pain from his face. But perhaps most importantly, the physicians knew what lay before him, on the other side of Seligman. They knew that the next day's race was a steep seventeen-hundred-foot climb to the mountain community of Williams. And so, seeing that the Hopi runner risked serious bodily injury if they allowed him to continue, the physicians forced Qömawunu to quit the Bunion Derby eight miles outside of Seligman. Neither Qömawunu or his trainer challenged this decision.

News that Qömawunu quit the derby spread throughout the nation. Sports writers expected the Hopi runner to excel on "Injun land," and they predicted that he would dominate the field in his home state. "After pounding the roads for nearly 500 miles," a writer for the *Los Angeles Times* observed, "the runners," including Qömawunu, began "dropping out like flies." "Some years ago," the *Times* recalled, "when The Times held a marathon in Los Angeles the Hopi Indians ran all the white boys off their feet; but the Indian couldn't hold the pace in this one." Referring to when Hopi runners Guy Maktima and Philip Zeyouma dominated the *Los Angeles Times* Modified Marathon of twelve miles in April 1912, the newspaper writer concluded: "I have an idea that the pace was too fast for the shuffling dog trot which made the Southwest Indians famous among the long-distance runners of the world."[69]

After Qömawunu dropped out of the race, Hubbell drove him to Flagstaff, and then farther east to Winslow. At Winslow, hundreds of Hopis from the reservation waited to greet him. There to cheer him as he ran across the high desert of Arizona, the group from Hopi did not expect their tribesman to enter Winslow in an automobile. Although they heard reports of his injuries, they expected him to have a strong performance near his home community. Even newspaper reporters acknowledged the ancient homelands of the Hopi people when the race neared Winslow. With a headline that read, "Runners in Hopi Indian Country," Leland C. Lewis of the International News Service noted that when the one hundred remaining runners left the previous day's stop at Two Gun Camp, they "advanced into Hopi Indian country . . . as they moved on to Winslow, twenty-six miles" away.[70] Years before, Hopis had used Winslow as a point of departure for the outside world. On this day, however, it served Qömawunu, perhaps unexpectedly, as a point of entrance back home to the Hopi mesas of northern Arizona.

Following his performance in the Bunion Derby, Qömawunu never regained his top standing in American distance running. His participation in the derby required him to become a "professional," which prevented him from competing in several races intended only for amateurs.[71] Unable to run in the upcoming Long Beach Marathon in New York due to his professional status, Qömawunu forfeited any opportunity to defend his title. Furthermore, since the American Olympic Committee chose that year's marathon to secure a candidate for the 1928 Summer Olympics in Amsterdam, Netherlands, Qömawunu also gave up a chance to be on the American Olympic team.[72] On May 19, 1928, nearly two months after Qömawunu quit the derby, a young yet highly accomplished runner named Joe "Joie" W. Ray won the marathon and clinched "his place on the American Olympic team." He completed the race in 2 hours, 35 minutes, and 13²/₅ seconds, more than 13 minutes faster than Qömawunu's record-breaking time a year before.[73] The next month the Hopi runner's trainer also announced that Qömawunu would not be competing alongside Hopi runners Arthur Pohequaptewa and Dan Comahungnioma in the Redwood Highway Indian Marathon from San Francisco to Grants Pass, Oregon.[74]

Even though race organizers had sent a promotional photograph of the Hopi runner to nearly every major news bureau in the United States, and newspaper writers greatly anticipated his participation in the nearly five-hundred-mile race, Qömawunu did not compete. The "fleet-foot of the Hopi tribe, isn't going to race . . . after all," the Los Angeles Times reported, "and the information is gladsome enough to make some of the other twenty-nine Indian runners sigh with relief, if not whoop with glee."[75]

In the early summer months of 1928, Qömawunu was not the only Native runner from the Southwest to forfeit a chance to compete for a slot on the American Olympic team. Prior to the Long Beach marathon in June,

A race promotional picture of Nicholas Qömawunu that organizers of the 1928 Redwood Highway Indian Marathon sent to news bureaus across the United States. Author's collection.

American trainer Mike Kirk, himself a former Olympic athlete, planned to enter three Zuni runners named Andrew Chimoney, Luti, and Leekahtee in the race to compete for a spot on the 1928 Olympic team. In April of the same year, all three had competed in the Southwestern Marathon Olympic race in Phoenix, Arizona.[76] The twenty-nine-year-old Chimoney won the event in 2 hours, 53 minutes, and 45 seconds, "five minutes faster" than a Hopi runner named Puhuguoptowa who took first place in the race the previous year. While Chimoney's victory guaranteed him the chance to compete in the Boston Marathon, an official Olympic trial race, he and his tribesmen decided not to go.[77]

Shortly after Chimoney won the Southwestern Marathon, he received a telegram that his wife had died. Chimoney was devastated. The "joy concerning his marathon victory," a writer for the *Arizona Republican* noted, "was almost immediately killed by the news of his wife's death."[78] A year earlier, while Chimoney competed in a different marathon, "word reached him that his baby daughter" had also died. This "sad occurrence," the Arizona newspaper went on to note, "was not considered at the time as a special hoodoo, but when his wife died as he was running in the regulation marathon at the Phoenix Greenway Field Day, the tribe felt that this was a sign from the Great Spirit that the Zuni Indians were not to compete in the white man's races." Although Kirk pleaded with his runners to change their minds, the Zunis held fast to their spiritual beliefs and refused to comply. Their days of running American footraces had ended.[79]

In the 1920s, Hopi runners Arthur Pohequaptewa, Ray Honkuku, and Nicholas Qömawunu competed during a time in history when Americans looked to Indian runners to reclaim the nation's standing in long-distance running. However, they also entered US competitions at a moment when Americans looked to other ethnic or marginalized groups to restore the nation's pride in various sports. "'Lo, the poor Indian' may be the means of regaining American Marathon prestige," a writer for the *Boston Globe* remarked, "just as other special racial talent—such as the Hawaiians in swimming and negroes in broad jumping—has added to the country's Olympic triumphs.[80] Although Hopi runners may not have thought much about how Americans used their success to "regain American marathon prestige," they nevertheless took advantage of these opportunities and competed for their own reasons. Some ran for off-reservation Indian boarding schools or various athletic clubs, while others ran simultaneously for their tribe and village communities.

After Qömawunu and his tribesmen ended their careers and Harry Chaca and Franklin Suhu completed their terms at Sherman Institute, Hopis also stopped dominating American distance competitions. In the years after 1933, Hopi runners won few major American marathons. Although Simon Polingyumtewa won the fifteen-mile marathon for the La Fiesta de Los Vaqueros in Tucson in February 1934, it was a small regional event consisting of only Indian runners.[81] Two years later, a Hopi runner named Cooch-wick-via, or "Little Eagle," won the Golden Gate Marathon, one of several events that city officials hosted to celebrate the grand opening of the Golden Gate Bridge in the San Francisco Bay.[82] More than forty years prior, nineteen men from Cooch-wick-via's community had arrived at the bay as prisoners on Alcatraz Island. In 1936, however, "Little Eagle" did not come to San Francisco to serve out a mandatory prison sentence or to be exposed to the civilizing influences of western society, but to compete in an American marathon. And for the next several years, this marathon also happened to be one of the last times a Hopi won another major American race.[83]

In December 1929, a writer for the *Santa Ana Register* remarked: "For unlike the oil-enriched plains Indians, the Hopi is not a motorist. He retains the transportation of his forefathers—fleet, sturdy legs which carry him untiringly over incredible distances."[84] However, by the mid- to late 1930s life had changed in American society and for the Hopi people. Visitors to Hopiland no longer depended solely on trains to bring them to the gateway towns of Winslow and Holbrook. With the creation of roads, which the Arizona Automobile Club and white traders heavily promoted in American newspapers, tourists journeyed to the mesas in their own cars.[85] Modern advancements in transportation had made their way to the reservation, and they increasingly became part of Hopi life. Older Hopis, however, lamented that their youth had become too dependent on automobiles and other modern conveniences.[86] And few, if any, Hopis continued the practice of running to Winslow and back just to "watch the trains go by." Even white individuals living on the reservation acknowledged the threat posed by modern influences on the long tradition of Hopi running. "They are known for their long distance running," remarked Principal J. H. Nylander of the Moencopi Day School in 1936. "Whether the younger men after contact with modern smoking, liquor and other such White influences will sustain this endurance is a question. Long may the Hopi run, but will he?"[87]

Although Hopis still came from a "tribe of racers," that tribe was no longer producing the kind of runners that once amazed white Americans at the turn of the twentieth century, or in the decades that followed. Newspaper accounts of Hopi runners during the late 1930s and 1940s focused on footraces that accompanied the Snake Dance on the reservation, and not American marathons. The era of Hopi running that began with

Louis Tewanima in 1907 had ended, and neither his people, nor others in American society, would see or experience anything like it again. But for Hopis who competed in American races, that era was never only about winning silver cups, bronze medals, or money. It was about representing their communities and the opportunity to continue the long tradition of distance running among their people.

Crossing the Terrain

Many years before Hopis competed in American races, or on a world stage at the Olympics, Hopi runners of long ago crossed the rugged terrain of their mesas to relay messages from village to village. They ran up and down cliffs to tend to their fields, to confront unexpected visitors, and to hunt. They did not run for silver cups and medals, or the pride and sense of accomplishment that came with it, but they competed on and below their mesas for the survival of their people. Hopi clan and ceremonial runners ran far beyond Hopi ancestral lands to entice the rain clouds to follow them back to their fields. To be blessed by the "cloud people," as Hopi cultural historian Leigh J. Kuwanwisiwma once remarked, "for the harvest, so we have a good life, a long life."[1] Other runners ran footraces for eagle feathers, which they used as prayers and offerings for rain.[2] Still others, existing only in Hopi legends, ran to teach the people life lessons and about the spiritual world of their ancestors.

When the Spanish conquistadors arrived on Hopiland in the 1500s, they entered a world of Hopi running. They came to the Hopi villages seeking gold and silver, but instead found a people deeply committed to their religious beliefs and practices. And they witnessed these people run, and recalled how they outdistanced even their horses.[3] Years after the Spaniards left Hopiland, a wave of military personnel, Christian missionaries, and US government officials also crossed through this dry and arid region. They did not come for precious metals, but to change the Hopis, to convince them to abandon their Indian ways, and to force them into compliance. Others arrived on the mesas to experience a world unlike their own. Having read about this world in American newspapers, they boarded trains on the East and West Coasts and arrived at the villages to witness religious ceremonies, but especially the Hopi Snake Dance. Flocking to Hopiland with cameras, pencils, and sketchbooks, these visitors came to record the Hopi and not to change them. They returned home and published their accounts in newspapers and in books. They wrote about the ceremonies in great detail, and many described the footraces that accompanied the dance.

While white Americans and other foreigners often came to Hopi country by rail, Hopis also used this mode of transportation to travel to distant lands and create a new reality for themselves at the turn of the twentieth century. In the late 1800s, a select number of Hopis boarded trains for destinations on the West and East Coasts. US government officials wanted these trips to broaden Hopi understandings of life beyond the mesas, to encourage Hopis to appreciate the supposed superiority of Western society, and to intimidate reluctant Hopi leaders into complying with government mandates. Hopis, however, had their own reasons and outcomes for boarding these trains. Following in a long tradition of migrating to distant lands, Hopis traveled throughout the United States to learn from the outside world, and to return home with knowledge that benefited their people. Others boarded trains to attend off-reservation Indian boarding schools, where they joined cross-country teams and used their ability to run to challenge white perceptions of Native people, to see the world beyond the mesas, and to develop themselves into modern runners.

When Hopis arrived at Indian schools, they came from a community of runners, but they also had to learn to run according to American rules and regulations. Although they had much experience running on dirt trails and rugged landscapes back home, they needed to be trained on how to run on clay and cinder tracks, mountain roads, and city pavements. "There is a great difference between running in the open country," described a newspaper writer after a Hopi runner's victory in New York City, "and dodging taxicabs in the heart of a metropolis."[4] And they had to learn to pace themselves in short and long races, follow instructions from their coaches and trainers, and focus amid the sounds of cheering spectators and the honking automobiles that polluted the routes with toxic exhaust.

Officials at Indian schools created sports teams to showcase the school, promote their athletic programs, and to teach their students to be competitive in the so-called white man's world. They also wanted their athletes to appreciate discipline, a sense of accomplishment, and a strong work ethic. Track and cross-country trainers at boarding schools possessed exceptional Hopi talent on their teams, and they wanted the American running community to know about it. They sought opportunities to enter Hopis in high-profile races, touted their prospects of qualifying for the Olympic Games, and served as their publicists for American newspapers. While school administrators and coaches used their athletic programs to promote their schools, city officials used Hopi victories to showcase their towns as places of business, leisure, and athletics. And powerful men in the American sporting community and the government used the success of Hopi runners to further US nationalism at home and abroad.

Beginning in the early 1900s, Hopis competed against the best runners in the nation and even the world. They ran against elite runners from across the United States and challenged runners from places as far away as Japan, Finland, and England. They competed on the streets of Los Angeles, the mountain roads of Colorado, and on the clay track of Madison Square Garden. Not all of these runners competed for schools. Some ran for city athletic clubs or for non-Indian race promoters. Some ran for themselves. Competing in American races allowed them to see the world beyond the mesas and to experience life in modern cities. It also allowed them to experience a sense of fame as their names graced the pages of American newspapers throughout the country. But their fame did not impress the older generation of Hopis who remained on the reservation. Victor Masayesva, Jr., once remarked that for Hopi people, "running is a traditional activity" with a "ritual function."[5] When the young Hopi runners returned to their villages as celebrated athletes, the people reminded them of the cultural significance of this "activity" and the "ritual function" of Hopi running. And in so doing they reminded them of their place in Hopi society.

But their society was always changing, never stagnant. And they had to collectively and individually decide how to embrace, confront, or reject the changes that came before them. For young Hopis who competed at Indian schools, they willingly and oftentimes eagerly donned modern track and cross-country uniforms and agreed to run according to American rules and expectations. Although government officials may have forced them to leave their homes and families for places such as Sherman Institute or the Carlisle Indian Industrial School, they did not require them to run on the school's athletic teams. Although white race promoters may have enticed nonstudent Hopi athletes with all-expense paid trips to the East and West Coasts or with prize winnings, they did not force them to leave their villages, board trains, or compete on the mountain roads of Colorado and the streets of New York City. Hopis ran in American races because they wanted to, choosing to live in the moment by taking advantage of opportunities to run as modern Hopi harriers in the twentieth century. And they did so because they were Hopi. And as such they were obligated to continue the tradition of footracing among their people while providing a historical and cultural link that still connects running with being Hopi today.[6]

Still Running

On a November morning at the Cave Creek Golf Course in Phoenix, Arizona, seven Hopi youth huddled together with their coach, Rick Baker, to hear his final instructions before the start of the 2015 Division IV Arizona State Cross Country Championship. "Get out there and own them today," he told his runners. "That last mile that's what we own, that's where you have to really dig down and run tough."[1] Members of the Hopi High School boys cross-country program, the youth arrived at the course to defend their title as Arizona's top Division IV high school cross-country team. Having won twenty-five consecutive state championships, the runners belonged to a program with a winning reputation, and none of them wanted to be known as the team that broke the quarter century–long streak. Just three days before, John Branch of the *New York Times* published a full two-page story on running in Hopi society, highlighted the team's accomplishments, and greatly anticipated their victory in the upcoming meet.[2] Much was at stake for their program, their school, and their people, and the runners knew it. The pressure was on.

A week earlier, however, the team had competed in Phoenix but "melted" in the desert heat, and some wondered, including Coach Baker, how they would perform in the race that mattered most. Furthermore, the team did not place first in three previous regular-season meets, which, as sports writer Mario Kalo observed, "potentially" left the "door open for another Division IV team to snatch its cross-country crown."[3] "Could this be the year," coaches from the other teams asked each other, "the year that Hopi will lose their title?" While cognizant of these questions and other realities, Coach Baker urged his runners to remain focused, to trust in their training, and to be "fearless and relentless."[4] Himself once a competitive distance runner at Winslow High School,[5] the Hopi coach knew that for them to succeed they needed to "relax" and race "hard," and he reminded them that "their minds should have already been made up" the night before on "how" they were "going to run."

When the race commenced, the seven Hopi youth joined over a hundred runners to begin the 3.1-mile route through the fairways of the Cave Creek Golf Course. During the first mile of the event some of the Hopi runners felt tightness in their muscles. This included junior Andre Lucas, as he positioned himself within the pack. Seeing this tension from the sidelines, Coach Baker called out to him to "relax," reassuring him that he would be "OK." As the race progressed, Coach Baker's words of encouragement took on an assertive and authoritative tone. "Darion," he shouted to Darion Fredericks, "wake up and go!" "Come on Iverson," he hollered to Iverson Qumyintewa, "It's almost over, go hard!" Others called out to runners in Hopi saying "Nahongvita'ay," a word used by members of the Hopi community to urge their runners to run strong; to run with strength. In the final stretch of the race, as hundreds of spectators cheered and screamed, Hopi runner and sophomore Diome Talaswaima and Navajo runner Zhariff Lee of Many Farms battled to the finish, with Lee clinching the individual title with a time of 16 minutes and 34 seconds.[6] Moments later, Hopi runners Lucas, Jihad Nodam, and Fredericks sprinted to the end. And when Qumyintewa crossed the finish line in twenty-fifth place, he clinched the twenty-sixth consecutive Division I State Cross Country championship for his team and school.[7] "I'm feeling pretty good," Coach Baker remarked to Crystal Dee of the *Hopi Tutuveni*. "The guys ran really well" and "exceeded our expectations."[8]

The team's victory reflects the runners' determination, training, and good coaching from Baker and Assistant Coach Juwan Nuvayokva, and it speaks to the continuity of running in Hopi society. Although this present work focuses on Hopi runners from the late 1800s to the mid-1930s, the tradition of distance running continued in the decades that followed. Throughout the 1940s and 1950s, a team of Hopis from Second Mesa regularly competed in the Inter-Tribal Ceremonial race in Gallup, New Mexico, a team who for many years had been coached by Wesley Poneona from the village of Musangnuvi.[9] And still other Hopis, such as Tino Youvella from Polacca, demonstrated their running abilities while members of teams at Indian high schools.[10] In the 1960s, for example, Hopi runners at the Phoenix Indian School dominated distance running in Arizona. In December 1967, the "Flying" Hopi harriers, Alfonso Gash, Clyde Nasafotie, Merrill Honyonwa, Gary Joshevama, Lauren Koinva, Alde Monongye, and Lawrence Namoki defeated "sixteen teams" to win the Class "A" State Cross Country Championship at Papago Park in Phoenix.[11] A day later, the team hosted a race against the Sherman Institute "Braves" to "find out who had the better team." While Hopi runner Ronald Takala of Sherman had led his "squad of two years to an undefeated season, the Sherman Hopi Team dropped a heartbreaking defeat" to the Indian school in Phoenix.[12] Eight years after Alfonso Gash and his teammates won the state championship, another Hopi runner named Arvis Myron began making a name for himself as a member of the "highly touted" Tuba City High School Cross Country team in northern Arizona. In October 1975, Myron outpaced runners from Kingman High School and his own teammates to win a 3.2-mile race at home in 16 minutes and 55 seconds.[13] During the 1980s, he left Northern Arizona to compete alongside Hopi runner Herman Sahneyah[14] on the cross-country team at Illinois State University (ISU) in the city of Normal.[15] "The biggest deciding factor for me attending ISU," Myron once remarked, "was the opportunity to get out of the state of Arizona and continue running, along with using running as a catalyst for my higher education."[16]

Similar to those early Hopi students who ran while receiving an education at off-reservation Indian boarding schools, Myron went to ISU first as a student, and then as an athlete.[17] And when asked to describe the highlights and challenges that he faced as a Hopi runner at ISU, Myron's answer reflects this reality. "My biggest highlight came in the second semester of my Freshman year as a student, and not as a runner," he explained, "when I carried a load of 18 credits and had a 3.5+ GPA for the semester, which gave me a chance to be inducted into the Honorary Freshman Society of Alpha Lambda Delta/Phi Eta Sigma." Focused more on his studies, Myron felt that he did not "excel" at running as much as his Hopi teammate Sahneyah. Part of this was due to his having shin splints early in his career, and the challenge for him to pile on the "mileage that was required to run at the Division I level." Although Myron noted that he worked hard to be a good runner at ISU, even running a 4:18 mile during his freshman year, his "biggest goal" was to be the first in his family to finish college.[18]

While Myron competed in Illinois, the long tradition of distance running continued with his people back in the Southwest. In August 1980, the All Indian Pueblo Council (AIPC) Tricentennial Commission organized a "symbolic relay run" to commemorate the role of Indian runners in the Pueblo Revolt of 1680.[19] At this time in Pueblo Indian history, Spanish conquistadors and Catholic missionaries had for years oppressed the people. But the people fought back, killed many of their oppressors, and temporarily removed the Spaniards from their communities. To relay information between the villages, including the villages at Hopi, the people relied on their messenger runners. Three hundred years later, Pueblo and Hopi runners, including Leon Nuvayestewa, Andy Martinez, and Ronald Laban, began the run in the village of Taos in northern New Mexico.[20] Over a four-day period, the runners ran to each of the Pueblo villages, traversed nearly three hundred miles west to Hopi country in Arizona, and returned to complete the run in the Pueblo village of Zuni.[21] In recalling his personal observations on the closing ceremony of the race, Peter Nabokov remarked: "The runners are still clad in modern track togs, and tomorrow tribal frictions and nine-to-five jobs will resume, but for a moment out of time the beleaguered Pueblo world has been knit together again by fast men on foot bearing the message of their essential separateness, their essential unity."[22]

In the late 1980s and the years that followed, Hopi runners continued running at Indian high schools and at local colleges and universities. One of these runners was fifty-eight-year-old Tom Cooka, who at the time was living in Joseph City near Holbrook, Arizona. In 1988, Cooka worked forty hours a week for the Santa Fe Railroad while maintaining 12 credit hours at Northland Pioneer College (NPC) in the town of Show Low, Arizona. Although he attended college to further his education, he also enrolled at NPC to compete on the school's cross-country team. At the same time that he ran for NPC, his twenty-year-old son, Terrence Cooka, competed in cross-country for Mesa Community College in Phoenix. In October of the same year, the two Cookas ran against each other at the Arizona Wildcat Meet in Tucson. Terrence Cooka placed thirty-sixth out of 150 runners, while his father, suffering from severe dehydration and fatigue, quit the race near the finish. "He's very good," Tom Cooka said about his son. "The last time I was able to beat him was three or four years ago, and then it was only a matter of seconds." But, as *Arizona Republic* writer Susan Kroupa once observed: "It doesn't bother Cooka that he is not a serious contender against many of the collegiate runners, most of them 30 or 40 years his junior." Regardless of his lack of competitiveness, Cooka served as an example to the younger Hopi and other Indian runners on the team. As their elder, he encouraged them to run with good hearts and reminded them of deep cultural reasons why Indian people run. "While he is not collegiately competitive in the sense that he'll be beating any of a team's top five runners," NPC cross-country coach Vernon Mays said about the elder Cooka, "his experience and discipline have been a real asset to the team."[23]

While Tom Cooka ran for NPC, another Hopi runner, Caroline "Kadoo" Sekaquaptewa from the village of Supawlavi (Shupawlavi), competed for the Hopi High School Cross Country Team from 1987 to 1992. In the same year that she joined the team, she and her teammates won their first Arizona state championship, an achievement that the Hopi High girls cross-country program would repeat twenty more times. Later in life she participated in a handful of marathons out West, and in 2012 she became the first Hopi to successfully complete the Ironman Triathlon. Furthermore, after qualifying in the Los Angeles Marathon, Sekaquaptewa competed in the highly coveted Boston Marathon in 2014, completing the race in 3:05:27.[24] "As I ran that last mile, a little on alert, the event of last year's bombing on my mind," Sekaqauptewa later recalled, "I began to thank people. I thanked God for getting me through the race safely. I thanked everyone at home for their prayers and support—so proud to be Hopi."[25]

Less than ten years after Sekaquaptewa won her last team championship at Hopi High, another Hopi runner, Juwan Nuvayokva from the village of Orayvi, began making a name for himself as a member of the cross-country team at Northern Arizona University in Flagstaff. Among his several accomplishments as a runner, Nuvayokva won the ten-thousand-meter race at the Big Sky Conference outdoor championship in 2001, which placed him as one of the top runners in the West. He also received the NCAI Division I All-American Award and helped carry the Olympic torch across Arizona in 1996. Furthermore, in 2009, Nuvayokva "signed a sponsorship agreement with Saucony, a designer and manufacturer of athletic footwear for men and women."[26] After signing with Saucony, Nuvayokva remarked: "This is an unimaginable status to reach. I have a gift of running that I will continue to use as long as I can. It is like I am just getting started again."[27] For the past several years, Nuvayokva has continued the tradition of running by serving as one of the coaches for the Hopi High School Cross Country Team and by founding and hosting the Hopi 10K & 5K event (formerly known as the Oraivi Footrace) at Orayvi in September of each year.

At the same time that Nuvayokva represented Hopi at NAU, Devan Lo-

Runners descending Third Mesa near Orayvi at the Oraivi Footrace, 2009. Photograph by author.

mayaoma from Polacca competed for the Hopi High School and Central Arizona College, and was a six-time state track and cross-country champion. He won the individual state cross-country championship for Hopi High School in 2001, and he was named an All-American runner at Central Arizona College. In recognition of his athletic accomplishments and his work with the youth running program Wings of America, Lomayaoma was one of the runners that carried the Olympic Torch across Utah in 2002. Following in the footsteps of Lomayaoma, Hopi runner Justin Secakuku eight years later led the Hopi High School cross-country team to its twenty-first consecutive state championship. Secakuku became the first Hopi High runner since Lomayaoma's 2001 title to win the individual state championship, with a time of 16:21:54. After graduating high school, Secakuku continued to run for Paradise Valley Community College, where he was named a cross-country academic all-American in 2011.

The aforementioned runners represent a small number of noted Hopi harriers who competed in American races after the 1930s. In addition to running in formal races, Hopis have also used running to bring awareness to issues threatening the Hopi community and all of humanity. None of these issues, however, has been more important or sacred to the Hopi people than the protection and preservation of water. As former Hopi chairman Ferrell Secakuku from Supawlavi once said: "Water is so sacred to the Hopi it is like a bloodline to our heart [and without it] our entire culture and people are at risk."[28] One of the occasions that Hopis used running to bring awareness to water took place on August 10, 2001, when a group of Hopi runners gathered at the site of the Peabody Energy Coal Mine on Black Mesa, a stretch of land that encompasses portions of the Hopi and Navajo Indian reservations.

In the 1960s, the Hopi Tribe had signed an agreement with Peabody that gave the coal company mineral rights to the land and allowed access to the Navajo Aquifer. Over the years, Peabody had pumped an enormous amount of pristine water from the aquifer to slurry coal 273 miles away to the Mohave Generating Station in Nevada for processing.[29] As the coal mining operations continued, and the aquifer levels dropped, the people noticed that their springs, some of which held ceremonial significance, and wells had dried up. And farmers found it increasingly difficult to irrigate their crops. Many Hopis concluded along with Secakuku and others that the depletion of their aquifer was having serious negative impacts on their community and traditional way of life. And so, when the Hopi runners gathered that fall day on Black Mesa, they embarked on a four-day and 265-mile run to downtown Phoenix, where they presented officials with the Bureau of Indian Affairs with a petition. "The petition was simple," Judd Slivka of the *Arizona Republic* observed. "End a Black Mesa coal mine's use of groundwater from an ancient aquifer" and "end coal mining there altogether when a nearby generating station's coal supply contract runs out."[30]

In the years ahead, Hopis continued to use their ability to run to advocate for the sacredness of water before local and even world audiences. On March 2, 2006, a group of twenty-five Hopi runners departed the village of Munqapi near Tuba City, Arizona, for an eighteen-hundred-mile run to Mexico City.[31] Running far beyond Hopi ancestral lands to participate in the World Water Forum, the Hopi runners ran to Mexico to demonstrate the "importance of water to Arizona as 5,000 scientists, diplomats, activists and government officials" met for the week-long gathering. "Our tradition is to carry important messages through running," Vernon Masayesva from Ho'atvela remarked. "That's what they're doing with this run, carrying a prayer for water to this important meeting."[32] Prior to the run, people across the United States and the world sent Masayesva and other organizers drops of water, which they combined with water from each of the Hopi villages. Of the twenty-five runners who left Munqapi, fifteen ran as primary runners. The remaining runners traveled with the group as alternates. Ranging from twelve to seventy-two years of age, the runners each ran ten miles per day while carrying a flask of the water that they had collected.[33] On their fourteen-day journey, the runners ran east to their villages, made their way to the Pueblo Indian communities in New Mexico, traversed over to El Paso, Texas, and then headed south toward Mexico City.[34] Vernon's younger brother, Victor Masayesva, Jr., also rode along with the group and filmed the run to produce a sixty-minute film called *Paatuaqatsi*, or *Water Is Life*.[35] The film and run to Mexico is closely connected to the Paatuaqatsi Trail Run of 31 miles (50K) that Bucky Preston from the village of Walpi organized to also bring attention to the sacredness of water to Hopi and non-Hopi people.

A year after the Hopi youth huddled at the Cave Creek Golf Course with Coach Baker, the Hopi High School cross-country team won its twenty-seventh straight Division IV Arizona State Cross Country Championship. However, their victory would be the last in a long and distinguished streak. On November 3, 2017, Northland Preparatory Academy of Flagstaff, Arizona, defeated the Hopi High School cross-country team at that year's state meet. The youth were devastated; the Hopi community was in shock. "There's nobody to blame," Coach Rick Baker remarked to the *Navajo-Hopi Observer*. "They all ran the best they could."[36] While Coach Baker expressed support for his runners and disappointment in the race outcome, Coach Missy Acker of Northland Prep used the opportunity to explain her team's philosophy of running the race, telling journalist Mark Brown that the "historic victory was achieved by a desire to run and have fun, and not by the sheer motivation of accomplishing a great, athletic achievement."[37] Northland Prep had indeed accomplished a "great, athletic achievement," and their victory served as a reminder, albeit a painful one, to the Hopi team about the deeply held cultural reasons why Hopi people run.

In American society, people run for a host of reasons that do not involve one's community or desire to bring awareness to the sacred. Many instead run to stay fit, have fun, relieve stress, clear the mind, or to feel younger.[38] They run to escape the busyness of life and the daily chaos that comes with it. For some, however, running is a chore, something they feel they have to do or face the dreaded consequences of weight gain and low self-esteem.[39] Still others run for recognition and proudly post their accomplishments on social media. But for Hopi runners who run in traditional or "cultural" races back home, the meaning of the races is and was much different. Devan Lomayaoma, an accomplished Hopi runner who competed for the Hopi High School and Northern Arizona University, once remarked, "running in cultural races is a lot different than running in high school or college." "In cultural races," he explained, "you never get recognition for it. They have a deeper meaning."[40] Hopi runners such as Lomayaoma remind us that for Hopi runners of the distant past, that "deeper meaning" was closely tied to the well-being of one's clan and village community. And this "deeper meaning" still resonates with Hopi runners today. Perhaps Coach Baker said it best: "These kids know that they are running more than for just a state title. They run for strength, they run for their lives, their villages, our tribe, and for water, and then our families."[41]

Louis Tewanima, Hopi (1882–1969)

About the Author: Benjamin H. Nuvamsa grew up with Louis and Blanche Tewanima at the Village of Songòopavi. Nuvamsa is a member of the Bear Clan and Kiikyam (village lead clan) of Songòopavi. Son of Peter, Jr., and Joan Nuvamsa, Ben is a former tribal chairman of the Hopi Tribe. Nuvamsa is President of KIVA Institute, LLC, dedicated to serving tribal nations throughout Indian Country.

Louis Tewanima, Hopi
(1882–1969)
Two-Time US Olympian: A Paradox
(The Untold Story)

Benjamin H. Nuvamsa

The story of Louis Tewanima, Hopi, a two-time U.S. Olympian, is a paradox of sorts: a contradiction between the policy of forced assimilation of Native peoples in America by the federal government, and the heroic feats of Tewanima who ably represented the United States; despite being held as "prisoner of war"; and while arguably, not a "legal" citizen of the United States.

"Tewanima" is a ceremonial name given him during the *Wuwtsim* ceremony (men's adulthood ceremony) by his ceremonial godfather. The traditional name, *Tewanima*, means *"Measures of the Sun"* and can be interpreted or translated appropriately as *"Setting a Goal or Setting a Mark."* Tewanima's godfather was a member of the Sun Clan, therefore the name given Tewanima is associated with the Sun.

Tewanima was born a *Piqöswungwa* (Hopi Bear Strap Clan) on the Hopi Indian Reservation. "Louis" was an English name given to him later by the federal government. As children, we called him *"Loos Kwa'a."* We could not pronounce the English name Louis. *"Kwa'a"* means grandfather.

Tewanima was, to a large degree, a product of the United States' policy of forced assimilation of Native peoples in America: a paradox of sorts. His feats and accomplishments as a US Olympian are well documented. Tewanima represented the United States in the 1908 London Olympics, where he placed ninth in the marathon. His silver medal in the 10,000 meters in the 1912 Stockholm Olympics set the record (32:06.6) for the United States, which stood for fifty-two years until another Native American, Billy Mills, a Lakota Sioux from the Pine Ridge Indian Reservation, broke the record when he won the gold medal at the 1964 Tokyo Olympics. Tewanima also placed sixteenth in the marathon at the 1912 Stockholm Olympics.

Tewanima won the Silver Medal in 1912, the same year of the statehood of the State of Arizona.

Associate Professor Matthew Sakiestewa Gilbert's (Hopi) article "Marathoner Lewis Tewanima and the Continuity of Hopi Running, 1908–1912"[1] in the 2012 *Western Historical Quarterly* describes the running feats of Tewanima.

Today, on every Labor Day weekend, the Hopi and Tewa people celebrate Tewanima's accomplishments at Songòopavi Village (Tewanima's hometown) at the Annual Tewanima Foot Races.

Tewanima was selected as one of 22 greatest US Track Olympians in 1954 in a ceremony held in New York City, and was the inaugural inductee to the Arizona Sports Hall of Fame in 1957. Sadly, the whereabouts of his trophies and medals are unknown. All that is available are limited copies of photographs.

Little is known of the historic events that led to Tewanima's (and other Hopìit) arrival at the Carlisle Indian School in 1907. Perhaps it is a sad history of the treatment of Native Americans that was conveniently not openly discussed. Tewanima and other Hopìit were transported to the Carlisle Indian School against their will as "prisoners of war" for refusing and objecting to attending a Bureau of Indian Affairs boarding school at Keams Canyon on the Hopi Indian Reservation. Other Hopi adults were arrested and transported to the island of Alcatraz. Young Natives from other tribes were also sent to Carlisle Indian School as part of the policy of assimilating Natives into the mainstream American society.

The goal of the federal government in the 1880s was to assimilate Natives away from their traditional ways into the mainstream American society by placing young Natives in institutions sanctioned by the federal government. Young Natives were forcibly removed from their homelands and families and placed in distant federal boarding schools and immersed in the values and practical knowledge of mainstream American society while being kept away from any traditional influences. Captain Richard H. Pratt's (founder of Carlisle Indian Industrial School) famous quote about "Kill the Indian, and save the man" echoed the federal government's assimilation policy.[2]

On the Hopi Indian Reservation, traditional Hopisinom (people) rejected the federal government's policy of forcibly removing Native children and placing them in boarding schools. Federal officials referred to them as "Hostiles." Other Hopisinom who were friendly and who cooperated with the federal government's policies were referred to as the "Friendlies."

In keeping with their traditional values and beliefs, Tewanima and others objected to doing away with their traditional ways. They were summarily rounded up and taken to a federal boarding school in Keams Canyon, Arizona, on the Hopi Indian Reservation as "prisoners of war." They were later transferred to Fort Wingate in New Mexico. Some were transferred to the Carlisle Indian School while others were sent to other federal boarding schools. Tewanima and others were transferred to the Carlisle Indian School in Pennsylvania. Hopi adults were arrested and sent to Alcatraz for objecting to sending their children to BIA schools.

Louis Tewanima, named *Tsöqahovi* as a child, was raised in the Hopi way with strong traditional values and principles. *Tsöqahovi* means "*Muddy Hips.*" His father was a member of the Snow Clan, thus the name related to snow and water. Tewanima was born in 1888 into the *Piqöswungwa* (Bear Strap Clan) and was destined to someday be a traditional leader. He participated in traditional ceremonies, tended to his corn fields and his family's livestock.

Like many young Hopìit, Tewanima was a great distance runner. There was always a friendly running competition among Hopi villages, especially during the women's traditional basket dances, where long and short distance races were the highlight of the dances. Hopìit are natural-born runners, thus Tewanima's famous quote "Me run fast good, all Hopis run fast good," as he allegedly told Coach Glen "Pop" Warner so he could be allowed to join the Carlisle track and field team.

To the Hopi, running is a tradition. It is a way of life. It is a culture. Running is an integral part of Hopi ceremonies. The Hopi run as a prayer for rain and the good things of life. In fact, before every ceremonial race can start, there is a call out to the spirits in all four directions to join the runners to the finish line at the village. This is a symbolic call for the rain clouds to bring rain and moisture as the run is a prayer for rain and moisture, and for the well-being of all mankind.

Every able young Hopi is expected to be a runner. During ceremonies, young runners are designated to run great distances to gather sacred water from distant springs for the ceremonies, and to deliver sacred prayer feathers (Paaho) to the distant shrines. This is considered an honor, one that is never declined. Winning a race is not as important as having the honor to participate in a ceremonial run. There are no medals, ribbons, trophies and certificates awarded in Hopi sacred ceremonial races. Instead the reward is life-sustaining sacred water that the runner can take to the corn field as a symbol of praying for rain and good crop. In the women's society races, runners are awarded with coiled traditional plaques and yucca baskets. Every runner is appreciated for his strength and endurance and his sacrifice for good things to come.

Today, young Hopìit carry on the long tradition of running. The local Hopi High School boys' cross country team holds an Arizona State high school record (and national record) of twenty-seven consecutive championship titles under the leadership of Coach Rick Baker (Hopi). The women's team is equally famous for winning several cross country championships. Several young Hopìit have been able to receive a college education on track scholarships.

Tewanima's love for running led to his joining the Carlisle's track and field team, and joining the famous Jim Thorpe (Sac and Fox). He joined the Carlisle track and field team after convincing Coach "Pop" Warner that he can be of value to the team. Never to lose his dignity, Tewanima laid aside his objection to being held "prisoner of war" at Carlisle Indian School because of his love for running and in keeping with the Hopi running tradition.

Tewanima returned home to Hopi after the 1912 Stockholm Olympics and resumed his traditional ways, tending to his corn fields, herding his sheep, and participating in traditional ceremonies. He married Omaw-mana (Blanche). They had one daughter, Rose, who attended the Sherman Indian boarding school in California but became very ill and was sent home. She later died of health complications in her early teens. Tewanima later became chief of the Antelope Society (Tsu'tsuvt), a post he held for many years. The Antelope Society is a clan responsibility of the Bear Strap Clan. The Antelope Society and Snake Society perform the traditional snake dance every other year in the summer.

He was initiated into the Two-Horn Society (Aa'alt) and played a key role in the kiva ceremonies. And it was during one of the evening kiva ceremonies in the winter of 1969 where, after the men finished their traditional smoking, he left to return home for the evening but mistakenly took a distant light from another village across the valley as the light from his house. He walked toward the light and fell several feet down the edge of the mesa to his death.

Louis Tewanima left a legacy as a great runner emblematic of the Hopi culture, a great role model for younger Hopìit. He also left a legacy as a traditional man living up to his tribal and clan responsibilities, and never strayed from his beliefs as a Hopi. He brought world recognition to the Hopi culture of running.

There is an irony, or a paradox, in the story of Tewanima. He was considered a federal "prisoner of war" yet he represented the United States in two world Olympics as a great "American" athlete. He never lost his dignity as a traditional Hopi. He represented Carlisle Indian School, the very institution where he (and many other Native youth) was held against his will as "prisoner of war" by the federal government. More ironic is how Tewanima and the famous Olympian Jim Thorpe represented the United States in the Olympics while arguably not considered as legal citizens of the United States. But it didn't matter because the United States was represented by great First American athletes. In fact, President Theodore Roosevelt once recognized Tewanima's accomplishments and told Tewanima that he was "extremely glad a real American Indian competed for America and represented the country abroad,"[3] not realizing the dilemma of citizenship of Native Americans.

Native Americans, although they are the original inhabitants of America, were not considered as legal citizens of the United States. It was not until the Indian Citizenship Act of 1924 (also known as the Snyder Act) that Native Americans became citizens of the United States.

While federal law recognized the legal status of Native Americans, many states, including the State of Arizona, refused to allow Native Americans the right to vote in state and national elections. It took a lawsuit in

1948 by two tribal veterans to allow Native Americans to vote in the State of Arizona.

So did he (and Jim Thorpe) legally represent the United States? Yes, because in his mind, he (and Jim Thorpe) had every right to represent his homeland. His love for running overshadowed the conditions under which he was institutionalized at Carlisle . . . a contradiction of sorts. In the end, Tewanima never lost his dignity. He was never assimilated. He never mastered the English language and never accepted the modern lifestyle. He remained true to his convictions and beliefs as a Hopi and became a traditional and religious leader. He is considered a hero and a role model by the Hopisinom and should be considered a national hero by the American people.

Nahongvita'ay!

Acknowledgments: Appreciation goes to Leigh Kuwanwisiwma and Owen Seumptewa, who started the Annual Tewanima Footraces. Thanks to Associate Professor Matthew Sakiestewa Gilbert for his continuing research into the life of Tewanima. And thanks to the many volunteers throughout the years, including the Louis Tewanima Association, for continuing to acknowledge the accomplishments of Louis Tewanima and for promoting the Hopi tradition of running. Finally, thanks go to another famous Native American Olympian, Billy Mills of the Oglala Sioux Tribe, for his friendship and participating at one of the Annual Tewanima Footraces.

"Are Moqui Runners World Beaters?"

Originally published in the San Francisco Chronicle, *October 5, 1902.*[1]

Look way down there on the desert plain, one, two, three, four, five miles to the eastward. Isn't the early morning air of Arizona wonderfully clear? Can you see that little dark patch, there? Take the field glass. Now you make it out. That is five miles from here. Cattle? No, those are Indian footracers. They are there preparing for the start. They will run clear across that stretch of dreary desert and then up to the top of these cliffs. Yes, it is a long race for any athlete. But watch those fellows. The outside world does not know it, yet these Moquis are probably the greatest distance runners on the face of the earth.

At 8 o'clock this morning, while you were sleeping profoundly and restfully, as a man will in such an atmosphere, a pueblo priest proclaimed this race from the top of one of those queer, ladder-entered adobe houses here on the mesa. At 4 o'clock the tall, dignified Moqui appeared again and repeated his chant. It was a strange, weird, romantic, lonely droning song, like the Moslem call to prayer.

He was directing the runners to leave their homes and go forth to the traditional starting place. You came out into this obscure part of Arizona to witness the annual snake dance of the Moqui Indians. You never heard that there were great footracers among these people. The snake dance is a wild, barbarous, religious ceremonial in which a group of painted Indian priests circle around holding venomous writhing rattlesnakes in their mouths, while all the people of the village perch on the near-by adobe houses and stand at a safe distance on the ground and become fanatically noisy over the uncanny sight. That is a remarkable aboriginal ceremony. But this race is really the more wonderful thing. A ceremony can be imitated by trained actors in a theater. But nobody can counterfeit the record performances of the world's greatest runner.

What? Are they lining up? Well, that means they are going to start. Let me have the field glass a moment. Yes, they are stretched out in a row. How much lighter it has grown! How beautifully crimsoned it is becoming on the horizon! You know they start this race when the priest out there with them signals that the sunrise flashlight has touched a certain clifftop in the middle mesa. One of the Indians is moving. It must be the priest. Oh, I know what that means. To north, to east, to south, to west, he raises a gourdful of water.

They're off! The priest has seen the first rising sunflash kiss the summit and he has dashed his gourd upon the ground. It is a ceremonial prayer for the god of rain to favor the land with abundant moisture everywhere. It gets terribly dry down here in Arizona.

Can you see them move? Take the glass. Doesn't it look like a lazy, creeping insect? That's the wonder of this atmosphere, the distinctness of things at great distances.

Keep the glass on them and I'll tell you how these Moquis came to be such marvelous runners. Sweep your glass back over the plain toward us and you'll make out other figures. Those are lesser priests stationed at certain intervals along the course. Before the Indians here can see with the unaided eye that the racers have started the word will be sent to them by relay signals from the priests.

Oh, I'll have time to talk while the race is on. A man does not go five miles like an express train. The world's record is 24:40. It was made in London in 1863 by J. White, a famous English professional runner of thirty years ago. But I have the world records here on a card: For Ireland, 25:21, in 1894, by Mullen, an amateur runner; for America, 25:22½, at Cambridge, in 1890, by Grant, a professional; and 25:23⅗, at New York, in 1887, by Carter, an amateur. Those are the best five-mile performances of which civilized man has any accurate knowledge since the world began. An athlete cannot go miles at a sprinting gait. The strain upon heart and lungs and vitality is terrible. Pace must be set to distance. College sprint racers have made 100 yards in 0:9 4-5, which is world's record time. Let's see. Well, at that rate a man would run a mile in 2:48. But the world's greatest record for a mile happens to be 4:12¾, made at London in 1886 by a professional named George. If a runner could keep up the mile-record speed for five miles that would be—yes, 21:03¾. The record happens to be three minutes and a half slower than that. They say it takes a man three-quarters of a minute longer to run five miles on turf than on a finely rolled cinder track. Just think what those poor panting devils down there are running on—barefoot, alternating patches of hardpan and shifting, desert sand, with no track at all, and then they have this long, final drag up the side of the mesa over the rocky trail.

Are they coming on at a good clip? Oh, no, they're not walking. Remember, that's five miles from here.

It was too dark last night for you to see much, and you were too tired after that hundred-mile stage ride across the desert from the railroad to be greatly interested in this mesa-land and its people. These Moquis are the most interesting of all the American Indian tribes. How they came to be living on the flat tops of these sterile, rocky, treeless tablelands no man knows. Even their own well-kept verbal traditions do not reach back through enough centuries to explain whence these people came. As long as their folk lore has existed the Moquis have been dwellers on these hilltops. This is the western mesa. That one out there behind the runners is the middle mesa. And there is another some miles beyond it called the east mesa. They are tablelands, each jutting out into the plain and naturally separated from the main bluffs of which they were a part in ages gone. Geological action and torrential rains of centuries have cut them off till they loom high and dry above the desert sands like monster ships left on the edge of a far-reaching, waterless sea. On the flat decks of these stranded mammoth hulks of the American desert the Moquis have made their homes for unknown centuries. They have built queer adobe houses, piled story on story in receding steps.

They're running in Indian file, are they? It just happens that way, for the faster men naturally assume a lead. Lend me the glass a minute. Not so bad. They're bunched in a close line. It'll be a beautiful race if they keep as near together as that.

The word Moqui means "peace-loving people." This tribe was not looking for fights. It has been trying for centuries to avoid trouble with its warlike neighbors. Some time in the dim past the forefathers of these Moquis sought the mesa lands as natural strongholds and built their villages upon them. To the northward have long dwelt the roving and treacherous Utes. Eastward are the Navajos, whose nomadic life made them ready for fights. On the south were the aggressive Spaniards. And off there to the west are deep and impassable canyons. The Moquis had either to get away from fighters or to fight. So they made their towns on the tablelands, where they could repel the enemy by simply defending the only trail up the sides of the precipitous mesa. The Spaniards got up here from Mexico nearly 400 years ago during Coronado's inland marches of conquest, and they tried to dislodge these fellows with guns. But the Moquis made it too hot for them with flocks of poisonous arrows every time the white-faced soldiers tried to come up the trail.

For 600 years, it is said, these Indians have held the annual snake dance. And the race at sunrise is a preliminary part of the ceremony. If you had been here at this time yesterday morning you would have seen the antelope race. It was like this, only the runners all wore the kilts and meager costumes of the Antelope Society. Then, in the afternoon, they had the antelope dance. This is the snake dance, and the runners are naked, bare feet and all. They are supposed to run like devils in this event. They want to travel as light as possible. When they finish up here on the mesa top you will have seen the fastest five-mile run of your life.

Look behind you at their houses. See the ascending ladders leading from lower to upper stories. Now glance down this trail to the level of the plain. Doesn't it look like a life of climbing? Think of the constant training these Indians get. Why, the little babies can scamper up the ladders on all fours, like monkeys, weeks before they can walk on the level. That's the sort of exercise that makes for good lungs and muscular legs. Men and women climb those ladders all their lives. The tribe is in unconscious training to produce a race of runners with great staying powers.

Where do you suppose these Moquis get the things they eat? They can't raise anything up here. Well, they are corn-eaters. They have corn patches two, three, five, six, eight, ten miles from here, along each side of a sort of dry stream. In the spring of the year there is a new assignment of the patches to the men of the tribe. While the corn is growing the Moqui goes down and tends his patch every day to protect it from birds and beasts. And how does he get out there, five miles from his home? He runs all the way, going and returning, not fast, but at an easy dog trot, and singing cheerfully to himself as he jogs along. Think of that daily exercise and the climb up that trail as a training for distance running, as a hereditary influence in producing a people that take naturally to distance running. Do you wonder the Moquis are great when it comes to a five-mile race?

Can you make out what they are doing? No, they're not stopping to rest. That is where they skirt the edge of one of the corn patches. Each yanks up a stalk of growing corn and quickly thrusts it through the string about his waist that holds up his simple loin cloth. They come in to the finish with that symbol of the coming crop.

This whole snake-dance business is just a big aboriginal prayer for rain. They always have it in August or September. There is no regular date. But early some morning the head priest crawls up to the housetop, and looking afar with solemn stare, piously proclaims that the snake dance will be celebrated sixteen sunsets from that day. This town of Oraibi gets the big snake dance only on the even years. The odd years it is held at Walpi, the biggest down on the East mesa, twenty miles from here. With sixteen days' notice the pueblo begins elaborate preparations for the biennial event. The women start to work cooking special things for the feasts. The priests of the pueblo retire into the sanctity of their secluded underground chamber and feast and perform strange rites. At sunrise of the eighth day the snake-catchers go forth to the northward with long forked sticks and cowhide bags in quest of rattlesnakes. One day they hunt to the north, one day they search to the eastward, one day they scour the plain to the south, and the fourth day they hunt rattlers on the desert to the west. They catch perhaps 200 of the vicious reptiles and bring them into the priests' chamber, where they are flung in a heap upon the floor and afterward handled in grewsome ceremonials, during which they are dipped into a sort of bath. The secret of the Moquis' successful handling of venomous rattlesnakes seems to be that they never permit the snake to coil ready for his fatal strike. When he coils they gently tickle him with a feather and coax him out of the dangerous pose. And when they pick a rattler up they do it with the rapidity of lightning, grabbing the snake a few inches back of the head.

You would naturally think that if these Moquis didn't get rain any one year they would be nearly starved out. The necessities of war ages ago taught these people to prepare for a famine and guard against a siege. To this day they have observed the traditions of their forefathers. Every house has a little storeroom under it. You go down into the place by a ladder. There, about the walls, is piled three years' supply of corn on the cob, and elsewhere each house keeps stored three years' supply of water. Poor devils, they have learned a hard lesson some time in the past, and it has taught them to be prepared against drought or against human enemies down on the plain, where they grow their corn. For two seasons now they have had very little rain and the corn crop has been miserably small. The result is that they are eating into their three years' supply. And they are seriously talking of migrating to old Mexico next year if they get a third successive dry season. If they do leave these mesas after all the hundreds of years they have lived on them the United States will lose its most interesting Indian tribe and Arizona will never see another snake dance.

Now you can see them coming on rapidly. The fellow ahead has a good lead, but the others are close up and well bunched. What would college athletes think of running on a course like that? It would create a sensation to have these Moqui runners at an intercollegiate field day. Let them have a good track and run to beat the world's record for three, four, five and six miles. I saw a cross-country run in Golden Gate Park, San Francisco. Washington's birthday of this year, with the best Olympic Club, Stanford University and Oakland High School distance runners competing for the speed and team trophies. Four miles on beautifully smooth, winding roadways, and the winner finished in 23:01, the record time of the year before. Both years it was a little high school runner that beat the maturer athletes. Practice and training counted most. But the remarkable part of the event was the marvelous performance of a fellow by the name of Garcia, a Californian, with Indian blood in his veins and a typical Indian physique. He was misdirected in the flagged course, and ran three-quarters of a mile too far when keyed up for a five-mile race. You should have seen him finish. He came down the driveway stretch like a fresh sprinter, so great was his reserve power. He would easily have won over the regular course in better than the record time. Indians are athletes of high order when properly trained. Do you remember how the famous Carlisle Indian football team came out from the East, two years ago, and defeated the most powerful eleven the University of California ever had?

In 1891, when they had the snake dance at Waipi, the winner of the five-mile course over there was timed in twenty minutes. The second runner finished in twenty-one minutes, and he was a mere boy of 15 years.

You will admit now that they are running all right. That's a powerful gait for such a long race.

What a perfect morning for a race! Generally, they say, this event comes too early for photographic light, and the camera has never before been able to catch the runners. Look at the spectators gathered on the edge of the mesa. Isn't that a picture for you? Look at those colored blankets and that sky line and those cliffs dashed with slanting sunlight! I wonder if the race of the ancient Greeks to the summit of Mount Olympus could have been any more spectacular than this is becoming.

It's a long way down there to the foot of the trail. It must take the heart out of a man to face that upward tug after his terrible barefoot race across the uneven floor of the desert.

What will they get? What prize? Just the glory of winning a manly athletic contest, the best possibly reward for a good sport. When the winner reaches the top of the mesa and runs to the "keva," or underground sanctuary of the priests, he will be given a little bowl of ground corn meal. That will be his reward. After he has had a breathing spell he will turn about and run back down this trail and way out to his corn patch, five or six miles, maybe and sprinkle the meal on the ground for the good crop it will bring, and then he will return on the run. That will make a five-mile trot to the start of the race, a straining five-mile race, and the perhaps ten or twelve miles of slower running in carrying the meal bowl. What college distance runner could stand any such trial as that? That would mean twenty or more miles of running in the early morning, including five miles of racing at highest speed.

To-morrow the trader who supplies most of the things that come into this pueblo will put up $20 for a special race of six miles. They say the winner will probably go over the triangular courses in twenty-five minutes. Guess what the winner is to receive. Just a measly $2 for running at six miles at world-record speed, and chasing up this long rocky trail for a finish.

Now you think they're running, don't you? The leader has struck the slope. Poor devil! what a climb before him. But see him come. Can't you hear his breathing? It sounds like the noise of a trotting horse panting down the homestretch. That's running for you. It's bad enough to run up that rail from a fresh start, but it must be nerve-taxing to tackle it after a race across the plain.

They'll never head him now. He has the pack shaken loose and beaten by an eighth of a mile. No, there come two fellows in between him and the rest. If he gets weak on the climb that second fellow may pass him. He's only fifty yards behind. It's a race, all right, among those in the bunch. One, two, three, four—not a fellow dropped out of the race. The whole thirteen are in at the finish. More than half the field would have quit if as many white athletes had started five miles on a cinder track.

Does that look like walking? Did you ever see a runner finish stronger than this fellow? Notice the way he runs erect and carries his arms swinging in unison with his legs, his fists clenched to help him along. It's a quarter of a mile up the slope from the bottom of the mesa, and that fellow is coming on as though it were but fifty feet of up-grade.

He's nearly here. Let's turn and sprint for the "keva" to see the finish. Did you ever hear such breathing?

He'll beat us. See him let out speed now. Same fellow that won the antelope race yesterday.

Whew! Where would we have been in the real race? Why, the second fellow has almost beaten us here. Look at his wide-open mouth and weary eyes. Gods, I'll bet he's had a terrible trip.

"Twenty minutes. Winner made it in twenty minutes."

Hear that shouting? And we forgot all about timing them when he ran to the finish. Those men stayed on the edge of the mesa and kept their watches in hand.

Twenty minutes for five miles! Could it be possible? But the winner was timed at Waipi in 1891 and ran the five-mile course there in twenty minutes, according to published report.

Could there have been a more beautiful finish for a long, hard race? That fellow is a physical wonder. He does not look to be more than 25. They told me that if he should win all three races, including the one to-morrow, he will probably be elected chief of the pueblo of Oraibi for next year in recognition of his prowess at this snake dance celebration of August 24, 1902.

Carlisle Town Council Resolutions

Carlisle Town Council Resolutions Concerning James Thorpe, Lewis Tewanima, and Glenn S. (Pop) Warner and the 1912 Summer Olympic Games

Whereas, In the Olympic games held during the present month at Stockholm, Sweden, James Thorpe, a student at the Carlisle Indian School, won the pentathlon and decathlon, and thereby became entitled to be called the world's greatest all-around athlete; and

Whereas, Lewis Tewanima, also a student at the same institution, participated with great credit in a number of running contests at said games and is justly entitled to be regarded as one of the world's greatest runners; and

Whereas, The victories of these men were won in competition with the most accomplished athletes of all the great nations of the world; and

Whereas, Glenn S. Warner, physical director at the same institution, by the exercise of his wisdom and counsel, has brought the aforesaid students to the high state of physical efficiency they have attained; and

Whereas, By their achievements Thorpe, Tewanima and Warner have not only acquired great personal renown, but have added to the splendid reputation of the great school in which they are being trained and educated, as well as spread abroad the fame of the town of Carlisle, already rich in the great accomplishments of the many notable men and women who in times past have lived therein, and

Whereas, There is a strong desire on the part of the citizens of Carlisle that the signal athletic triumphs of Thorpe and Tewanima should be fitly recognized in some public way; therefore,

It is resolved by the Town Council of the Borough of Carlisle, to honor

James Thorpe, Louis Tewanima, and Glenn S. Warner by this official recognition of their great victories and a public acknowledgement of the
indebtedness of citizens of Carlisle to them for upholding with distinguished credit the fame and glory of one of its great education institutions; and further,

It is resolved that, that five engrossed copies of the foregoing preamble
and resolution, duly certified under the corporate seal of the borough, be
presented respectively to Thorpe, Tewanima, Warner, the Carlisle Indian
School and the Hamilton Library, by the President of the Council on the
occasion of the public demonstration to be held in their honor by the citizens of Carlisle.[1]

A Hopi Runner and His Marathon Trophy

Matthew Sakiestewa Gilbert
Originally Published on *Beyond the Mesas* Weblog
June 28, 2010

Most people who visit the Sherman Indian Museum in Riverside, California, see this first-place trophy without knowing who won it. Marathon officials did not engrave the athlete's name on the trophy, but they did include the date and the event, which was the Vallejo Pre-Olympic National Marathon held in California on December 22, 1929.

At one point in the school's history, the students at Sherman Institute knew who won this award. But as time passed, the trophy, one of the largest in the Museum's collection, became disassociated from its owner.

The trophy belongs to Hopi runner Harry Chaca from the village of Polacca on First Mesa. He was among the great Hopi runners of the twentieth century. Chaca attended Sherman in the 1920s and early 1930s and he earned several marathon honors while a student at the school.

I wrote about Chaca and his victory of the 1929 Vallejo Pre-Olympic National Marathon in my article "Hopi Footraces and American Marathons, 1912–1930" (*American Quarterly*, March 2010). I note that prior to this event, Chaca had won other prestigious marathons and his reputation as a great runner spread far beyond the United States.

In Japan, for example, a runner named Yoshikio Sudsuki heard that Chaca was the best runner in America and so he traveled to the United States for the sole purpose of competing against the Hopi from Polacca. But at the 1929 Vallejo Pre-Olympic National Marathon, Chaca's speed

First-place trophy that Hopi runner Harry Chaca of Polacca won at the Vallejo Valley Pre-Olympic National Marathon, December 22, 1929. Trophy is on display at the Sherman Indian Museum, Riverside, California.

and endurance proved too much for the forty-nine-year-old runner from Tokyo. In my article I write that the

> Hopi runner ran at a "killing pace to win" the full marathon in two hours, forty-one minutes, and twenty-five seconds, a "full second better than the performance of Alpien Stenroos" in the 1924 Olympic Games in Paris. One of the fifty thousand spectators of the marathon recalled that Chaca's "victory" was "all the more noteworthy for his sensational finish. After trailing for twenty-three miles it was at that mark that he applied a final burst of speed that sent him ahead" of Hopi runner Franklin Suhu. In addition to winning the race, Chaca set a new American marathon record, which immediately confirmed his place as the top long-distance runner in the nation.

Shortly after Chaca's marathon victory, school officials took his trophy and displayed it in a large cabinet located in Sherman's administration building (now the Sherman Indian Museum). According to school administrators, all individually won trophies belonged to the school.

At times Hopi students attempted to obtain their trophy cups after their terms at Sherman had expired. During the 1940s, for example, Hopi runner Philip Zeyouma asked the school's superintendent if he could reclaim his trophies (pictured on the front cover of *American Quarterly*), but school officials refused to honor his request.

More than eighty years after Chaca won the Vallejo Pre-Olympic National Marathon, his trophy remains at the Sherman Indian Museum. Although government officials consider the award to be property of the Bureau of Indian Affairs, the trophy will always belong to Harry Chaca and his family.

Notes

PREFACE

1. Over the years I have worked on several research projects with the HCPO. In March 2010, HCPO issued me a permit to conduct research on the Hopi Reservation for this book and related articles. For information on the history and purpose of the HCPO, see Leigh J. Kuwanwisiwma, "The Collaborative Road: A Personal History of the Hopi Cultural Preservation Office," in *Footprints of Hopi History: Hopihiniwtiput Kukveni'at*, ed. Leigh J. Kuwanwisiwma, T. J. Ferguson, and Chip Colwell (Tucson: University of Arizona Press, 2018), 3–15.

2. Amby Burfoot, *The Runner's Guide to the Meaning of Life* (New York: Skyhorse Publishing, 2011), 5.

INTRODUCTION: TO THE FENCE AND BACK

1. Victor Masayesva, Jr., is a pioneering experimental Hopi filmmaker and photographer perhaps best known for his 1992 feature-length documentary, *Imagining Indians*. His other films include *Hopiit, Itam Hakim Hopiit, Ritual Clowns*, and a documentary on Hopi running and the sacredness of water called *Paatuwaqatsi: Water, Land & Life*. He has taught visual arts in Ho'atvela and his work has been exhibited internationally. See Victor Masayesva, Jr., *Husk of Time: The Photographs of Victor Masayesva* (Tucson: University of Arizona Press, 2006).

2. As Teresa L. McCarty and Sheilah E. Nicholas persuasively argue, "we use the term Indigenous to represent original peoples and languages, marking it with a capital 'I' to signify a 'nationality parallel' (King and Benson 2008: 343). Ultimately, the names Indigenous peoples call themselves are the most precise identifiers." See McCarty and Nicholas, "Indigenous Education: Local and Global Perspectives" in Marilyn Martin-Jones, Adrian Blackledge, and Angela Creese, *The Routledge Handbook of Multilingualism* (New York: Routledge, 2012), 146.

3. Hopi scholar and linguist Sheilah E. Nicholas correctly observes that the word "Hopis" is a "Western pluralization of the ethnic label Hopi." The word "Hopiit" is the plural form of "Hopi" in the Hopi language. It is the preferred term used by today's Hopi speakers. Although my understanding of the word Hopìit is still evolving, I use the term "Hopis" knowingly here and elsewhere to remain consistent with how it is used in the majority of my sources, includ-

ing my prior scholarship. Sheilah E. Nicholas to Matthew Sakiestewa Gilbert, email communication, May 5, 2018.

4. Anthropologist Peter Nabokov once observed: "Gods and animals ran long before Indian men and women ever did. Thereafter the gods told the people to do it, and the animals showed them how." See Peter Nabokov, *Indian Running: Native American History and Tradition* (Santa Fe, NM: Ancient City Press, 1981), 23. Also, in their book on traditional Hopi stories, Ekkehart Malotki and Ken Gary retell a story about how a boy from Orayvi once turned into a deer. The boy, who wanted to be known for his speed, had been told that if he killed the fastest deer in the herd, he would "acquire his swiftness." See Ekkehart Malotki and Ken Gary, *Hopi Stories of Witchcraft, Shamanism, and Magic* (Lincoln: University of Nebraska Press, 2001), 191, 192. Furthermore, writing about Hopi runners, Walter Hough once remarked: "Nothing in the whole realm of animal motion can be imagined more graceful than the movements of one of these runners as he passes by in the desert." See Walter Hough, *The Hopi Indians* (Cedar Rapids, IA: Torch Press, 1915), 109. Finally, in his book on a global history of running, Thor Gotaas describes a Chinese running coach named Ma Junren, who wanted his female runners to study the running motions of the ostrich: "Ma Junren studied the running techniques of the ostrich and considered the combination of running and hopping to be extremely effective. The women should have a short stride with minimal lifting of the knees." See Thor Gotaas, *Running: A Global History* (London: Reaktion Books, 2009), 323.

5. Danny Abshire with Brian Metzler, *Natural Running: The Simple Path to Stronger, Healthier Running* (Boulder, CO: VeloPress, 2010), 11.

6. Louise Udall, *Me and Mine: The Life Story of Helen Sekaquaptewa* (Tucson: University of Arizona Press, 1969), 228, 229.

7. Kit Fox, special projects editor for *Runner's World* magazine, describes a similar account about a runner named Mauricio Díaz. During a 5K run on the Tohono O'odham Nation in southern Arizona, Díaz asked an older Hopi runner how many miles Hopis ran during the Snake Dance ceremony. "The man started laughing, then responded, 'Measuring distance and taking time is something white men invented, for we only chase after the fastest of the group.'" See Kit Fox, "These Ultramarathoners Tackle Epic Trail Runs to Connect with Indigenous Populations, *Men's Journal*, November 2017, https://www.mensjournal. com/adventure/meet-aire-libre-a-group-of-ultrarunners-connecting-with -native-tribes-w509387/.

8. See, for instance: Ed Eyestone, "6 Rules to Determine How Many Miles a Week to Run," *Runner's World*, July 5, 2016: 228–229, https://www.runnersworld .com/running-tips/6-rules-to-determine-how-many-miles-a-week-to-run; Erin Strout, "The 6 Reasons You Need to Do Speedwork," *Runner's World*, June

29, 2017, https://www.runnersworld.com/running-tips/the-6-reasons-you-need-to-do-speedwork; Heather Mayer Irvine, "How I Broke 20 Minutes in the 5k (and Why I Wanted To), *Runner's World*, May 30, 2017, https://www.run nersworld.com/5k/how-i-broke-20-minutes-in-the-5k-and-why-i-wanted-to.

9. One high-end example of this is the Garmin fēnix® 5X, which comes equipped with GPS, various monitors, and "outdoor navigation features," https://buy .garmin.com/en-US/US/p/560327.

10. In their insightful book on foot injuries and the ways running has evolved for humans over the centuries, historians and avid runners Peter Larson and Bill Katovsky observed that "Today's runners wear technical polyester fabrics rather than animal skins; they consume energy bars, gels, and sports drinks instead of meats, roots, vegetables and fruits; they log miles for fun or out of a desire to compete, often following detailed workout plans, instead of ne- cessity for survival; they run for the most part on concrete and asphalt instead of rock, sand, and dirt; and they are almost always shod in cushioned shoes rather than running in their bare feet." See Peter Larson and Bill Katovsky, *Tread Lightly: Form, Footwear, and the Quest for Injury-Free Running* (New York: Sky- horse Publishing, 2012), 51, 52.

11. The techniques Hopi runners relied on to navigate their landscape evoke the seafaring technologies Pacific Islanders used to populate Oceania and to maintain trade, clan, and political linkages among islands. Navigators in the Caroline Islands relied on two principles to find their way: *etak*, the notion that it is the islands that move as the canoe remains stationary, and *pookof*, a mental inventory of the creatures indigenous to each island, their travel habits and behavior, the character of clouds, currents, and stars, and even an island's smell. Vicente Diaz has argued that the survival and revival of these practices provide an "indigenously-oriented, anti-colonial praxis" that can furnish a critique of political programs "centered firmly on nation-state based claims of sovereignty." Vicente M. Diaz, "Voyaging for Anti-Colonial Recovery: Aus- tronesian Seafaring, Archipelagic Rethinking, and the Re-mapping of Indige- neity," *Pacific Asia Inquiry* 2, no. 1 (Fall 2011): 21, 26–27.

12. Robin Harvie, *The Lure of Long Distances* (New York: Perseus Books Group, 2011), 7.

13. I explain this concept further in Matthew Sakiestewa Gilbert, "A Second Wave of Hopi Migration," *History of Education Quarterly* 54, no. 3 (August 2014): 356– 361.

14. For detailed accounts of Hopi migration and emergence stories, see Alfred Hermequaftewa, *The Hopi Way Is the Way of Peace* (Santa Fe, NM: Friendship Press, 1953), and Edmund Nequatewa, *Truth of a Hopi: Stories Relating to the Or- igin, Myths, and Clan Histories of the Hopi* (Flagstaff, AZ: Northland Publishing, 1994), 1–15. For an anthropological examination of Hopi migrations, see Pat-

rick D. Lyons, *Ancestral Hopi Migrations* (Tucson: University of Arizona Press, 2003).

15. In their edited collection on hemispheric Indigenous education, historians Brenda J. Child and Brian Klopotek remarked: "Travel near and far provided knowledge of the land, its resources, its peoples, and its history, and groups developed deep and abiding ties between their land, religion, their history, their values, and their culture." Brenda J. Child and Brian Klopotek, "Introduction: Comparing Histories of Education for Indigenous Peoples," in *Indian Subjects: Hemispheric Perspectives on the History of Indigenous Education*, ed. Brenda J. Child and Brian Klopotek (Santa Fe, NM: School of Advanced Research Press, 2014), 3.

16. Thomas E. Sheridan, Stewart B. Koyiyumptewa, Anton Daughters, Dale S. Brenneman, T. J. Ferguson, Leigh Kuwanwisiwma, and Lee Wayne Lomayestewa, eds., *Moquis and Kastiilam: Hopis, Spaniards, and the Trauma of History Volume I, 1540–1679* (Tucson: University of Arizona Press, 2015), 23.

17. The word used to describe *runner* in Hopi is "warik'aya." It is especially descriptive of "one who runs," or "one who represents others." A *fast runner* is "höngiwarik'aya." See Kenneth C. Hill, Emory Sekaquaptewa, and Mary E. Black, eds., *Hopi Dictionary Hopìikwa Lavàytutuveni: A Hopi-English Dictionary of the Third Mesa Dialect* (Tucson: University of Arizona Press, 1998), 844.

18. Alexander M. Stephen, *Hopi Journal*, 2 vols. (Mansfield Centre, CT: Martino Publishing, 2005), 2: 780.

19. See my discussion of this journey in Chapter 2. Leigh J. Kuwanwisiwma interview, March 21, 2006, Paaqavi, Arizona, Hopi Reservation. Herman J. Viola, *Diplomats in Buckskins: A History of Indian Delegations in Washington City* (Norman: University of Oklahoma Press, 1995), 113.

20. Polingaysi Qoyawayma, as told to Vada F. Carlson, *No Turning Back: A Hopi Indian Woman's Struggle to Live in Two Worlds*, 9th printing (Albuquerque: University of New Mexico Press, 1996), 50.

21. For excellent histories of these two schools, see Diana Meyers Bahr, *The Students of Sherman Indian School: Education and Native Identity Since 1892* (Norman: University of Oklahoma Press, 2014), and Linda F. Witmer, *The Carlisle Indian Industrial School: Carlisle Pennsylvania, 1879–1918*, 3rd ed. (Carlisle: Cumberland County Historical Society, 2002).

22. See: Keith R. Burich, *The Thomas Indian School and the "Irredeemable" Children of New York* (Syracuse, NY: Syracuse University Press, 2016); John R. Gram, *Education at the Edge of Empire: Negotiating Pueblo Identity in New Mexico's Indian Boarding Schools* (Seattle: University of Washington Press, 2015); Clifford E. Trafzer, Matthew Sakiestewa Gilbert, and Lorene Sisquoc, eds., *The Indian School on Magnolia Avenue: Voices and Images from Sherman Institute* (Corvallis: Oregon State University Press, 2012); Matthew Sakiestewa Gilbert, *Education beyond the*

Mesas: Hopi Students at Sherman Institute, 1902–1929 (Lincoln: University of Nebraska Press, 2010).

23. "What the Government Schools Are Doing for the Indian," Arizona Republican, May 11, 1903, 2.

24. John Bloom, To Show What an Indian Can Do: Sports at Native American Boarding Schools (Minneapolis: University of Minnesota Press, 2000), xiv.

25. See "The Origins of the Common Language of Sport and the Invention of Athletic Technology," in Mark S. Dyreson, Making the American Team: Sport, Culture, and the Olympic Experience (Urbana: University of Illinois Press, 1998), 17–20. Also, in his essay on early modern accounts of Kenyan long-distance running, John Bale observed that while Africans had been running since "time immemorial," they had to learn modern ways of athletic competition that connected them to other runners in the world. "Most significant," Bale notes, "is that modern sport is structured by rules and regulations that are global in their application and acceptance (Stovkis 1992). In this sense the results of modern running form a kind of global 'currency', understood and adhered to in most nations of the modern world." See John Bale, "Kenyan Running before the 1968 Olympics," in East African Running: Towards A Cross-Disciplinary Perspective, ed. Yannis Pitsiladis, John Bale, Craig Sharp, and Timothy Noakes (New York: Routledge, 2007), 12.

26. Hopi High School Cross Country Coach Rick Baker once noted that when Hopis run, they are "Dancing on Mother Earth." See Rick Baker, "Native American Runners," 6, www.nacoach.org/uploads/Baker1.pdf. In his essay on strategies for running on various terrains, Sage Canaday, an accomplished long-distance trail runner, once remarked: "A smooth dirt doubletrack can feel like a paved road, where as a rock-laden singletrack up a mountain can feel more like an obstacle course. . . . As you gain balance, agility, and confidence, amp up your speed. Take small, quick steps and adjust your stride on the fly like you're 'dancing' with the terrain." See Sage Canaday, "Scratch New Surfaces," Runner's World, May 2018, 9–11.

27. N. Scott Momaday, House Made of Dawn (New York: Harper Perennial, 2010).

28. In Hopi ways of thinking, the lack of rain represented bad hearts and thoughts, and so when the people ran with "good hearts" it ensured rain for the entire community. Stephen, Hopi Journal, 2: 796.

29. "Indians Return," Saturday Evening, May 28, 1927, 5. Issued by the Associated Press.

30. Modern-day sneakers originated with Charles Goodyear's 1844 patent of vulcanization, the process of melting rubber and fabric together, which enabled him to create rubber-soled shoes with a molded tread. Reebok, initially known as Boulton, was founded in the United Kingdom in 1890 and began marketing the first spiked running shoes in 1905. Keds were launched in the

United States in 1916 by the Goodyear and US Rubber Company as a rubber-soled sneaker, with a line of basketball shoes called "Pro-Keds" released the following year. Converse released its "All Star" line the following year, the first sneakers designed specifically for basketball. See Yuniya Kawamura, *Sneakers: Fashion, Gender, and Subculture* (New York: Bloomsbury, 2016), 53–54. For a terrific history of the athletic running shoe, see Larson and Katovsky, *Tread Lightly*, 79–105.

31. Special Agent Julian Scott observed that in the early 1890s, Hopis made their moccasins with either deer or cow hides: "The moccasins are of plain buck or cow skin, either of a natural color or dyed black or brick red; the vamp reaches to the ankle, the quarters or sides extend a little higher and pass across the front; the button fly folds over the outer quarter and fastens just above the heel." See Julian Scott, "Report of the Moqui Pueblos of Arizona," in *Extra Census Bulletin: Moqui Pueblos of Arizona and Pueblos of New Mexico*, ed. Thomas Donaldson (Washington, DC: US Census Printing Office, 1893), 52.

32. Howard W. Angus, "Philip Zeyouma Will Run Again," *Los Angeles Times*, December 25, 1914, III1.

33. Here I am referring to Hopi runner Nicholas Qömawunu (Quomawahu) from the village of Orayvi, Arizona. At the time Qömawunu was competing in the 1928 Bunion Derby, a race that stretched from Los Angeles to New York City. He quit the race near Seligman, Arizona, as a result of numerous physical ailments. He did not compete after this race, partly as a result of the toll the derby had taken on his body, and partly as a result of his new status as a "professional," which prohibited him from competing in numerous races intended only for "amateurs" including the Olympic Games. I cover Qömawunu's participation in the Bunion Derby in Chapter 6.

34. In his comprehensive book on running, James F. Fixx describes:

> Watch a child play. It runs for a while, rests, runs again. Now it runs quickly, now slowly, now briefly, now for a long time. After we enter school our running becomes more institutionalized. We run a few yards on a football field or ninety feet on a baseball diamond. Once out of school we hardly run at all—our style of living slowly squeezes the running out of us. Yet the need to run never leaves us, and we are the poorer if we do not somehow find a way to keep at it.

See James F. Fixx, *The Complete Book of Running* (New York: Random House, 1977), 23.

35. In the early 1930s, Sherman Institute cross-country coach Bert Jameison commented on the daily routine of his runners, saying: "These boys run ten miles every morning and then ten miles before supper for exercise alone." See Ralph W. Callahan, "Morning Musing," *Anniston (Alabama) Star*, May 22, 1931, 14.

36. See "Outing Record—Carlisle Industrial School" in "Tewanima, Louis," file 3766, box 79, Carlisle School Files (CSF), Records of the Carlisle Indian Industrial School, Carlisle, PA, Records of the Bureau of Indian Affairs, 1793–1989, Record Group 75, National Archives and Records Administration (Washington, DC).

37. Historian Philip J. Deloria notes that even as Louis Tewanima was making waves in the 1912 Olympics, "everyone back at Hopi knew runners with better wind and faster legs." Tewanima's seamless post-retirement transition to farmer and Antelope Society priest and his decision to give away his medals, Deloria suggests, indicate an "everydayness" to Native running that began to wilt under the heat of postwar America's mass culture of athletic celebrity. Philip J. Deloria, *Indians in Unexpected Places* (Lawrence: University Press of Kansas, 2004), 132, 133.

38. The spiritual and cultural significance of rain in Hopi society is extremely important. Nearly all of the Hopis' many ceremonies involve some ritual or supplication for rain to water their crops. For the Hopi, rain was much more valuable to the people than trophy cups or medals. See, for instance: Richard O. Clemmer, *Roads in the Sky: The Hopi Indians in a Century of Change* (New York: Routledge, 1995), 19.

39. Deloria, *Indians in Unexpected Places*, 132, 133.

40. *Sherman Bulletin*, November 27, 1907, 3. Sherman Indian Museum, Riverside, California.

41. Ibid.

42. Dyreson, *Making the American Team*, 29.

43. Ralph C. Wilcox, "The Shamrock and the Eagle: Irish Americans and Sports in the Nineteenth Century," in *Ethnicity and Sport in North American History and Culture*, ed. George Eisen and David K. Wiggin (Westport, CT: Praeger, 1995), 71.

44. Pamela Cooper, *The American Marathon* (Syracuse, NY: Syracuse University Press, 1998), 2.

45. Henry J. Furber, Jr., "A New Era for Athletics," *Crittenden Press*, February 27, 1902, 6.

46. Women's National Indian Association employee Mabel W. Collins, who lived with the Hopis for three years during the late 1890s, once observed: "The Moquis are like little children, having to be taught over and over again in the most simple style." See Mabel W. Collins, "Curious Customs of Moqui Indians," *Democrat and Chronicle*, April 29, 1900, 13.

47. "Harry M'Lean for Celebration Races," *Arizona Republican*, September 18, 1911, 1.

48. William H. Freeman, *Physical Education, Exercise, and Sport Science in a Changing Society*, 8th ed. (Burlington, MA: Jones and Bartlett Learning, 2013), 177.

49. Steven A. Riess quoted in ibid.

50. "Many Prizes for Marathon," *Los Angeles Herald*, December 13, 1908, Part III, 3.

51. In the early 1900s, United States newspapers regularly published stories of Indian runners who competed in American races. Even before Hopis arrived on the American and international running scenes in 1908, other Native runners attracted attention from major news outlets across the nation. One of these runners was Tom Longboat, an Onondaga Indian from the Six Nations Reserve in Canada who won the Boston Marathon in April 1907. Longboat's remarkable accomplishments in distance running, and the excitement he generated in the sporting community, greatly influenced the way Americans understood Hopi and other Indian runners who came after him. His victories, especially against white American athletes, caused Americans to reconsider their opinion of Indian people and their notion of sport and American exceptionalism. "Wasn't it Uncle Sam who said 'the only good Indian is a dead Indian?,'" asked a sport columnist following the Onondaga's big win in Boston. "But that was before Tom Longboat put the dust of his flying feet all over the 'Americans.'" See "Sport," *Nanaimo Daily News*, April 30, 1907, 2.

52. Stephen, *Hopi Journal*, 1: 589, 1: 658–659, 2: 780, 2: 817, 2: 850–853.

53. J. Walter Fewkes, "The Wa-Wac-Ka-Tci-Na, a Tusayan Foot Race," *Bulletin of the Essex Institute* 24 (1892): 113–133.

54. Mischa Titiev, "Hopi Racing Customs at Oraibi, Arizona," *Papers of the Michigan Academy of Science, Arts and Letters*, vol. 24, part 4 (1939): 33–42.

55. Ibid., 33.

56. Although I focus my discussion here on Hopi runners, a great amount of literature has been written on the topic of running in general. For an excellent resource, see Roger Robinson, *Running in Literature: A Guide for Scholars, Readers, Runners, Joggers, and Dreamers* (Halcottsville, NY: Breakaway Books, 2003).

57. Nabokov, *Indian Running*.

58. Nabokov situates Hopi and other Indian runners within an American sport society in his chapter entitled "In the White Man's Arena." See Nabokov, *Indian Running*, 177–193.

59. Richard L. Lutz and Mary Lutz, *The Running Indians: The Tarahumara of Mexico* (Salem, OR: Dimi Press, 1989).

60. Michael Ward, *Ellison "Tarzan" Brown: The Narragansett Indian Who Twice Won the Boston Marathon* (Jefferson, NC: McFarland, 2006).

61. Brian S. Collier, "'To Bring Honor to My Village': Steve Gachupin and the Community Ceremony of Jemez Running and the Pike's Peak Marathon," *Journal of the West* 46, no. 4 (2007), 62–71.

62. Ben Fogelberg, "Saul Halyve, Forgotten Hopi Marathon Champion." *Colorado Heritage* 26, no. 4 (2006): 36–47.

63. Christopher McDougall, *Born to Run: A Hidden Tribe, Superathletes, and the Greatest Race the World Has Never Seen* (New York: Vintage, 2009). In 2010, I also began

publishing accounts of Hopi runners at Sherman Institute and the Carlisle Indian Industrial School. See Matthew Sakiestewa Gilbert, "Hopi Footraces and American Marathons, 1912–1930," *American Quarterly* 62, no. 3 (2010): 77–101, and Matthew Sakiestewa Gilbert, "Marathoner Louis Tewanima and the Continuity of Hopi Running, 1908–1912," *Western Historical Quarterly* 43, no. 1 (Autumn 2012): 324–346.

64. Mark S. Dyreson, "The Foot Runners Conquer Mexico and Texas: Endurance Racing, *Indigenismo*, and Nationalism," *Journal of Sport History* 31, no. 1 (Spring 2004): 1–31.

65. Some contemporary Hopi runners who deserve attention from scholars and nonscholars alike are Caroline Sekaquaptewa, Trent Taylor, Steve Ovah, and Anthony Masayesva. See Toyacoyah Brown, "4 Native Runners Finish Boston Marathon," *Powwows.com*, April 27, 2015, http://www.powwows.com/4-native-runners-finish-boston-marathon/.

66. Stephen, *Hopi Journal*, 2: 780.

CHAPTER 1: A WORLD UNLIKE THEIR OWN

1. "Mokis and Zunis Are Snake Dancing in Wildest Arizona," *St. Louis Post-Dispatch*, August 6, 1899, A9. Many Indian people throughout the Southwest have historically used kivas for ceremonial and social purposes. In his book *Runner in the Sun*, Salish Kootenai writer and activist D'Arcy McNickle describes a Southwest Pueblo Indian kiva as a

> circular room without windows, could be entered only by the square opening in the roof, at one a smoke hole and a doorway. This was the meeting place for the men of the clan, but it was more than that. In it, Salt and boys of his own age, and boys before his time, were taught the art and skills of manhood. History and legend were told here, and the manner in which a man should stand before the world was proclaimed in many long speeches.

See D'Arcy McNickle, *Runner in the Sun*, illus. by Allan Houser, 3rd printing (New York: Holt, Rinehart and Winston, 1962), 14.

2. Construction of the Santa Fe Railroad approached sixty miles to the south of Hopiland by 1881. As historian Peter Iverson suggests, although the tracks did not go near Hopi villages, "the reality of the railroad forced the federal government to come to terms with the reality of the Hopis." Peter Iverson, "The Enduring Hopi," in *Hopi Nation: Essays on Indigenous Art, Culture, History, and Law*, ed. John R. Wunder (Lincoln: Digital Commons, University of Nebraska–Lincoln, 2008), 147. David F. Myrick, *Railroads of Nevada and Eastern California*, vol. 2 (Berkeley: Howell-North Books, 1963), 763.

3. See Leah Dilworth, "Representing the Hopi Snake Dance," *Journal for the An-*

thropological Study of Human Movement 11, no. 4, and 12, no. 1 (Fall 2001/Spring 2002): 453–496.

4. The complete name of MacNeil's sculpture is *The Moqui Runner (The Moqui Prayer for Rain—The Returning of the Snakes)*. Over the years, MacNeil produced several of these sculptures, one of which is currently on display at the Art Institute of Chicago. See Andrew J. Walker, "The Aesthetics of Extinction: Art and Science in the Indian Sculptures of Hermon Atkins MacNeil," in *Perspectives on American Sculpture before 1925*, ed. Thayer Tolles (New York: Metropolitan Museum of Art, 2003): 106, 107.

5. "Delirious Rites: Weird Arizona Snake Dance for Penance," *Columbus Journal*, December 16, 1896, 1.

6. In the 1900s, some Native people would publically challenge "popular notions of Indianness" that cartoonists published in American newspapers. See Frederick E. Hoxie, ed., *Talking Back to Civilization: Indian Voices from the Progressive Era* (Boston: Bedford, 2001), 108–115.

7. "The Grotesque Snake Dance of the Moquis," *Daily Review*, March 30, 1902, 14.

8. "Snake Dance of the Moki Indians," *(Philadelphia) Times*, January 29, 1899, 21.

9. "Hopi Chief Makes Prayer to Ocean," *Los Angeles Times*, October 18, 1925, B14.

10. Ruth DeEtte Simpson once observed: "Religion is an integral part of Hopi life: it is the core about which life evolves; it is the great directing, motivating influence back of each Hopi's deed and thought." See Ruth DeEtte Simpson, *The Hopi Indians*, 3rd ed. (Los Angeles: Southwest Museum, 1971), 32.

11. "Saw the Great Snake Dance," *Philadelphia Inquirer*, October 3, 1897, 26.

12. Edward Holland Spicer, *Cycles of Conquest: The Impact of Spain, Mexico, and the United States on the Indians of the Southwest, 1533–1960* (Tucson: University of Arizona Press, 1976), 189.

13. Much of this information comes from Castanedas's account in Harry C. James, *Pages from Hopi History* (Tucson: University of Arizona Press, 1974), 36.

14. Henry W. Haynes, "Early Explorations of New Mexico," *Spanish Exploration and Settlements in America from the Fifteenth to the Seventeenth Century*, vol. 2, ed. Justin Winsor (Boston: Houghton Mifflin, 1886), 484.

15. Robert P. Porter, *Report on Indians Taxed and Indians Not Taxed in the United States (Except Alaska) at the Eleventh Census, 1890* (Washington, DC: US Census Printing Office, 1894), 172.

16. Ibid., 173–174. See also "Lieutenant Ives Meets Moqui Guides, Moqui Pueblos, May 11, 1858," in Donaldson, *Extra Census Bulletin*, 30–31.

17. See John Wesley Powell, *The Exploration of the Colorado River and Its Canyons* (New York: Dover Publications, 1961); Donald Worster, *A River Running West: The Life of John Wesley Powell* (Oxford: Oxford University Press, 2001).

18. Powell, *Exploration of the Colorado River*, 117–119.

19. C. A. Behm, "Stood Guard over Brigham with Major Powell in Grand Canyon," *Weekly Journal-Miner*, April 22, 1903, 2.

20. At this time, Hopis tended to be very superstitious, and visitors to Hopiland often wrote about the people's beliefs in spirits, goblins, or other supernatural beings. For example, in the US Eleventh Census of 1890, Expert Special Agent Thomas Donaldson observed that "No people, no race, is free from superstitions. Thought breeds and develops them. The [Moqui and Pueblos of New Mexico] fills the mountain cañon, the roaring, leaping river, the cave in the rock, the mountain top with its tall trees, and the distant valley with mysterious life, with strange people, giants, dwarfs, and witches." See Donaldson, *Extra Census Bulletin*, 4.

21. C. A. Behm, "Exploring with Powell," *Weekly Journal-Miner*, May 6, 1903, 3. Over the years, scholars and other writers have published extensively on the physical and mental benefits of exposing one's body to cold water after strenuous exercise, including running. See Sandra Uckert, *Cold Application in Training & Competition: The Influence of Temperature on Your Athletic Performance* (Indianapolis: Meyer & Meyer Sport, 2014).

22. C. M. Robinson III, ed., *The Diaries of John Gregory Bourke Volume 5* (Denton: University of North Texas Press, 2013), 277.

23. Quoted in Matt Fitzgerald, *Run: The Mind-Body Method of Running by Feel* (Boulder: VeloPress, 2010), 47.

24. Heinrich R. Voth, "The Oraibi Summer Snake Ceremony," *Field Columbian Museum Publication* 3, no. 83 (1903): 324.

25. During an interview for a film on Hopi running, Hopi High School coach Rick Baker once remarked: "These kids know that they are running more than for just a state title. They run for strength, they run for their lives, their villages, our tribe, and for water, and then our families." Scott Harves, *Run Hopi*, ESPN SportsCenter, https://vimeo.com/179251785.

26. Simpson, *The Hopi Indians*, 26.

27. Robinson, *The Diaries of John Gregory Bourke*, 277.

28. In his comprehensive study of Indian running, anthropologist Peter Nabokov provided examples of women runners from various tribes, including the Chippewa, Chiricahua and Mescalero Apache, Navajo, Maidu, and many others. See Nabokov, *Indian Running*, 85–87, 93, 108, 123, 139–142, 144, 167, 171.

29. Stephen, *Hopi Journal*, 2: 850–851.

30. Tsakaptamana, "The Racers at Tsikuvi," in *Hopi Voices: Recollections, Traditions, and Narratives of the Hopi Indians*, ed. Harold Courlander (Albuquerque: University of New Mexico Press, 1982), 85, 86.

31. Donald L. Fixico, *"That's What They Used to Say": Reflections on American Indian Oral Traditions* (Norman: University of Oklahoma Press, 2017), 43.

32. Harold Courlander, *People of the Short Blue Corn: Tales and Legends of the Hopi Indians* (New York: Harcourt Brace Jovanovich, 1970), 96–109.

33. For another example of how Pueblo people use running as a way to represent their village, see Collier, "To Bring Honor to My Village," 62–71.

34. Courlander, *People of the Short Blue Corn*, 100.

35. James, *Pages from Hopi History*, 194–195.

36. Walter Hough, "Biographical Memoir of Jesse Walter Fewkes, 1850–1930," in *National Academy of Sciences of the United States of America: Biographical Memoirs, Volume XV—Ninth Memoir* (Washington: National Academy of Sciences, 1932), 263. Fewkes died on May 31, 1930. In its brief announcement about his death, the Associated Press noted: "He was the first man to make use of the phonograph in the recording of Indian music. He was initiated into the secret ries [sic] of the Hopi Indians, who called him 'Medicine Bowl' because they said he was always pouring information into them." See "Dr. Fewkes, Friend of Hopi Indians, Dies," *Star Tribune*, June 1, 1930, 10. Issued by the Associated Press.

37. J. Walter Fewkes, "The Wa-Wac-Ka-Tci-Na, a Tusayan Foot Race," *Bulletin of the Essex Institute* 24 (1892): 1.

38. "The Only Good Indian," *New York Times*, March 22, 1896, 25.

39. David Nelson has argued that college football has been at its heart a "game of change," having made more rule changes during the first eighty years of the twentieth century than any other major American team sport. Nelson, *The Anatomy of a Game: Football, the Rules, and the Men Who Made the Game* (Newark: University of Delaware Press), 153.

40. "Mexican Runners," *Cincinnati Enquirer*, July 27, 1901, 12. Originally published in the *New York Sun*.

41. G. Wharton James, "Are Cruel Savages: The Seri Indians and Their Pacific Island Home. Physically They Are the Superiors of All Other American Aborigines—Unequaled as Hunters and Runners," *Phillipsburg (Kansas) Herald*, February 8, 1900, 6.

42. There is no evidence in the Spanish colonial record to indicate that the Seri ever practiced cannibalism. Rather, according to anthropologist Thomas Sheridan, the myth of Seri cannibalism was apparently invented by the US press in the late 19th century and has lingered in popular portrayals of the group since then. Thomas E. Sheridan, *Empire of Sand: the Seri Indians and the Struggle for Spanish Sonora, 1645–1803* (Tucson: University of Arizona Press, 2016), 6.

43. Schweickhardt's, also known as the Cottage, was a restaurant and saloon located inside Forest Park on land leased from the city of St. Louis. It was operated by Charles Schweickhardt from 1885 through 1904. From 1891 through 1904, Schweickhardt had the exclusive right to sell refreshments in the park. The restaurant was torn down to make way for the Louisiana Purchase Expo-

sition in 1904. "Will Prof. M'Gee Bring His Cannibals Here? What's Eating Him?," *St. Louis Post-Dispatch*, August 2, 1903, 15. Caroline Loughlin and Catherine Anderson, *Forest Park* (St. Louis: Junior League of St. Louis, University of Missouri Press, 1986), 30–31, 43–45.

44. Harry B. Hawes was the police commissioner of St. Louis, and thus his "fat emissaries" were police officers. By 1903, when this article appeared in the *Post-Dispatch*, Hawes had been involved in several high-profile news stories including a controversial expansion of the city's police force and taking an active role in putting down the St. Louis Streetcar Strike of 1900, so Hawes would have been a familiar name for many of the paper's readers. "Harry Bartow Hawes," in *History of Missouri, A Compendium of History and Biography for Ready Reference*, vol. 3, ed. Howard L. Conard (New York: The Southern History Company, 1901), 205.

45. The artist who created this cartoon was Oscar Charles Chopin, who was a well-reputed editorial cartoonist for the *St. Louis Post-Dispatch*. Chopin was the son of proto-feminist author Kate Chopin. Laura Wexler, "The Fair Ensemble: Kate Chopin in St. Louis in 1903," in *Haunted by Empire: Geographies of Intimacy in North American History*, ed. Ann Stoler (Durham, NC: Duke University Press, 2006), 285.

46. As John Coward suggests, media representations such as these, in addition to more romantic characterizations of Indigenous people, were omnipresent in the American media of the nineteenth century. This "newspaper Indian," Coward writes, "was a product of newspapers aligned with both government and business interests, a view that saw Indians as obstacles to economic growth and national expansion" as well as being shaped by the desire of journalists and editors to produce popular, and often sensationalist, copy. John Coward, *The Newspaper Indian: Native American Identity in the Press, 1820–1890* (Urbana: University of Illinois Press, 1999), 38–39.

47. The regulation against gambling mentioned here may have been specific to this unit. The 1891 edition of the *Instructions for Courts Martial* lists only the "reduction and forfeiture" of $5 for noncommissioned officers who encourage gambling. "White against Red," the *Wyandott Herald* (Kansas City, Kansas), October 22, 1891, 1. Arthur Murray and Wesley Merritt, *Instructions for Courts-Martial* (Saint Paul, MN: Headquarters Department of Dakota, 1891), 62.

48. "Speedy Indians: They Can Easily Outrun Uncle Sam's Cavalry," *Coleman Voice* (Coleman, TX), December 17, 1891, 2.

49. "Immortalizing the Features of a Vanishing Race," *San Francisco Chronicle*, September 30, 1900, 32.

50. David Hurst Thomas, *Skull Wars: Kennewick Man, Archaeology, and the Battle for Native American Identity* (New York: Basic Books, 2000), xxx, xxxi.

51. In his fascinating history of Hopis and photography during the late nineteenth and early twentieth centuries, Erin Younger noted that "by the late 1890s, a growing number of amateur and avocational photographers converged on the Hopi mesas. Embracing the popularly held notion that Indians were a 'vanishing' race, some had come to document the rapidly changing Hopis; others sought to reconstruct what they imagined traditional Indian life to be." See Erin Younger, "Changing Images: A Century of Photography on the Hopi Reservation," in *Hopi Photographers: Hopi Images*, ed. Victor Masayesva, Jr., and Erin Younger (Tucson: Sun Tracks & University of Arizona Press, 1983), 17.

52. "Back from among the Moqui Indians," *San Francisco Call*, September 15, 1902, 8. Special Agent Scott was similarly impressed with the Snake Dance footrace held at Walpi in August 1883, writing "it is a most exciting scene, and in their running great endurance is exhibited, for they (the racers) have fasted for 4 days previous, partaking of nothing but a decoction prepared by the chief priest or priestess of the order as an antidote to the rattlesnake bite in case any may be bitten during the ceremonies. This antidote is only known to the chief priest and the priestess, and the secret is only imparted to their successors." Donaldson, *Extra Census Bulletin*, 41.

53. In an interview with Hopi archivist Stewart B. Koyiyumptewa, Leigh J. Kuwanwisiwma noted that the term "Moqui" originated with Spanish explorers who adopted the Zuni name for Hopi people, *Amookwe'eh*. The term translates literally to "it's a clown (*mokweh*)" but was meant to signify that the Hopi people had "finished their migrations, established their villages, established their ceremonial cycles, and were now exercising as stewards" of the mesas. Sheridan, et al., *Moquis and Kastiilam* (Tucson: University of Arizona Press, 2015), 177.

54. "Are Moqui Runners World Beaters?," *San Francisco Chronicle*, October 5, 1902, A3.

55. Today the driving distance between Orayvi and Tuba City is about fifty miles. In this account, Hopi runner Talashyatua may have decreased the distance between the two locations by taking a more direct path.

56. Reprinted in "Wonderful Hopi Runners," *Boston Daily Globe*, October 5, 1902, 32.

57. Walter Hough once observed that Hopi runners preferred to wear moccasins while running in the sand: "The Indians say that moccasins are the best footwear for travel over sandy country, as the foot, so clad, presses loose the sand into a firm, rounded bunch, giving fulcrum for the forward spring, but the naked feet scatters the sand, and this, on experiment, was found to be true." See Hough, *The Hopi Indians*, 109.

58. The energy cost expended in running on sand has been measured at 1.8 times the energy cost of running on a paved road. William D. McArdle, Frank I.

Katch, and Victor L. Katch, *Essentials of Exercise Physiology* (Baltimore: Lippin-cott Williams & Wilkins, 2006), 280.

59. Reprinted in "Wonderful Hopi Runners," *Boston Daily Globe*, October 5, 1902, 32.

60. "Wonderful Hopi Runners," *Indian's Friend* 16, no. 2 (October 1903): 10, 11. The "flour" referenced here may have actually been corn meal. The *Indian's Friend* newsletter was published by the Women's National Indian Association, Philadelphia, PA.

61. See Julian H. Steward, *Theory of Culture Change: The Methodology of Multilinear Evolution* (Urbana: University of Illinois Press, 1955).

62. Julian H. Steward, "Notes on Hopi Ceremonies in Their Initiatory Form in 1927–1928," *American Anthropologist* 33, no. 1 (March 1931): 56–58.

63. Ibid., 58.

64. Samuel Travers Clover, *On Special Assignment: Being the Further Adventures of Paul Travers; Showing How He Succeeded as a Newspaper Reporter* (Boston: Lothrop Publishing, 1903), 117.

65. Ibid., 118.

66. Another example of this took place in 1907, when an individual from Lancashire, England, named Oliver H. Haslam visited the Hopi village of Orayvi (by way of Tuba City), remarked on the running abilities of the people, and published his account in the *Bolton Journal and Guardian*: "The people—the Hopis or Moquis (the latter the name given them by the Spaniards)—are supposed to be the most civilized of all the Indian tribes, and are not a war-like people. They are great runners, thinking nothing of sixty miles at once, and in a rough country beating a horse and rider in a distance of seven or ten miles." See Oliver H. Haslam, "Amongst the Indians in Arizona," *Bolton Journal and Guardian* (April 26, May 3, and May 10, 1907): 5, 6. Northern Arizona University, Cline Library, Colorado Plateau Digital Archives, Flagstaff, Arizona.

67. "Is a Moki Chief," *Boston Daily Globe*, March 6, 1904, 38.

68. "News of the Morning," *(Sacramento) Record-Union*, May 21, 1880, 2.

69. Clement Powell, "The Powell Expedition," *Chicago Tribune*, February 23, 1873, 2.

70. H.M.W., "Arizona," *Chicago Tribune*, April 11, 1879, 9.

71. "Snake Dancing," *Brooklyn Daily Eagle*, November 2, 1889, 1. Originally published in the *St. Louis Globe-Democrat*.

CHAPTER 2: DIRT TRAILS AND STEEL RAILS

1. Walter Hough indicates only that this incident took place "one morning about seven o'clock," but it would have occurred sometime between his initial visit to Hopiland as a field assistant for J. Walter Fewkes in 1896 and the publication of Hough's *The Hopi Indians* in 1915. Neil M. Judd, "Walter Hough: An Appreciation," *American Anthropologist* 38, no. 3 (1938), 471–481, 474.

2. In the early 1890s, the Atlantic & Pacific Railroad line that passed through Winslow functioned as a joint subsidiary of the St. Louis & San Francisco Railway and the Atchison, Topeka & Santa Fe Railway. All three companies went into receivership following in 1893, and the Santa Fe Pacific Railroad emerged in 1897 to take control of the line. Myrick, *Railroads of Nevada and Eastern California*, vol. 2, 763, 788.

3. Hough, *The Hopi Indians*, 108, 109.

4. At the turn of the twentieth century, non-Indian people still relied on Indian runners to deliver messages throughout the Southwest: "As long-distance runners [Yaquis] have excelled for hundreds of years. While carrying mail to the distant mining camps, the young men used as runners can cover eight miles an hour and keep the pace steady for half a day at a stretch. They run with the free stride of the English cross-country runner, and not with the flat trot of the Indian. Wearing only a breech cloth and a serape, they skim lightly over the ground, always taking hills and sandy washes at points of least resistance." See "Yaquis Unconquered," *Washington Herald*, August 2, 1908, 9.

5. As Philip Deloria has argued, "a significant cohort of Native people engaged the same forces of modernization that were making non-Indians reevaluate their own expectations of themselves and their society." See Deloria, *Indians in Unexpected Places*, 6.

6. Leech Lake Ojibwe scholar Scott Richard Lyons has written a fascinating essay on the complexities surrounding Indians and modernity wherein he rightly pushes back against the long-used phrase employed by scholars (and others) who describe Indian people as being "torn between two worlds." He writes: "In the context of Native American studies, subjects fitting this general description have typically been characterized as 'torn between two worlds,' Indian and white, but it seems more accurate to find them experiencing the same historical moment as others; to discover them feeling and responding in similarly human ways to the dramatic onset of modernity's ceaseless cycles of destruction and renewal, even though that modernity was undeniably entangled with settler colonialism, racism, and disproportionate loss." See Scott Richard Lyons, "Migrations to Modernity: The Many Voices of George Copway's *Running Sketches of Men and Places, in England, France, Germany, Belgium, and Scotland*," in *The World, the Text, and the Indian: Global Dimensions of Native American Literature*, ed. Scott Richard Lyons (Albany: State University of New York Press, 2017), 144, 145.

7. Women's National Indian Association employee Mabel W. Collins, who lived with the Hopis for three years during the late 1890s, once described how a person would travel by train and then horse to reach the Hopi villages: "The Moqui reservation is located in the northeastern part of the state and is about eighty-five miles from the Santa Fe railroad station in Holbrook, A. T. [Apache

Territory]. To reach this place it is necessary to go by team over a sandy desert country to the Keam's Canon, where there is a government boarding school. Then begins the climb to the mesa where the Indians hide themselves shyly from the eyes of the whites and know no more about the doings of the world beyond their mountain home than did Alexander Selkirk on his desert island." See Collins, "Curious Customs of Moqui Indians," 13. Alexander Selkirk was a Scottish naval officer who was marooned on an uninhabited island in the South Pacific Ocean from 1704 to 1709. His story about how he survived the ordeal became legendary. See John Howell, *The Life and Adventures of Alexander Selkirk* (Charleston, SC: Bibliolife, 2009). Originally published in 1829.

8. E. Charles Adams, *Homol'ovi: An Ancient Hopi Settlement Cluster* (Tucson: University of Arizona Press, 2002), 3.

9. The Hopi delegation left Fort Defiance, Arizona, for Gallup, New Mexico, on Tuesday, June 17, 1890. See "Five Moqui Chiefs: Indian Agent Vandever and Party of Indians Reach Terre Haute," *Terre Haute Evening Gazette*, June 20, 1890, 1. In 1929, a second delegation of five different Hopi chiefs would return to Washington, DC, to speak with Vice President Charles Curtis to express their concern about the lack of water and poor sanitary conditions on the Hopi Reservation. See "Five Hopi Chiefs, on Way to See Vice-President, Stop Here," *Baltimore Sun*, April 10, 1929, 32.

10. Deloria, *Indians in Unexpected Places*, 143.

11. C. E. Vandever to Commissioner of Indian Affairs, "Report of Moqui Pueblo Indians, Navajo Agency," Fifty-Ninth Annual Report of the Commissioner of Indian Affairs to the Secretary of the Interior (Washington, DC: Government Printing Office, 1890), 171, 172.

12. On December 16, 1882, President Chester A. Arthur by Executive Order officially established the Hopi Reservation. See James, *Pages from Hopi History*, 100, 101.

13. Years later in 1941, soldiers at Fort Leavenworth remembered the Hopi people as being great long-distance runners. See "Runs to Smash Army's Theory," *Daily Press*, February 3, 1941, 1. Issued by the Associated Press.

14. *Who Owns the Past*, directed by Jed Riffe, Berkeley, CA: Berkeley Media, DVD, 2002.

15. "Purely Personal," *Saturday Evening Mail* (Terre Haute, Indiana), December 29, 1888, 8.

16. *Saturday Evening Mail*, June 21, 1890, 7. See also Tom Roznowski, *An American Hometown: Terre Haute, Indiana 1927* (Beverly, MA: Quarry Books, 2009), 51, 52.

17. Henry C. Bradsby, *History of Vigo County, Indiana with Biographical Selections* (Durham, NC: S. B. Nelson, 1891), 490–498.

18. Gordon M. Bakken and Alexandra Kindell, eds. *Encyclopedia of Immigration and Migration in the American West*, vol. 1 (Thousand Oaks, CA: Sage Publications, 2006), 306, 307.

19. E. S. Clark, "Report on the Moqui Pueblos of Arizona," in Donaldson, ed., *Extra Census Bulletin*, 1893, 50. This rainfall figure is an average for most parts of the Hopi and Navajo reservations. Some parts of Hopi and Navajo receive smaller or larger rainfall totals, such as at the Chuska Mountains at Navajo, which have an average annual rainfall of twenty-five inches. Arizona Department of Water Resources, "Climate of the Eastern Plateau Planning Area," last modified March 27, 2014, http://www.azwater.gov/AzDWR /StatewidePlanning/WaterAtlas/EasternPlateau/PlanningAreaOverview /Climate.htm.

20. "Five Moqui Indians," *Washington Post*, June 27, 1890, 1. Other buildings or landmarks that the Hopis likely saw on their tour include the Treasury; State, War and Navy; the Patent Office; the Pension Bureau; Dead-Letter Office; the Navy Yard; Smithsonian and National Museum; Corcoran Art Gallery; the Soldiers' Home; Arlington; Mount Vernon; and Alexandria. Charles B. Reynolds, *The Standard Guide, Washington: A Handbook for Visitors* (Washington: Foster & Reynolds, 1898), 5.

21. "The Five Moqui Chiefs," *Washington Post*, June 28, 1890, 8.

22. Ibid.

23. "The Moquis Eat Ice-Cream," *San Francisco Call*, July 11, 1890, 2. Originally published in the *Washington Sunday Herald*. The newspaper article noted that the Hopi chiefs attended the opera "Thursday night," which would mean that the chiefs saw *Amorita* on Thursday, July 10, 1890.

24. "Amusements," *Evening Star*, June 21, 1890, 16. See also "Plays and Players," *Philadelphia Inquirer*, September 21, 1890, 10.

25. "The Moquis Eat Ice-Cream," 2.

26. The chiefs also assured those at the reception that when "white people" visited them on the Hopi Reservation, the chiefs and "all the [Hopi] people" would give them a "hearty welcome." Ibid.

27. Ibid.

28. At this time, newspaper reporters often referred to Indians who stayed at the Tremont House as "Tremont Indians." The Tremont was a "temperance hotel" located at the corner of Second Street and Indiana Avenue. The Department of the Interior's (DOI) partiality to it may be due to an incident in 1874 when on an earlier visit to the city Red Cloud and Spotted Tail were lodged at the Washington House. According to the *Indianapolis News*, the Washington "supplied [the party] with all the liquor they could drink, and a party of sharpers took them to the worst haunts in the city, where they spent night after night in debauchery with the vilest women." The DOI was presented with a bill of $1,400 in extra charges, which included doctors' and druggists' bills. When in 1875 the returning Sioux delegation was refused the opportunity to return to the Washington, most of its members staged a walkout, although

Red Cloud and Spotted Tail elected to remain at the Tremont. "The Wicked Red Man," *Indianapolis News*, May 25, 1875, 1. Wm. H. Boyd, *Boyd's Directory of the District of Columbia* (Washington, DC: John Polhemus, 1881), 716.

29. "Eastern News," *San Francisco Chronicle*, May 25, 1875, 3.

30. Robert W. Larson, *Red Cloud: Warrior-Statesman of the Lakota Sioux* (Norman: University of Oklahoma Press, 1997), 162–169.

31. "Arrival of Indians," *Washington Post*, April 12, 1880, 1.

32. For an excellent discussion on Hampton Institute, see James D. Anderson, *The Education of Blacks in the South, 1860–1935* (Chapel Hill: University of North Carolina Press, 1988), 33–78.

33. The report in the *Washington Post* was very racist and derogatory in its reporting of the Sioux children, describing them as "unpromising looking," "hideous," and "unwholesome spectacles"; "Seventeen Little Indians," *Washington Post*, October 24, 1881, 1.

34. At the time, Carlisle enrolled nearly 700 Indian pupils (296 girls and 385 boys). See "Number of Scholars at the Indian School," *Evening Sentinel* (Carlisle, Pennsylvania), May 9, 1890, 1.

35. Historian John Troutman has argued that the US government built schools such as Carlisle to "remove children from the 'uncivilized' surroundings of their families and reservation communities and to educate Native children in what it considered the proper arts, language, literature, and labor of the American citizenry. This instruction included the shunning of tribal affiliations; forbidding the use of tribal languages; dressing and grooming the children to look as 'non-Indian' as possible; teaching jingoistic American history; celebrating American holidays such as the Fourth of July, Washington's birthday, and even their own 'Indian Citizenship Day'; and subsuming their religious life into strict interpretations of Christianity." See John W. Troutman, *Indian Blues: American Indians and the Politics of Music 1879–1934* (Norman: University of Oklahoma Press, 2009), 7.

36. "Civilization for Indians," *New York Times*, March 1, 1896, 26.

37. C. E. Vandever to Commissioner of Indian Affairs, "Report of Moqui Pueblo Indians, Navajo Agency," 171, 172.

38. Some of the first references to Carlisle's track team began to appear in American newspapers in the early 1900s. Coach Glenn "Pop" Warner likely established the track team after he started coaching at Carlisle in 1899. See "Carlisle Indian Track Team," *Philadelphia Times*, April 1, 1901, 8.

39. Daniel Honahnie, "After 1000 Years Hopi We Stand: An Overview of Hopi History," in *Hopihiniwtipu: Significant Events for Hopi People*, ed. Anita Poleahla and Kristin Harned (Polacca, AZ: Mesa Media, 2012), 121, 122.

40. Leigh J. Kuwanwisiwma interview, March 21, 2006, Paaqavi, Arizona, Hopi Reservation.

41. The US government's Eleventh Census of the seven Hopi pueblos in 1890 was 1,996. See Donaldson, *Extra Census Bulletin*, 15.

42. "Planting the Seeds for Our Children's Future," Hopi Education Endowment Fund website, http://www.hopieducationfund.org/multimedia.html.

43. According to a US government report, Chief Loloma had initially opposed the mandatory enrollment of Hopi children in western schools but changed his mind and thought more favorably of the idea after he returned from his trip to Washington and saw "so many wonderful things" of the outside world. See Donaldson, *Extra Census Bulletin*, 56.

44. "The Chiefs at Carlisle," *New York Times*, February 16, 1891, 1.

45. Collectively, the students in Carlisle's Outing Program earned about $18,000 per season (summer months only). See "Civilization for Indians," *New York Tribune*, March 1, 1896, 26.

46. Kevin Whalen, *Native Students at Work: American Indian Labor and Sherman Institute's Outing Program, 1900–1945* (Seattle: University of Washington Press, 2016), 16.

47. The "hole" was likely one of the underground kivas at Orayvi.

48. "Trouble in the Moqui Tribe," *Boston Daily Globe*, November 20, 1894, 5.

49. Expert Special Agent Thomas Donaldson noted that "Intelligence was sent to us from Oraibi of the seizure and imprisonment of La-lo-la-my, which was the crowning act of his opponents; but coming to a realizing sense of their mistake they released him." Donaldson, *Extra Census Bulletin*, 60.

50. Leigh J. Kuwanwisiwma, "Why Were Hopi Men Sent to Alcatraz Prison?," in Poleahla and Harned, *Hopihiniwtipu: Significant Events for Hopi People*, 114.

51. George H. Guy, "Mastering the Moqui," *Los Angeles Times*, January 27, 1895, Part 2, 17.

52. The Hopi prisoners began their return home by rail from Alcatraz Island on September 23, 1895. Four armed soldiers accompanied the men on this trip to Gallup, New Mexico. After they reached Gallup, the group traveled by wagon more than thirty miles to Fort Defiance. See "Transferring Indians," *San Francisco Call*, September 21, 1895, 8. See also James, *Pages from Hopi History*, 115, 116; Pierre Odier, *The Rock: A History of Alcatraz Island, the Fort, the Prison* (California: L'Image Odier [self-published], 1982), 227. Former historian of the Hopi Cultural Preservation Office Wendy Holliday has written a brief history on Hopis whom government officials sent to Alcatraz. See Wendy Holliday, "Hopi Prisoners on the Rock," https://www.nps.gov/alca/learn/historyculture/hopi-prisoners-on-the-rock.htm.

53. "A Batch of Apaches," *San Francisco Chronicle*, January 4, 1895, 5. The *Chronicle* misidentified the Hopi prisoners as Apaches because of Fort Wingate's location and recent history. The fort was situated between Navajo and Chiricahua Apache Territory (AT). After 1868, its primary responsibilities consisted of

"patrols, military surveys, and escort functions," but the Fort Wingate troops had also conducted military campaigns against the Chiricahua Apache alongside Navajo scouts during the 1880s. Harold L. James, "The History of Fort Wingate," in *Guidebook of Defiance-Zuni-Mt. Taylor Region Arizona and New Mexico* (Albuquerque: New Mexico Geological Society, Eighteenth Field Conference, 1967), 158. Patricia Janis Broder, *Shadows on Glass: The Indian World of Ben Wittick* (Savage, MD: Rowman & Littlefield, 1990), 55.

54. Guy, "Mastering the Moquis," 17.

55. "A Batch of Apaches," 5.

56. "Alcatraz Island," *San Francisco Chronicle*, February 26, 1894, 10.

57. "Punishments in Army Are Hard," *Philadelphia Inquirer*, February 10, 1903, 4.

58. "Teaching the Red Man," *Pittsburgh Daily Post*, June 2, 1895, 19.

59. John E. Skinner, "An Historical Review of the Fish and Wildlife Resources of the San Francisco Bay," Water Project Branch Report No. 1, Department of Fish and Game, Sacramento, CA, June 1962, 23–55.

60. "Alcatraz Island," 10.

61. At this time prison officials on Alcatraz regularly sent prisoners to the mainland, including San Francisco, to work on various construction projects. It is possible that the Hopi prisoners had other opportunities to experience the city as a result of these mandatory labor assignments. See ibid.

62. "Visiting Indians," *San Francisco Chronicle*, February 10, 1895, 19.

63. "San Francisco's Fair Dome," *Washington Post*, April 14, 1895, 21.

64. "Visiting Indians," 19.

65. "In a Bad Fix," *San Francisco Chronicle*, February 15, 1895, 5.

66. "Hopi Chief Makes Prayer to Ocean," *Los Angeles Times*, October 18, 1925, B14.

67. These pilgrimages are deeply rooted in Hopi history. In 1968 Charles Lummis wrote that early twentieth-century Hopi travelers who visited California made excursions to the Pacific, "a tradition among them for a thousand years back, but which they had never seen, and which they treated with such reverence as it does one's heart good to see in this irreverent age." Charles F. Lummis, *Bullying the Moqui* (Prescott, AZ: Prescott College Press, 1968), 38–39. Don Talayesva, a Hopi student at Sherman Institute from 1906 to 1909, also recalls making a visit to the Atlantic Ocean, and a prayer he made when he reached it: "Our Mother of the Ocean, I have arrived from afar to pray to you. I thank you for all your blessings and have come to tell you about life among the Hopi. We have been suffering from much sickness. Please drive off all disease so that our people will increase. Notify your spirit people to hasten with clouds and give us moisture for our crops. Let them arise and go ahead of me over the mountains, drop rain on Oraibi, and refresh my people so they will be in good health when I return. I ask this in the name of my God, the Sun. May our lives be good." He then splashed water toward his home four times, rubbed

his hand over his heart, and smoked to send a message to the Six Point Cloud People. Don C. Talayesva, *Sun Chief: The Autobiography of a Hopi Indian*, 2nd ed. (New Haven, CT: Yale University Press, 2013), 416.

68. "A Real Live Injin," *San Francisco Chronicle*, May 18, 1873, 8.

69. "A Disgusted Indian," *San Francisco Chronicle*, February 11, 1874, 1.

70. Frederick E. Hoxie, *Parading through History: The Making of the Crow Nation in America, 1805–1935* (New York: Cambridge University Press, 1995), 362.

71. "State and Nation," *San Francisco Chronicle*, July 10, 1891, 2.

72. See Matthew Sakiestewa Gilbert, "Foreword to the Second Edition," in Talayesva, *Sun Chief*, xii–xiii, and Homer Cooyama's recollections of Voth in Courlander, *Hopi Voices*, 124–126.

73. Clemmer, *Roads in the Sky*, 65, 66.

74. In November 1903, Mennonite missionary Heinrich Voth took a Hopi man from Orayvi named Qoyawayma (father of Polingaysi Qoyawayma, who attended Sherman Institute from 1906 to 1909) on a train to Albuquerque, New Mexico. After a short visit in Albuquerque, the men proceeded by rail to Newton, Kansas, and then Chicago, Illinois, to help Voth with his "ethnological research." See "An Hopi Indian in Newton," *Evening Kansas-Republican*, November 24, 1903, 1.

75. Margaret D. Jacobs, "A Battle for the Children: American Indian Child Removal in Arizona in the Era of Assimilation." *Journal of Arizona History* 45 (2004): 34.

76. Julian Scott, "Report on the Moqui Pueblos of Arizona," 60.

77. See also Sakiestewa Gilbert, *Education beyond the Mesas*, 1, 2; and Sakiestewa Gilbert, "A Second Wave of Hopi Migration," 358, 359.

78. Nequatewa, *Truth of a Hopi*, 3, 46, 47.

79. David Wallace Adams, *Education for Extinction: American Indians and the Boarding School Experience, 1875–1928* (Lawrence: University Press of Kansas, 1995), 97.

80. James, *Pages from Hopi History*, 115, 116. For a detailed analysis of the Hopi division, see Peter M. Whiteley, *Deliberate Acts: Changing Hopi Culture through the Oraibi Split* (Tucson: University of Arizona Press, 1988).

81. In an article in the *Santa Fe New Mexican*, Hopi filmmaker and farmer Victor Masayesva, Jr., remarked about these two imposed names: "They called our ancestors 'hostiles,' and the people who stayed were called 'friendly' because they were willing to go along with the government programs . . . I guess we would be considered terrorists today." See Paul Weideman, "Drawing Down Rain from the Devil's Claw," *Santa Fe New Mexican*, August 18, 2006, ZO51.

82. Historians Jon Reyhner and Jeanne Eder have provided an excellent overview of the tensions surrounding the school issue at the Hopi mesas during this period. See *American Indian Education: A History*, 2nd edition (Norman: University of Oklahoma Press, 2017), 184–188.

83. Historian James F. Brooks provides a fascinating account of the many tensions and other complexities leading up to and involving the Orayvi Split. See Brooks, *Mesa of Sorrows: A History of the Awat'ovi Massacre* (New York: W. W. Norton, 2016), 126–141.

84. I go into great detail on Tawaquaptewa and the story of how Hopi students arrived at Sherman Institute in Sakiestewa Gilbert, *Education beyond the Mesas* (2010).

85. "Things May Be Doing in the Moqui Country," *Albuquerque Journal*, November 3, 1906, 7. As Peter M. Whiteley once noted to me, these kinds of newspaper accounts tended to be unreliable. Therefore, this account should also be read alongside written US government documents provided in Whiteley's two-volume book on the Orayvi Split. See Peter M. Whiteley, *The Orayvi Split: A Hopi Transportation, Part 2: The Documentary Record* (New York: American Museum of Natural History, 2008), 977–987, 1019–1024.

86. "Things May Be Doing in the Moqui Country," 7.

87. "Indian Tribe Is under Arrest," *Los Angeles Herald*, November 16, 1906, 1.

88. There is some uncertainty as to Tewanima's exact age when he was arrested in January 1907. Hal Boyle of the Associated Press noted that Tewanima was eighty-two years old when he visited New York City in 1954. If this estimate is correct, then Tewanima would have been born in 1872, which would have made him around thirty-four years old at the time of this arrest. See Hal Boyle, "The Globe and Guys," *Santa Cruz Sentinel*, October 14, 1954, 19.

89. In a newspaper article entitled "What Carlisle Has Done for the Hopis," the writer noted that Tewanima was part of a band of Hopis from Orayvi who arrived at the school in January 1907: "Half a dozen years ago the Hopi Nation was causing considerable trouble in Arizona. Internecine strife had divided the tribe, and a troop of United States cavalry was sent post-haste to the Keams Canyon region to restore peace. After pow-wows and conferences, in which the Indian leaders sternly refused to adopt the white man's education, 12 of the most obstinate 'standpatters' were taken as prisoners of war and sent from the Moqui agency in Arizona to the Carlisle Indian School, the party arriving there January 26, 1907. All of these Indians were members of the Oraibi band of the Hopi Nation. Among them were several priests and head men of the tribe." See "What Carlisle Has Done for the Hopis," *Baltimore Sun*, February 25, 1912, 21.

90. Superintendent Theodore G. Lemmon to Commissioner of Indian Affairs Francis E. Leupp, March 16, 1906. Letter located at the Theodore Lemmon Papers at the Los Angeles County Natural History Museum. Commenting on this letter in his two-volume book on the Orayvi Split, Peter M. Whiteley notes: "The events of February–March, 1906, that eventuated in the relocation of Second Mesa Hostiles to Orayvi, can only be pieced together with difficulty from

Lemmon's available correspondence. Lemmon reported a conflict at Song-òopavi [Shungopavi] on February 26, 1906, in which one man was killed, and another clash there on February 28th, leading to the departure of Second Mesa Hostiles for Orayvi in early March 1906." It is believed that Tewanima was among the hostile Hopis at Songòopavi who went to Orayvi in March 1906, which is further supported by a letter that Lemmon sent Leupp on September 20, 1906. See Whiteley, *The Orayvi Split: A Hopi Transportation*, Part II, 977–987, 1019–1024.

91. "Carlisle Indian Industrial School Descriptive and Historical Record of Student," 31 August 1912, 2, and "Tewanima, Louis," CSF. See also Nequatewa, *Truth of a Hopi*, 62, 63, 113n53, and "Hopi Students," in *(Carlisle) Red Man*, 248. The remaining Hopi prisoners included William Navongva, Ponaqua Tewa, Andrew Hermequatewa, Edward Tewane (Tuwanomitiwa), Joshua Hermeyesva (Humiyesva, Sun Clan), and Archie Quamala. Peter M. Whiteley suggests that Commissioner of Indian Affairs Francis E. Leupp allowed the Hopi prisoners to choose which off-reservation boarding school they would attend, and the Hopis chose Carlisle. See Whiteley, *The Orayvi Split: A Hopi Transformation; Part II*, 1063. There appears to be confusion on the exact number of Hopis who enrolled at Carlisle on January 25, 1907. For example, in a newspaper article in the *New York American*, which was republished in the *(Carlisle) Red Man*, the author notes that at this time, twelve Hopis enrolled at Carlisle. Two of the twelve Hopis listed are "Tala Yamtewa" and "Washington Talyumptewa." However, I believe that both names refer to the same individual, Washington Talyumptewa. Furthermore, photographic and National Archives and Records Administration (NARA) evidence suggest that only eleven Hopis enrolled at Carlisle in January 1907. "Hopi Students," 248, and "Talayamtewa, Washington," file #3751, box 79, CSF. Also, the *Philadelphia Inquirer* noted: "Eleven Hopi Indians from Fort Wingate, New Mexico, arrived here yesterday in charge of Lieutenant J. A. Lewis, United States Army, to enter the Carlisle Indian School. All were boys." See "State Notes," *Philadelphia Inquirer*, January 26, 1907, 3.

92. Glenn S. (Pop) Warner, "Eskimo Indian Makes Good on 'Pop's' Team; in Game at Harvard He Takes out Huskey Rival Center in Neat Style,'" *Des Moines Register*, January 17, 1928, 7.

93. Government officials had initially sent Indian students to off-reservation boarding schools to weaken or destroy their Native identities and to encourage them to leave their old Indian ways behind. Native students, however, often made strategic decisions ("turn the power") to use this experience and education to better prepare themselves for living and working in an increasingly modern American society. Many of them had been encouraged by their parents or other community members to do well in school and to learn skills that would help them in life. While at times students may have looked

at schools such as Carlisle as prisons, especially since students could not normally come and go as they pleased, they nevertheless looked for ways to take advantage of the situations or predicaments that they found themselves in. For Hopi students, they knew that learning about the world beyond the mesas would ultimately prove useful and helpful to them later in life.

CHAPTER 3: HOPI OLYMPIAN

1. "American Athletes Sure of Success," *New York Times*, July 12, 1908, Part 4, S1; "Physical Record," December 3, 1908, "Tewanima, Louis," CSF. See also "Hopi Students to Preach Culture to Sun Worshipers: From the *New York American*," reprinted in *(Carlisle) Red Man* 5 (February 1913): 248.

2. "The Olympic Games," *(London) Times*, July 25, 1908, 8.

3. US Olympic coach Mike Murphy had originally assigned Neil McCarthy to cycle beside American runner Mike Ryan. When Ryan quit the race after the eleven-mile mark, McCarthy sought out Tewanima and remained with him to the finish. See "Bill Henry Says," *Los Angeles Times*, December 8, 1935, 17.

4. According to Tewanima's teammate Joseph Forshaw, who ran alongside Tewanima for the first twenty miles of the marathon and ended up winning a bronze medal, the Hopi runner was "suffering from bad knees" and sore feet. Forshaw also recalled that Tewanima had a difficult time understanding his pacesetter Neil McCarthy, due to his inability to comprehend much English. Christine Forshaw O'Shaughnessy, "Joseph Forshaw, Marathon Runner," *Journal of Olympic History* 12 (May 2004): 12.

5. "The Olympic Games," 8. See also John Bryant, *The Marathon Makers* (London: John Blake, 2008), 217. Mississauga Ojibwa runner Frederick Simpson from Canada also competed in the 1908 Olympic marathon. He finished in sixth place, three places ahead of Tewanima. Tewanima completed the course in 3 hours, 9 minutes, and 50.8 seconds. His US teammate John Hayes won a gold medal by finishing in 2 hours, 55 minutes, and 18.4 seconds. See Bill Mallon and Ian Buchanan, *The 1908 Olympic Games: Results for All Competitors in All Events, with Commentary* (Jefferson, NC: McFarland, 2000), 65.

6. Deloria, *Indians in Unexpected Places*, 113, 114, and Norm Frauenheim, "Lewis Tewanima: Running for a Reason: Hopi Legend's Rain Cloud Had Silver Lining," *Arizona Republic*, December 16, 1999, C3.

7. See Nabokov, *Indian Running: Native American History and Tradition*; Brian S. Collier, "'To Bring Honor to My Village,'" 62–71; Dyreson, "The Foot Runners Conquer Mexico and Texas," 19–49; and Darcy C. Plymire, "The Legend of the Tarahumara: Tourism, Overcivilization and the White Man's Indian," in *Native Americans and Sport in North America: Other People's Games*, ed. C. Richard King (New York: Routledge, 2008), 17–29. For a nonscholarly but very compelling book on Tarahumara runners, see McDougall, *Born to Run* (2009).

8. Joseph B. Oxendine, *American Indian Sports Heritage* (Lincoln: University of Nebraska Press, 1995), vii, 87, 89; Bloom, *To Show What an Indian Can Do*, xvii, 24, 72, 73, 90, 151; Bill Crawford, *All American: The Rise and Fall of Jim Thorpe* (Hoboken, NJ: John Wiley & Sons, 2004), 72; Sally Jenkins, *The Real All Americans: The Team That Changed a Game, a People, a Nation* (New York: Doubleday, 2007), 270; and Jim Hinckley, *Backroads of Arizona: Your Guide to Arizona's Most Scenic Backroad Adventures* (St. Paul, MN: Voyageur Press, 2006), 65.

9. Steven W. Pope, *Patriotic Games: Sporting Traditions in the American Imagination, 1876–1926* (Knoxville: University of Tennessee Press, 2007), 49, and Dyreson, *Making the American Team*, 5, 10, 199.

10. There is confusion among scholars and other writers as to when Hopis became US citizens. Some have argued that Hopis became citizens in 1924 with the Indian Citizenship Act, although there is evidence to suggest that it technically took place much earlier, in 1848. See Donaldson, *Extra Census Bulletin*, 9; Porter, *Report on Indians Taxed and Indians Not Taxed in the United States*, 164; and Treaty of Guadalupe Hidalgo, 2 February 1848, *Perfected Treaties, 1778–1945*, Record Group 11, General Records of the United States Government, 1778–1992, National Archives, accessed 29 November 2011, http://www.ourdocu ments.gov/doc.php?flash=old&doc=26.

11. Warren King Moorehead, *The American Indian in the United States, Period 1850–1914* (Andover, MA: Andover Press, 1914), 201. For additional information on the founding and purpose of Carlisle, see Jacqueline Fear-Segal, *White Man's Club: Schools, Race, and the Struggle of Indian Acculturation* (Lincoln: University of Nebraska Press, 2007), 25–27.

12. When Tewanima was not training or competing in races, he honed his skills as a tailor, learned English, and worked in the school's Outing Program. While he had a modest academic record, he was most admired by his peers for his ability to run long distances. See "Outing Record—Carlisle Industrial School" in "Tewanima, Louis," CSF, and "Favor Worcester to Win B.A.A. Meet," *Boston Journal*, February 15, 1909, 9. For an examination of Carlisle's famous football team, see David Wallace Adams, "More Than a Game: The Carlisle Indians Take to the Gridiron, 1893–1917," *Western Historical Quarterly* 32 (Spring 2001): 25–53.

13. Gerald R. Gems, *The Athletic Crusade: Sport and American Cultural Imperialism* (Lincoln: University of Nebraska Press, 2006), 9.

14. Peyton Reavis, "Great Little Hopi: Lewis Tewanima," unpublished manuscript, 1990, "Lewis Tewanima," LAB BIO-229, Labriola Indian Data Center, Department of Archives and Special Collections, University Libraries, Arizona State University, Tempe.

15. "Indian Is a Great Runner," *Des Moines Register*, March 21, 1909, 14.

16. The official newspaper at Carlisle went by several names, including *Eadle*

Keatah Toh, *School News*, the *Morning Star*, the *Red Man*, the *Carlisle Indian Boys'* *and Girls' Friend*, the *Indian Helper*, the *Arrow*, the *Carlisle Arrow*, and the *Indian Craftsman*. See "Newspapers and Periodicals," Carlisle Indian Industrial School, http://carlisleindian.historicalsociety.com/resources/newspapers/.

17. Stephen, *Hopi Journal*, 2: 780. See also Nabokov, *Indian Running*, 27, 28.

18. From at least the early 1980s, writers have claimed that Tewanima was Tuwangyam (Sand Clan). I thank his family members Sheilah E. Nicholas and Benjamin H. Nuvamsa, both from Songòopavi, for providing me with his correct clan—Piqöswungwa (Bear Strap Clan).

19. Collier, "To Bring Honor," 62–71. One newspaper writer affirmed Tewanima's running past by noting that he had been "taught running in the school where running is a necessity and for years he was a runner among his people, and his duty was to carry messages from post to post and from village to village." "Lewis Tewanima," *Trenton Evening Times*, February 23, 1909, 15.

20. After the London Olympics, Tewanima and other US team members traveled to France to participate in a series of exhibition games. They returned to the United States on the American Line steamer *New York* on August 15, 1908. See "More Olympic Athletes Back," *New-York Tribune*, August 16, 1908, 8. Frank Mount Pleasant was Tewanima's teammate at Carlisle. He competed in the 1908 Olympics and placed sixth in the broad jump and the triple jump events. See Mallon and Buchanan, *1908 Olympic Games*, 83–87. The reception took place sixteen days after they returned from Europe on August 31, 1908. See "President Greets Olympic Athletes," *New York Times*, September 1, 1908, 5.

21. "Athletes Visit Sagamore Hill," *Gazette-Telegraph* (Colorado Springs, Colorado), September 1, 1908, 1.

22. In 1912, the *Ogden Standard* (referencing the *Evening Bulletin* of Philadelphia) commented on how focused Tewanima was when he competed, and how carefully he followed the instructions of his coach, Glenn Warner: "It made no difference to Lewis how many people stared at him when he was on the mark waiting for the start of a race. He was even cooler than the proverbial cucumber. The word 'excited' was one totally unknown to Tewanima. He was never afflicted with stage fright nor scared by the ability of any runner, because he never paid any attention to any other runner in the race. They could run as they pleased; he always ran as Glen Warner told him. And Glen pretty nearly knew what every one in the race could do and what the little Hopi could do." See "Carlisle Runner Is Cool One," *Ogden Standard*, September 25, 1912, 2.

23. "Carlisle School Runner Is Another Willie Day," *Spokane Press*, February 4, 1909, 6.

24. "Tewanina Was Too Busy to Bother about His Prize," *Evening World*, January 26, 1909, 12, and "Indian Tewanina Wins 10-Mile Race," *New York Times*, January 26, 1909, 10.

25. "Carlisle School Runner Is Another Willie Day," 6. For information on the number of contestants and spectators, see "Tewanima Won," *Sentinel* (Carlisle, Pennsylvania), January 27, 1909, 4. Coach Warner would later explain more details about how he helped Tewanima win the race: "Once I took him to New York for a 10-mile competition in Madison Square Garden, and after looking at the track . . . he turned to me and said: 'Me afraid get mixed up go round and round. You tell me front man and I get him.' About the middle of the race I managed to catch his eye and point out the runners who led him, and one by one he picked them up, finally finishing in a burst of speed that established a new world's record." See Edwin McDowell, "Famous Hopi Runner Louis Tewanima, Olympic Medal Winner, 'Doing Fine,'" *Arizona Republic*, September 8, 1968, 6. A newspaper writer for the *Ogden Standard* later remarked that at some point in the race, Tewanima bumped into another runner, "but not enough to interfere with the stride of the pale face." When the other runner caught back up to Tewanima, he spit in the Hopi runner's face. The writer noted that "Tewanima did not even look up; in fact, he paid not the slightest attention to the insult." See "Carlisle Runner Is Cool One," 2.

26. "Tewanini Wins Marathon Race," *New York Times*, February 22, 1909, 2, and "From Other Schools," *Native American* (Phoenix Indian School), March 13, 1909, 180. For additional information on the *Native American*, see Robert A. Trennert, *The Phoenix Indian School: Forced Assimilation in Arizona, 1891–1935* (Norman: University of Oklahoma Press, 1988), 82.

27. Whiteley, *Deliberate Acts*, 300, and Moses Friedman to Washington Talayamptewa, 25 September 1908, "Talayamtewa, Washington," File #3751, Box 79, CSF.

28. "It's No Wonder Tewanina Can Run," *Globe and Commercial Advertiser*, March 13, 1909, in "Tewanima, Louis," CSF. Newspaper reporters spelled Tewanima's last name in various ways, including Tewanina, Tewanini, and Tewauina. On his school records, officials at Carlisle recorded his name as "Lewis Tewani." See "Carlisle Indian Industrial School Descriptive and Historical Record of Student," CSF.

29. "Indian Snake Dance Draws Big Crowds," *Coconino Sun* (Flagstaff, Arizona), August 23, 1912, 1, and Theodore Roosevelt, "The Hopi Snake Dance," *Outlook* 105 (October 1913): 364–373.

30. Brendan Hokowhitu, "Tackling Māori Masculinity: A Colonial Genealogy of Savagery and Sport," *Contemporary Pacific* 16 (Fall 2004): 270.

31. "Tewanima First in Running Race," *Trenton Evening Times*, September 26, 1910, 11; "Win Bailey Is Now Ten-Mile Champion," *New York Times*, November 6, 1910, C5. See also "'Win' Bailey First Home," *New-York Daily Tribune*, November 6, 1910, 11; "Indian Wins Marathon: 1,000 Start," *San Francisco Call*, May 7, 1911, 46; "Tewanima Again a Winner," *Washington Post*, December 3, 1911, S3;

"Race Too Swift for Gallagher," *Washington Post*, November 29, 1912, 9; and partial newspaper clipping, *Washington Star*, December 6, 1911, in "Tewanima, Louis," CSF.

32. See Joseph K. Dixon, *The Vanishing Race: The Last Great Indian Council and the Indian's Story of the Custer Fight* (Glorieta, NM: Kessinger Publishing, 1973), and Deloria, *Indians in Unexpected Places*, 9.

33. "American Marks Best," *Morning (Portland) Oregonian*, January 26, 1912, 8, and Dyreson, *Making the American Team*, 156.

34. Jack Newcombe, *The Best of the Athletic Boys: The White Man's Impact on Jim Thorpe* (Garden City, NY: Doubleday, 1975), 179, and "To Begin Work for Olympics," *Washington Post*, March 15, 1912, 8. For a critical discussion on the term "redskin," see Suzan Shown Harjo, "Fighting Name-Calling: Challenging 'Redskin' in Court," in *Team Spirits: The Native American Mascot Controversy*, ed. C. Richard King and Charles Fruehling Springwood (Lincoln: University of Nebraska Press, 2001), 190. For Sullivan's comments on Tewanima, see "United States Athletes Sail," *Washington Post*, June 15, 1912, 8, and "Lewis Tewanima Looks Good for the Marathon," *Augusta (Georgia) Chronicle*, April 28, 1912, 3.

35. Tom Derderian, *Boston Marathon: The History of the World's Premier Running Event* (Champaign, IL: Human Kinetics Publishers, 1994), 63. Historian Joseph B. Oxendine observed that Tewanima earned a place on the US team based on his past performances "in spring meets," and not by competing in an American Olympic Committee–sanctioned event. Joseph B. Oxendine, *American Indian Sports Heritage* (Lincoln: University of Nebraska Press, 1995), 216.

36. "United States Athletes Sail," 8, and James Edward Sullivan, *Olympic Games: Stockholm 1912* (New York: American Sports Publishing, 1912), 37. See also George Retzer, "Retzer Tells of Long Trip," *Los Angeles Times*, September 13, 1912, III1. Six months after the Olympics, the *Allentown (Pennsylvania) Democrat* published a short story about how Tewanima "saved" his fellow teammates with his ability to sew, a skill he supposedly learned at Carlisle: "While he was at the Carlisle Indian school, Lewis Tewanima, the long distance runner, learned the tailor's trade, and his knowledge along these lines saved more than one of America's Olympic athletes a trying situation during the trip to Stockholm last summer. Whenever there was a tear or a rip in a coat or pants the athletes would cry, 'Where's Lewis?' This Little Hopi was always equal to the emergency and always refused compensation, no matter in what form it was offered. 'No, no! Are you not my friend?' the little aborigine asked when his teammates offered something in the way of reward." See "Tewanima Saved Men Lots of Trouble," *Allentown (Pennsylvania) Democrat*, January 20, 1913, 6. It should also be noted that Tewanima came from a society where men traditionally wove. So Tewanima likely already had skills in some form of sewing prior to his attendance at Carlisle.

37. Bill Mallon and Ture Widlund, *The 1912 Olympic Games: Results for All Competitors in All Events, with Commentary* (Jefferson, NC: McFarland, 2002), 82, 83. See also "Olympic Events Find Americans in Front," *Times-Picayune* (New Orleans), July 8, 1912, 2, and "The 10,000 Meters," *Rhodesia Herald* (Harare, Zimbabwe), July 12, 1912, 12.

38. Lars Anderson, *Carlisle vs. Army: Jim Thorpe, Dwight Eisenhower, Pop Warner, and the Forgotten Story of Football's Greatest Battle* (New York: Random House, 2008), 242. Tewanima did not compete in the 5,000-meter race at the 1912 Olympic Games. For an official list of the 5,000-meter starters and winners, see Mallon and Widlund, *1912 Olympic Games*, 80–82.

39. "Americans Take All in 800 Event," *Chicago Daily Tribune*, July 9, 1912, 14, and Sullivan, *Olympic Games, Stockholm 1912*, 77. Lars Anderson notes that Tewanima was not "at his peak" on the day of the race and that the "transatlantic voyage had given him a severe case of seasickness, and his internal compass was still a tick off." Anderson, *Carlisle vs. Army*, 242. Tewanima also competed in the 1912 Olympic marathon and finished in sixteenth place while his Carlisle teammate Andrew Sockalexis came in fourth. See "Marathon Won by South African; American Is Close Third," *Albuquerque Morning Journal*, July 15, 1912, 1.

40. "Contributions of Celebration Fund," *Carlisle Evening Herald*, July 26, 1912, 1.

41. "Council Acts on Carlisle Triumph in the Olympiad," *Carlisle Evening Herald*, July 26, 1912, 1.

42. "Carlisle Honors Her Olympic Victors on the Return from Stockholm," *Carlisle Arrow*, September 13, 1912, 1, and "Parade Escorts Victors to the Campus and Great Reception Follows," *Carlisle Arrow*, September 13, 1912, 3.

43. "Parade Escorts Victors," 3.

44. "Kohlemainen Gives Jolt to Pride of United States Athletic Booster by His Victories at Stockholm, in Olympics, and Successes since on These Shores," *Washington Post*, December 29, 1912, S2; Oxendine, *American Indian Sports Heritage*, 277. American runner Louis Scott did not finish the 10,000-meter final event, and William Scott, also a runner from the United States, did not qualify to compete in the same event. See Mallon and Widlund, *1912 Olympic Games*, 82.

45. "Praises American Olympics," *New York Times*, August 11, 1912, 2. Charles Otway quote originally published in the *London Sporting Life*.

46. In the 1980s, Tewanima's family began a "nationwide search" for his lost medals. Then assistant director of the Hopi Health Department Leigh Jenkins (Kuwanwisiwma) said: "What the family really wants is to see those medals back here on Hopi land so they can be housed at the tribal museum. . . . We want to collect as many as we can find to include in a Louis Tewanima memorial." See Joe Schroeder, "Hopis Search for Medals Won by Fastest Native Son," *Arizona Republic*, July 28, 1984, G1. Furthermore, in 1964, Tewanima allowed

1924 American Olympic wrestler Bryan Hines of Flagstaff, Arizona, to borrow some of his medals so they could be "displayed around Arizona" to help raise money for the 1964 US Olympic team. It is not known whether Hines returned all or any of the medals to Tewanima. See Frank Gianelli, "Happy Hopi Lends Hand," *Arizona Republic*, June 27, 1964, 52.

47. "Notes of the Game," *Chicago Daily Defender*, September 21, 1912, 7; "Tewanima to Marry and Quit Athletics," *Washington Times*, September 13, 1912; Newcombe, *Best of the Athletic Boys*, 189; and "Tewanina Was Too Busy to Bother about His Prize," 12.

48. Deloria, *Indians in Unexpected Places*, 133. In his remarkable book on Native runners, anthropologist Peter Nabokov notes that Hopi artist Fred Kabotie once told him that he and his father saw Tewanima compete in a marathon in Winslow, Arizona. Tewanima was outpaced by Zuni and other Hopi runners and ultimately failed to complete the race. Also, Nabokov suggests that Tewanima won first place in the 1925 Bunion Derby from New York City to Los Angeles but was "disqualified for an infraction of the rules." Nabokov, *Indian Running*, 182. However, this account, which may have come from Nabokov's interview with Kabotie, appears to be in error in two ways. The first Bunion Derby took place in 1928 and the race stretched from Los Angeles to New York City. Cherokee runner Andy Payne won the event. A second, and far less popular, Bunion Derby took place in 1929 and the path went from New York City to Los Angeles. For more information on the Bunion Derby, see Charles B. Kastner, *Bunion Derby: The 1928 Footrace across America* (Albuquerque: University of New Mexico Press, 2007).

49. Friedman to Louis Tewanima, October 1, 1913, "Tewanima, Louis," CSF. Historian David Wallace Adams notes that Friedman was "so despised by students that on various occasions he had been hooted and jeered and even made the target of such epithets as 'old Jew,' 'Christ-Killer,' and 'pork-dodger,' perhaps out of resentment to the superintendent's penchant for calling students 'savages.'" See Adams, *Education for Extinction*, 324.

50. LeRoy Berman, "Jim Thorpe's Teammate 'Doing Well' at Shongopavi,'" *Albuquerque Journal*, November 8, 1968, 34.

51. "S.F. Features Indian Fiesta," *San Bernardino Daily Sun*, August 26, 1924, 4.

52. There is some uncertainty as to Tewanima's exact age when he competed at Carlisle. Hal Boyle of the Associated Press noted that Tewanima was eighty-two years old when he visited New York City in 1954. If this estimate is correct, then Tewanima would have been born in 1872, which would have made him thirty-eight years old at the time of the 1910 Madison Square Garden 10-Mile Race, and forty years old when he competed in the 1912 Olympics. See Boyle, "The Globe and Guys," 19.

53. McDowell, "Famous Hopi Runner Louis Tewanima," 6.

54. Ray Silvius, "Aged Hopi Runner Enters New Era," *Arizona Republic*, October 10, 1954, Section 4, 3.

55. "Veteran Hammer Thrower to Display His Wares at Greenway Meet Tomorrow," *Arizona Republican*, April 13, 1928, Section 2, p. 10.

56. Ibid. Tewanima would see Gillis again two months later at a fundraiser in Phoenix, Arizona, to benefit the "1956 Olympic fund." Officials in charge of the event flew Tewanima from Winslow to Phoenix to participate in the gathering. See "Olympics to Benefit," *Arizona Republic*, December 10, 1954, 3.

57. In his article on Tewanima's visit to New York City, newspaper writer Ray Silvius included a black-and-white photograph of Tewanima shortly after arriving in the city. See Silvius, "Aged Hopi Runner Enters New Era," 3. Hal Boyle of the Associated Press also included a picture of Tewanima standing in his Hopi attire with American model Frances White in New York City with skyscrapers in the background. Tewanima had likely just arrived in town because his luggage was at his side in the photograph. See Hal Boyle, "Gotham's Tall Tepees Leave Tewanima Cold," *Star-Gazette* (Elmira, New York), October 14, 1954, 21. Furthermore, when Tewanima attended the awards banquet, one newspaper reporter noted: "The sage of Shungopavi, Tewanima was dressed in Hopi clothes—deep blue velveteen shirt, white duck pants, buckskin leggings and moccasins, and red headband to further add to his own natural color of long hair and deep tan." See "Hopi Wears Honor Well," *Arizona Republic*, October 14, 1954, 37.

58. McDowell, "Famous Hopi Runner Louis Tewanima," 6.

59. Boyle, "The Globe and Guys," 19.

60. The same reporter noted that at the banquet, Tewanima was "flanked at the head of the table by department store head Bernie Gimbel and Charles Bacon, president of the New York chapter of the U.S. Olympics," and that the next evening Gimbel and Roy Rogers and his wife, Dale Evans, took the old Hopi runner to see a rodeo at Madison Square Garden. See "Hopi Wears Honor Well," 37.

61. In addition to being inducted in the Arizona Sports Hall of Fame, Tewanima was inducted into the American Indian Athlete Hall of Fame—nearly three years after his death. The honor took place at a banquet dinner at the University of Kansas in Lawrence on November 25, 1972. See "Indian Hall of Fame Will Induct 14 Tonight," *Kansas City Times*, November 25, 1972, 48. Issued by the Associated Press.

62. "Indian School Star Succumbs," *Evening Sentinel* (Carlisle, Pennsylvania), January 21, 1969, 1. In an article on Louis Tewanima's relative, Milfred Tewanima, a talented runner in the late 1980s and early 1990s, newspaper writer Norm Frauenheim noted that Louis ran "because there was no other mode of transportation to Winslow or to the cornfields below the mesas. With the arrival of

internal combustion, the Native American began to ride where he once ran."
See Norm Frauenheim, "Legends of the Land Are Long-Running," *Arizona Republic*, June 16, 1991, D1, D11. The Seri Indians in Mexico were also known to run down rabbits: "Now, I suppose you are aware that the jack rabbit is considered a very fleet animal. Yet these Indians are accustomed to catch jack rabbits by outrunning them. . . . For this purpose three men or boys go together. If the rabbit ran straight away from its pursuer, it could not be taken; but its instinct is to make its flight by zigzags. The hunters arrange themselves at short distances apart. As quickly as one of them starts a rabbit, a second Indian runs as fast as he can along a line parallel with the course taken by the animal. Presently the rabbit sees the second Indian and dashed off at a tangent. By this time the third hunter has come up and gives the quarry another turn. After the third or fourth zigzag the rabbit is surrounded, and the hunters quickly close in upon him and grab him. . . . It is an odd fact that this method of catching jack-rabbits is precisely the same as that adopted by coyotes, which work similarly by threes. By this strategy these wild dogs capture the rabbits, though the latter are more fleet by far." See "They Are Sprinters: Swift-Footed Indians Who Can Catch Jack Rabbits," *Evening Star* (Washington, DC), January 5, 1895, 19.

63. Boyle, "The Globe and Guys," 19. In October 1929, a Hopi runner named Kwa Qa'uah, or Flying Eagle, attempted to outdistance a nine-year-old "western cow pony" called "Boss" in a one-hundred-mile race in Roswell, New Mexico. Taking place on a dirt oval track, the race received modest attention from various newspapers throughout the United States. With a headline that read "Noted Hopi Runner Loses Race against Cow Pony," a reporter for the St. *Louis Post-Dispatch* observed that at the "end of the forty-third mile," Kwa Qa'uah "fell exhausted" and race officials immediately took him to an "emergency hospital. "Flying Eagle is one of the best known of the famed Hopi runners," the *Post-Dispatch* noted, and he was recently used "in the long search through the Hopi mesas for the lost air liner City of San Francisco." See "Noted Hopi Runner Loses Race against Cow Pony," St. *Louis Post-Dispatch*, October 10, 1929, 3.

64. Caleb Carter, "How the Nez Perces Trained for Long Distance Running, 1911," in *Recovering Native American Writings in the Boarding School Press*, ed. Jacqueline Emery (Lincoln: University of Nebraska Press, 2017), 104–106.

65. "How an Indian Runs Down a Deer," *Los Angeles Herald*, August 23, 1908, 40.

66. The article goes on to note: "They not only rout out the 'cotton tails,' and club them to death, but run down the large jack rabbits and make them captive.'" See "Indians Run Down Rabbits," *Ottawa Daily Republican* (Ottawa, KS), November 26, 1906, 3.

67. Byron S. Harvey III, *Ritual in Pueblo Art: Hopi Life in Hopi Painting* (New York:

Museum of the American Indian, 1970), 49, 50, figure 115. For a detailed explanation of clowns in Hopi society, see Barton Wright, *Clowns of the Hopi: Tradition Keepers and Delight Makers* (Walnut, CA: Kiva Publishing, 2004), and Emory Sekaquaptewa, "One More Smile for a Hopi Clown," in *The South Corner of Time: Hopi, Navajo, Papago, Yaqui Tribal Literature*, ed. Larry Evers (Tucson: University of Arizona Press, 1980), 14.

68. "Famed Tewanima Dead," *Arizona Republic*, January 21, 1969, 55.

69. "Arizona Senate Pays Tribute to Tewanima," *Arizona Republic*, January 31, 1969, 5.

70. Historian Pamela Cooper has argued that when runners, especially those from underrepresented ethnicities, succeeded in marathons, they enhanced the "honor of an entire group." Cooper, *The American Marathon*, 2.

71. "Indian Race, Perishing, Gives Nation Men of Influence," *Evening Standard* (Ogden, Utah), December 28, 1912, 11, and Bloom, *To Show What an Indian Can Do*, 74. Another newspaper writer described Tewanima and the other Hopi prisoners as "savages" and "Wild Hopi Indians." See "Wild Hopi Indians," *Colfax (LA) Chronicle*, April 20, 1912, 6.

72. For more information on the Annual Louis Tewanima Footrace, visit *Annual Louis Tewanima Footrace*, http://www.tewanimafootrace.org/. Also, the race at Hopi was not the only race established in Tewanima's honor. In October 1976, the Carlisle Army War College, situated on the former Carlisle Indian School grounds, hosted the first annual Carlisle Army War College Louis Tewanima 15 Mile Marathon. Race organizers used Tewanima's name in this race "because of the natural tie Tewanima" had with the "Carlisle Barracks." See "Carlisle War College Planning Tewanima 16 Mile Marathon Run," *Evening Sentinel* (Carlisle, Pennsylvania), October 2, 1976, 11.

CHAPTER 4: A TRIBE OF RACERS

1. In a few instances, newspaper writers referred to Harry McLean as being Pima Indian. Since newspapers noted that McLean's home was in Sacaton, Arizona, which is part of the Gila River Indian Reservation (Pima), it is possible that McLean had some social or familial association with the Pima. See "Attractions of the Fair," *Mohave County Miner* (Mineral Park, Arizona), September 21, 1912, 5, and "Hopi Runner Home Again," *Arizona Republican*, August 24, 1909, 1. In the *Arizona Republican*, McLean was referred to as a "full-blood Hopi Indian." See "The Winner of Marathon," *Arizona Republican*, July 13, 1909, 1. Also, it should be noted that Harry McLean was named after Mary McLean, a Christian missionary who worked on the Hopi Reservation in the early 1900s. After his conversion to Christianity, Harry demonstrated his appreciation of Mary and took her last name as his own. See "Hopi Missionary," *Arizona Republican*, April 6, 1910, 11. Also, at the time the Maricopa and Phoenix Railroad boasted that it only took seventeen hours to carry passengers from Phoenix to

Los Angeles. See "Maricopa Route," *Native American* 10, no. 29 (September 11, 1909): 299.

2. Several newspaper articles refer to this as the P.A.A. meet during the Elks' Convention. The marathon was one of many events held during the convention, and not necessarily the main one. The official title was "Full distance marathon and wrestling championship of the Pacific Athletic association of the Amateur Athletic Union of America, under auspices of the Los Angeles Athletic Club"; from "Official Program Los Angeles Show," *Arizona Republican*, July 10, 1909, 4. It was also referred to as "the field meet" during the Elks' Carnival and Convention at "Los Angeles, under the management of the Southern California Athletic Club," in "Phoenix Athletes Go to Los Angeles," *Arizona Republican*, June 19, 1909, 7. The Amateur Athletic Association of the Pacific Coast paid for the Phoenix Indian School runner's registration fees and transportation costs. See "Phoenix Athletes Are All Registered," *Arizona Republican*, July 5, 1909, 4.

3. "Phoenix Athletes Go to Los Angeles," 7.

4. "The Winner of Marathon," 1. See also "Phoenix Athletes Go to Los Angeles," 7.

5. "Official Program Los Angeles Show," 4. Race officials presented the top three finishers with medals that had the Elks' emblem embossed on it. See "Good Prizes Up for Elk's Marathon," *Los Angeles Herald*, July 3, 1909, 12.

6. "Marathon Runner Fine," *Arizona Republican*, June 29, 1909, 6.

7. "Phoenix Athletes Go to Los Angeles," 7.

8. The term "pink of condition" was often used to describe people (or animals) who were healthy, who had a "pink" or salmon-colored hue to them. Origins of this term can be traced to Shakespearean literature. See Julia Cresswell, ed., *Little Oxford Dictionary of Word Origins* (New York: Oxford University Press, 2014), 131.

9. "Indian Marathon Runner Is Fast," *Arizona Republican*, June 21, 1909, A6.

10. "Hopi Runner Home Again," 1.

11. "Indian Marathon Runner Is Fast," A6.

12. A year before attending the Phoenix Indian School, Harry McLean briefly visited Sherman Institute in Riverside, California. See "From Other Schools," *Native American* 9, no. 21 (May 30, 1908): 208.

13. Bloom, *To Show What an Indian Can Do*, 4.

14. "Official Program Los Angeles Show," 4.

15. "The Winner of Marathon," 1.

16. Ibid.

17. "Indian Runner Is a Surprise at Two Miles," *San Francisco Chronicle*, July 15, 1909, 8.

18. "Trainer J. E. Lewis on Harry M'Lean: The Fleet Hopi Will Shortly Undertake to Outrun a Two-Man Relay for Five Miles," *Arizona Republican*, July 26, 1909, 4.

19. "Indian Runner Is a Surprise at Two Miles," 8.

20. "Athlete's Interest in Harry M'Lean," *Arizona Republican*, July 24, 1909, 8.

21. "An Old Time Runner of the Maricopas," *Arizona Republican*, July 14, 1909, 2. The term "old-time Indian runner" was a popular phrase that newspaper writers used to describe older Indian runners who made names for themselves for their abilities to run long distances, whether it be in competitive or noncompetitive races. "Old Time Indian Runner Is Dead," a headline read in the *Plain Speaker*. "Tom Longboat, the lank Onondaga Indian, was buried yesterday not far from the reservation where he began his career as a fabulous distance runner. He was laid to rest to the tribal chant of Iroquois funeral rites." See "Old Time Indian Runner Is Dead," *Plain Speaker* (Hazleton, Pennsylvania), January 12, 1949, 7.

22. Present-day Arizona was referred to as the Arizona Territory from 1863 until it received statehood on February 14, 1912. See Thomas E. Sheridan, *Arizona: A History* (Tucson: University of Arizona Press, 1995), 178.

23. "Trainer J. E. Lewis on Harry M'Lean," 4.

24. For a discussion on the health risks, including skin conditions, associated with training horses in hot climates, see Danny W. Scott and William H. Miller, *Equine: Dermatology*, 2nd ed. (Philadelphia: Saunders, 2010), 459.

25. "Trainer J. E. Lewis on Harry M'Lean," 4.

26. Officials at Sherman Institute did not have to work hard to convince people that California's climate was ideal for athletics. At times, businesses even connected California's climate to athletics to promote their products. For example, an advertisement for Wieland's Beer read: "The splendid climate makes California ideal in sport and athletics the year round. Whether you wish to excel in the various games of brawn and muscle, or whether you only indulge in them for the love of the sport and the healthy exercise you obtain, you need healthy food and drink to sustain you." See "Wieland's Wherever You Are," *San Francisco Chronicle*, May 12, 1910, 3.

27. Trennert, *The Phoenix Indian School*, 102.

28. Ibid., 103.

29. "Trainer J. E. Lewis on Harry M'Lean," 4.

30. Ibid.

31. "Phoenix Is the Best Town in America," *Arizona Republican*, September 9, 1900, 5.

32. For a detailed account of the early history of the BPOE, see Meade D. Detweiler, *An Account of the Origin and Early History of the Benevolent and Protective Order of Elks of the U.S.A.* (Harrisburg, PA: Harrisburg Publishing, 1898).

33. "Fast Run on Slow Track: Harry M'Lean Does Two Miles in 10:70 3-4," *Arizona Republican*, August 28, 1909, 4, and "Plan Welcome for President," *Los Angeles Times*, August 30, 1909, 13.

34. "Ballard Wins the Providence Race," *Boston Post*, February 23, 1909, 11.

35. McLean also noted that race officials had made him go twenty-one laps, and not twenty. "I might have made better time," he told the reporter, "but I feel that I made a world's record, for I ran twenty-one laps instead of twenty for the five miles. Everyone was excited as Bellairs and I took turns in the lead, and the judges forgot when the referee failed to warn us at the first lap of the last mile. What the judges said goes with me, for I know that I ran twenty-one better than anyone else, and Bellairs knows it too." See "Hopi Runner Home Again," 1.

36. "Harry M'Lean Made Failure," *Arizona Republican*, October 18, 1909, 1.

37. "The Indians Failure," *Arizona Republican*, October 19, 1909, 2.

38. In the early 1900s, the US government had taken millions of acres of Indian lands through the General Allotment Act (also known as the Dawes Severalty Act) of 1887. The government intended for the act to privatize Indian land holdings, force Indians to become farmers, make way for the selling of excess Indian lands to white ranchers and other businessmen, and provide a path for Indian (US) citizenship. For more information on the act, and the federal policies that surrounded it, see C. Joseph Genetin-Pilawa, *Crooked Paths to Allotment: The Fight over Federal Indian Policy after the Civil War* (Chapel Hill: University of North Carolina Press, 2014).

39. One example of this took place among the Pima Indians in southern Arizona. In 1901, the Gila River above the Pima Indian Reservation was diverted by white Americans who used it for agricultural purposes. The Pimas, and other white sympathizers, asked Congress for help, but no assistance came from Washington. One newspaper writer noted: "Some years ago the white settlers began to divert the waters of the Gila river above the land of the Pima Indians; they were even encouraged to do so by the government. There has not been enough water for both, and as the Indians are not citizens but only wards of the government, their rights have been totally neglected. . . . So the Indians are going on retrograding, being forced to become beggars, thieves and government paupers, where once they own farms, reared their own families and had their own tribal government." See "The Gila River Dry," *Weekly Republican-Traveler* (Arkansas City, Kansas), June 27, 1901, 4. Originally published in the *Interstate Manufacturer*.

40. "The Indians Failure," 2.

41. "Tewanima Moqui Indian," *Indianapolis Star*, September 19, 1909, 31.

42. "Danish Champion on Indian's Trail," *Arizona Republican*, March 21, 1910, A1.

43. "Long Distance Runners Would Come for Fair," *Arizona Republican*, September 8, 1910, A1.

44. Ibid.

45. "Attractions of the Fair," *Arizona Republican*, September 7, 1912, 10. The fifteen-mile modified marathon was for "professionals only," which gives

further support that McLean was likely not running for (or enrolled at) the Phoenix Indian School at this time. See "Tempe Athletes at the State Fair," *Arizona Republic*, November 2, 1912, 10.

46. "Hopi Missionary," 11.

47. "Do You Remember?" *Arizona Republic*, September 19, 1949, 6, and "Do You Remember?" *Arizona Republican*, August 26, 1929, 18.

48. One newspaper writer spelled Halyve's name as "Sayl Haylne." See "An Indian Runner," *Arizona Republican*, June 6, 1909, 10.

49. "Teaching Savage Minds," *Detroit Free Press*, April 9, 1893, 13.

50. While at this time in American society "Marathonitis" had swept the country and attracted the attention of young people such as Halyve and his school-mates, some individuals, including those in the medical profession and sport authorities, decried its supposed dangers. In an opinion piece first published in the *Newark News* entitled "Danger in the Marathon Fad," the author sharply criticized the sport and parents who allowed their children to participate in it. The author noted that unlike boxing or bicycling, two popular sports of the period, to be a "juvenile Marathon" runner was "within the privileges of thousands of boys." "They can race after school hours," the author remarked, and if they "can't go out into the country, they can plan a course around a half dozen or more city blocks, and can speed away and continue running till they win the goal or drop from exhaustion." Citing a study published in *American Medicine* that claimed that running long distances damaged a person's body, the author in the *Newark News* concluded by arguing that many youth competing in marathons are doing "themselves irreparable injury, creating in their youthful bodies the conditions that are likely to develop into chronic indigestion, consumption, and heart failure." The writer even suggested that the "Marathon should be barred to all boys under the age of 18." Although a small percentage of people agreed with these concerns, the sport remained extremely popular with American youth, including Indian youth, and adults in US society. See "Edegren First to Call Attention to Marathon Danger—Sullivan," *Evening World*, March 29, 1909, 12, and "Danger in the Marathon Fad," *Asbury Park (NJ) Evening Press*, April 9, 1909, 4. Originally published in the *Newark News*.

51. Ben Fogelberg, "Saul Halyve, Forgotten Hopi Marathon Champion," *Colorado Heritage* 26, no. 4 (Autumn 2006): 38.

52. Fogelberg, "Saul Halyve, Forgotten Hopi Marathon Champion," 43.

53. Charles E. Burton had served as "Agent to the Moqui Reservation" in the early 1900s. His tenure as "Agent" among the Hopi was fraught with abuse and controversy. He may have brought Halyve, Atokuku, and other Hopi students with him when he began serving as superintendent at Teller Institute. See James, *Pages from Hopi History*, 123–129.

54. L.B.C., "The Indian as an Athlete," *Reading (Pennsylvania) Times*, January 8, 1910, 5.
55. Ibid.
56. Fogelberg, "Saul Halyve," 44.
57. "Erxleben Again Loses to Indian at Denver," *St. Louis Post-Dispatch*, June 21, 1909, 10. A newspaper article entitled "Indian Wins Marathon" that was published in several American newspapers noted that Halyve won the marathon in 3 hours, 14 minutes, and 53 seconds. See "Indian Wins Marathon," *Albuquerque Journal*, June 21, 1909, 3.
58. "Moqui Indian May Run at Athens Marathon," *El Paso Herald*, June 26, 1909, 23.
59. Fogelberg, "Saul Halyve," 44.
60. Ibid., 45.
61. "Indian Runner Marries Indian School Girl," *El Paso Herald*, March 13, 1911, 6.
62. In the summer of 1917, Reverend Lee I. Thayer of the American Baptist Home Mission Society mentioned Halyve in an article he wrote on Hopi religion. In it he remarked that Hopis "have great physical endurance as shown in their foot races. The runners frequently follow a course in which they wish the water to run, and thus make the race a prayer for water. Saul Halyve is a Christian Marathon runner. His record for 10 miles is 59 minutes; for 26¼ miles, 3 hours, 1 minute and 10 seconds." See Lee I. Thayer, "The Hopi Indians and their Religion," *Missionary Review of the World*, July 1917, 509.
63. Amy G. Adams, "The Hopi Indian Runner," *Carlisle Arrow* 8, no. 40 (June 14, 1912): 3.
64. Ibid.
65. Albert F. Warden, "Long-Distance Running Growing in Popularity," *Salt Lake Tribune*, June 25, 1916, 3.
66. Fogelberg,"Saul Halyve," 47.
67. "Indian Runners Dash through City to Park," *Arizona Republican*, February 8, 1914, 9.
68. Winning a sweater in Phoenix may not appear to be a very appropriate or useful prize. However, temperatures in Phoenix during February tend to be in the low 70s (high) and high 40s (low). A sweater would have kept the winner warm in the cool February mornings.
69. Ibid.
70. "Hopi Boy Breaks State Mile Record to 44:42½," *Arizona Republican*, November 18, 1915, 2. Eighteen-year-old Lakota runner Billy Mills ran this same distance in 4:22.8 while a student at Haskell Institute in Lawrence, Kansas. See Lyle Schwilling, "Indian Runs Mile in 4:22.8," *Evening Republican* (Columbus, IN), May 7, 1957, 10. For reference of Talayumptewa being from Bacavi, see "Sakiestewa Hopi Head," *Gallup Independent*, December 2, 1959, 1.
71. "Indian Runs Mile in 4:42 1-2," *El Paso Herald*, November 19, 1915, 10. After

winning a five-mile footrace at the Phoenix Fairgrounds in December 1911 with a time of 27:26:30, his trainer John E. Lewis remarked to a reporter for the *Arizona Republican* that Swiggett would "make a greater man than [Harry] McLean, the Indian distance runner who ran away from the crowd of athletes at Los Angeles two years ago and came near being sent as the Western distance runner to Europe to compete in the Olympic games two years ago." See "Training for World Honors," *Arizona Republican*, December 26, 1911, 1, 2.

72. "Hopi Boy Breaks State Mile Record," 2.

73. "Sportitorial," *Arizona Republican*, November 21, 1920, 14.

74. "Handsome Diamond Studded Medal for Gardner Marathon," *Arizona Republican*, November 7, 1920, 18.

75. "Sportitorial," 14.

76. "Marathon First, Dinner Second, Then Football," *Arizona Republican*, November 25, 1920, 11.

77. "Gordon Coola Wins Gardner 10-Mile Race," *Arizona Republican*, November 26, 1920, 15.

78. The 1921 Gardner Marathon was held on "Decoration Day" (Memorial Day) on May 30, 1921. See "Two Phoenix Athletes Entered in National A.A.U. Championship Track and Field Meet July 2–5," *Arizona Republican*, June 14, 1921, 7.

79. Robert Edgren, "Deerfoots on Cinder Path; Through Camera's Eye," *El Paso Herald*, November 21, 1921, 6.

80. Robert Edgren, "Mexican Youths May Be World's Best Athletes," *El Paso Herald*, November 9, 1921, 6.

81. "General Closing of All the Stores in Phoenix Today," *Arizona Republican*, May 30, 1923, 6.

82. "No Mail Delivery at the Postoffice on Memorial Day," *Arizona Republican*, May 30, 1923, 6.

83. "Phoenix and Valley Pay Tribute Today to the Soldier Dead," *Arizona Republican*, May 30, 1923, 1.

84. "Speakers Urge Vets to Carry On Battle for True Citizenry," *Arizona Republican*, May 31, 1923, 1.

85. "Memorial Day," *Los Angeles Herald*, May 24, 1892, 5.

86. "Local Weather Yesterday," *Arizona Republican*, May 31, 1923, 6.

CHAPTER 5: LAND OF ORANGES

1. Owen R. Bird, "Many Entrants Received for Big Marathon," Los Angeles Times, March 10, 1912, 10.

2. *Sherman Bulletin*, April 24, 1912, 3, Sherman Indian Museum, Riverside, California.

3. Howard W. Angus, "Philip Zeyouma Will Run Again," *Los Angeles Times*, December 25, 1914, III1.

4. In Hopi culture, the people have long believed in "flying snakes," creatures often depicted in drawings and told about in oral traditions. After an excavation of a kiva at the ancient Hopi settlement of Awatovi, Chief Wilson Tawaquaptewa of Orayvi explained a painting of a flying snake that the expedition had uncovered: "The creature on the Front wall of Room 240 (fig. 43, b), which has already been discussed in the section on Birds, was regarded by a Hopi informant, Wilson Tewaquaptewa of Oraibi, as the Water Serpent. He added that the red and orange might be sunlight, and that the animal itself was a 'very powerful snake, a flying snake, a racer snake,' and was called Tawataho, a pet of the Sun." The "flying snake" depicted on Philip Zeyouma's shirt was most likely Tawataho, the "racer snake." See Watson Smith, *Kiva Mural Decorations at Awatovi and Kawaika-a: With a Survey of Other Wall Paintings in the Pueblo Southwest* (Cambridge, MA: Peabody Museum Press, 2006), 215. See also *Sherman Bulletin*, April 24, 1912, 3.

5. *Sherman Bulletin*, April 24, 1912, 3.

6. Ibid.

7. Ibid.

8. A writer for the *San Francisco Call* noted that the world's "record for 12 miles is 1:02:00, but this, however, was made on a prepared track, and officials of today's race declared the Indian's time had never before been equaled." See "Zeyouma Takes Marathon Run," *San Francisco Call*, April 21, 1912, 70.

9. *Sherman Bulletin*, April 24, 1912, 3.

10. Ibid. Coach Shoulder took the two Hopi runners to Los Angeles to register for the race on Sunday, April 14, 1912. Owen R. Bird for the *Los Angeles Times* remarked that when race officials were in a meeting, "two more entries came in. The first was from the Sherman Indian School in Riverside and he goes by the high sounding name Guy Maktima of the Hopi tribe, he will be a running mate for Philip Zeyuma, these two original citizens of the U.S. will run as a team from Sherman, and, Joseph Scholder, manager of athletics at the school, says in his letter, that these boys are right having been in training for the race ever since the middle of March." See Owen R. Bird, "Starting the Big Marathon," *Los Angeles Times*, April 15, 1912, 19.

11. *Sherman Bulletin*, April 24, 1912, 3.

12. Although it may have been Zeyouma's first time to ride in an automobile, he had previously traveled to Los Angeles with Coach Shoulder and Guy Maktima to register for the marathon, and both runners certainly had past experiences with streetcars. As early as 1902, the city of Riverside operated a streetcar on Magnolia Avenue that regularly brought visitors to the front gate of Sherman Institute. The tourists, local community members, and government officials who often made visits to the school required a convenient mode of public transportation. See William Oscar Medina, "Selling Indians at Sherman Institute" (Ph.D. diss., University of California, Riverside, 2007).

13. Owen R. Bird, "The Marathon Starts Tomorrow Afternoon," *Los Angeles Times*, April 19, 1912, III1.

14. Stewart Nicholas, *Hopi Tutuveni*, Kiiqòtsmori, Arizona, August 31, 2006, 3.

15. *Sherman Bulletin*, May 8, 1912, 1.

16. Ibid.

17. Ibid.

18. Ibid.

19. Robert Trennert observed that Native "athletes became campus heroes and were held up as examples" for the students to "follow." Trennert, *The Phoenix Indian School*, 131.

20. *Sherman Bulletin*, May 8, 1912, 4.

21. "Philip Zeyouma Easily Beaten," *Los Angeles Times*, May 15, 1912, 30.

22. Nearly three weeks after the two-mile race at Sherman, Philip Zeyouma and Albert Ray competed against each other in the Pasadena–Los Angeles Modified Marathon of 12½ miles. Once again, Ray defeated the Hopi runner with a time of 1 hour, 12 minutes, and 3 seconds, more than 4 minutes ahead of Zeyouma. See "Indian Won a Lively Race," *Arizona Republican*, June 3, 1912, 5.

23. *Los Angeles Times*, "Sherman Institute Has Bright Athletic Future," July 22, 1913, IV4.

24. Ibid.

25. Moses Friedman to Frank M. Conser, May 14, 1912, "Zeyouma, Philip," Box 402, RG-75, Sherman Indian High School Student Case File (SIHSCF), NARA, Laguna Niguel, California.

26. There is some uncertainty whether the American Olympic Committee actually fulfilled its obligation to extend an invitation to Zeyouma to be part of the 1912 US Olympic team. On May 22, 1912, Superintendent Frank Conser of Sherman Institute replied to the letter Moses Friedman had sent him on May 14 of the same year. In it Conser stated: "It would be very pleasing indeed to have Philip represent the Pacific coast and Louis the Atlantic. I rather doubt, however, Philip being selected as there apparently seems to be a desire to have another selected and Philip will not be selected unless it is found to be an absolute necessity." Frank Conser to Moses Friedman, May 22, 1912, "Zeyouma, Philip," SIHSCF.

27. D. H. Biery To Whom It May Concern, August 17, 1945, "Zeyouma, Philip," SIHSCF.

28. Wayne Dennis, *The Hopi Child* (New York: John Wiley & Sons, 1965), 38.

29. For detailed discussion on the complex relationship between parents and Indian pupils who attended boarding schools, see Reyhner and Eder, *American Indian Education*, 168–204.

30. Frank M. Conser to Horton H. Miller, June 11, 1909, "Masaquaptewa, Herman," Box 232, RG-75, SIHSCF, NARA, Laguna Niguel, California.

31. Although the Hopi and Pueblo Indians of New Mexico technically received US citizenship through the Treaty of Guadalupe Hidalgo in 1848, certain rights did not apply to them until Congress passed the Indian Citizenship Act in 1924. See Donaldson, *Extra Census Bulletin*, 9.

32. James, *Pages from Hopi History*, 191.

33. Bill Mallon, "Louis Tewanima," in *Native Americans in Sports*, vol. 2, ed. C. Richard King (Armonk, NY: Sharpe Reference, 2004), 296.

34. *Sherman Bulletin*, October 30, 1912, 4.

35. Al G. Weddell, "Famous Marathoners Beaten on the Desert," *Los Angeles Times*, November 19, 1912, III3.

36. "Beat Olympic Winner," *New York Times*, February 1, 1913, 9. See also *Sherman Bulletin*, October 10, 1912, 4. The *New York Times* noted that Tewanima spoke to the older men in English. However, Tewanima most certainly responded to the men in Hopi, saying, "Um itamuy pevewne', um itamumi naamataqtani," or, "If you doubt us, get in and show what you can do." I thank Stewart B. Koyiyumptewa of the Hopi Cultural Preservation Office and Hopi scholar Sheilah E. Nicholas for providing me with the Hopi translation.

37. "Beat Olympic Winner," *New York Times*, February 1, 1913, 9.

38. In an interview by anthropologist Peter Nabokov, Hopi runner Bruce Talawema noted that "running was something the elders used to preach to us," saying, "anytime you go somewhere on foot, you should try to run. It is a big part of our life. Even when you are old, as long as you can race or trot, at whatever pace, it makes you feel younger." See Nabokov, *Indian Running*, 100, 101.

39. Joshua Hermeyesva to Friedman, October 28, 1913, "Hermeyesva, Joshua," file #3732, box 78, CSF.

40. *Sherman Bulletin*, May 27, 1927, 5.

41. Bert C. Smith, "Red, White, Black Lads Mix in Dressing-Room," *Los Angeles Times*, April 20, 1913, Part VII, 10.

42. "Indian Runners Are Tutored in Riding," *Los Angeles Times*, April 27, 1913, Part VII, 12.

43. Angus, "Philip Zeyouma Will Run Again," 23.

44. Albert Ray won the Sierra Madre Mount Wilson Climb Marathon in 1 hour, 19 minutes, and 54 seconds. Hopi runner Guy Maktima, also from Sherman Institute, came in third place with a time of 1 hour, 26 minutes, and 27 seconds. See "Indian Winner in Annual Climb of Mount Wilson," *Santa Ana Register*, April 30, 1913, 1.

45. Shortly after Azul won the Ocean Park Marathon, a writer for the *Los Angeles Times* observed: "Crossing the finishing line four minutes ahead of W. J. Churchill, William Azul of the Sherman Indian School won first place in the L.A.A.C. first annual Marathon race today, running the 14 4-5 miles in 1h. 32m. Though there was a broad grin on his face as he made the last few yards

of his run, Azul was in bad condition for several hours after he finished." See "Azul Wins the Marathon," *Los Angeles Times*, May 31, 1919, Part II, 9. See also, "Speedy Pima Indian Runner Will Enter Gardner Marathon," *Arizona Republican*, May 15, 1921, A3.

46. "Azul, Indian, Winner," *Modesto Evening News*, May 25, 1920, 5.

47. Geoff Williams, *C. C. Pyle's Amazing Foot Race: The True Story of the 1928 Coast-to-Coast Run across America* (New York: Rodale, 2007), xi.

48. Cooper, *American Marathon*, 65, 66.

49. "Nurmi to Race Hopi Indians," *Logansport Pharos-Tribune*, April 25, 1925, 9.

50. The other Indian runners included Garnet Billy (Navajo), Cecil Begay (Navajo), Anthony Barney (Navajo), Harry Arthur (Navajo), and California Indian Roy Arenas (Mission). See "Eight Braves to Battle with Paavo Nurmi," *Morning Sun* (Pittsburg, Kansas), April 25, 1925, 1. Issued by the Associated Press.

51. Braven Dyer, "Nurmi Thrills 45,000 Track Fans," *Los Angeles Times*, April 26, 1925, 41.

52. Ibid., 47.

53. For a detailed description of Paavo Nurmi's remarkable running career, see Gotaas, *Running*, 154–165.

54. "Indians Lose to Speedy Finn," *Salt Lake Telegram*, April 26, 1925, 34. One newspaper writer also noted the similar strides of Nurmi and Hopi runners: "Nurmi doesn't run up on his toes. He has a smooth, low, gliding run, almost if not entirely flat-footed. . . . There is nothing strange about this. Probably the messenger runners and long distance runners of ancient times, who covered such wonderful distances in a day or night, ran just as Nurmi does, in a natural manner and without any highly developed artificial form. I have seen some of the Indian runners, and they run like Nurmi. The Hopi Indians for hundreds of years have held ceremonial races covering long distances across the deserts. Their runners today can outravel a horse and they run flat-footed, in the easiest, most natural way without strain." See Robert Edgren, "Remarkable Endurance of Famous Finn Surprising," *Salt Lake Telegram*, January 18, 1925, 6. Also, a few weeks after competing in Los Angeles, and during his return trip to the East Coast, Nurmi had planned to stop in Albuquerque, New Mexico, to race against three Hopis and three Zuni runners at the "University of New Mexico's quarter mile course" on May 8, 1925. See "Finn vs. Indians," *Petaluma Argus-Courier*, April 23, 1925, 1. Issued by the United Press.

55. Harry Chaca's last name has three spellings: Chaca, Chauca, and Chacca. I have chosen to privilege the spelling that his family currently uses on the Hopi Reservation. However, when he was competing in American races, he apparently "insisted" that newspaper reporters spell his name "Chacca." See "Mercury Squad off for Meet," *Los Angeles Times*, June 29, 1929, 11. Also, one newspaper spelled his last name "Chadea" from the village of "Polarca, Ar-

izona." See "Harold Buchanan Wins Marathon Race," *Hartford Courant*, April 22, 1928, 39. Another spelled his name "Ochauca"; see "Hopi Indian Wins Pre-Olympic Race," *Eau Claire Leader*, June 16, 1929, 6. Issued by the Associated Press.

56. "Indian Runners in Long Race," *Hutchinson News*, April 21, 1928, 2.

57. "Arizona Indian Runners Place," *Arizona Daily Star*, April 22, 1928, 10. Issued by the Associated Press.

58. McRae, "By the Way," *Morning Call*, May 14, 1929, 3.

59. "Indians 6-Mile Race Mark under Official Probe," *Salt Lake Telegram*, May 7, 1929, 4. Issued by the Associated Press.

60. Braven Dyer, "Carter Conger May Run Again," *Los Angeles Times*, May 6, 1929, 11.

61. "De Mar Beaten in Race," *New York Times*, June 16, 1929, S7.

62. Clarence De Mar was born in Melrose, Massachusetts, which explains the name "Melrose Marvel." James F. Fixx provides a short biography of De Mar in his comprehensive book on running. See Fixx, *The Complete Book of Running*, 47, 48.

63. Cooper, *American Marathon*, 70.

64. Braven Dyer, "Chauca Wins 'Times' Marathon Race," *Los Angeles Times*, June 16, 1929, A1.

65. Relman Moran, "The Start, the Finish, and the Winner of the First Pre-Olympic Marathon," *Los Angeles Times*, June 16, 1929, A1.

66. De Mar Beaten in Race," S7.

67. "Jap Athlete Training to Beat Harry Chacca," *Sherman Bulletin*, December 6, 1929, 2. The Japanese also have a long tradition of distance running. For more information on this topic, see Adharanand Finn, *The Way of the Runner: A Journey into the Fabled World of Japanese Running* (New York: Pegasus Books, 2015).

68. "Harry Chauca Race Favorite," *San Bernardino (California) County Sun*, December 22, 1929, 22.

69. "Jap Athlete Training to Beat Harry Chacca," 2.

70. Gems, *The Athletic Crusade*, 37.

71. Eiichiro Azuma, *Between Two Empires: Race, History, and Transnationalism in Japanese America* (New York: Oxford University Press, 2005), 9.

72. "Passes Bill to Bar Japanese Students," *New York Times*, February 5, 1909, 1.

73. Allen Guttmann and Lee Thompson, *Japanese Sports: A History* (Honolulu: University of Hawai'i Press, 2001), 118.

74. Eriko Yamamoto observed that in 1932, 70 percent of the 138,834 Japanese on the "mainland United States" lived in Southern California. See Eriko Yamamoto, "Cheers for Japanese Athletes: The 1932 Los Angeles Olympics and the Japanese American Community," *Pacific Historical Review* 60, no. 33 (August 2000): 404.

75. Ibid., 403.

76. Ibid., 414.

77. "Harry Chaca Makes New American Record," *Sherman Bulletin*, December 27, 1929, 3.

78. Bill Tobitt, "Chaca Takes Suisun—Vallejo Marathon," *Oakland Tribune*, December 23, 1929, D19.

79. Dyreson, *Making the American Team*, 55.

80. Ibid., 158.

81. "Indian Athletes Train Diligently for 'The Times' Pre-Olympic Marathon Run," *Los Angeles Times*, June 2, 1929, A3; "Injuns Forsake Warpath for Cinderpath," *Los Angeles Times*, May 3, 1931, F3.

82. Maynard Tahbo to Matthew Sakiestewa Gilbert, personal e-mail communication, October 25, 2008. Maynard Tahbo is the grandson of Harry Chaca.

83. Guy Maktima to F. M. Conser, August 13, 1916, "Maktima, Guy," Box 222, RG-75, SIHSCF, NARA, Laguna Niguel, California.

84. Nick Brokeshoulder interview, Hopi Cultural Center, Second Mesa, Arizona, the Hopi Reservation, March 26, 2006.

85. Mrs. Philip Zeyouma to F. M. Conser, April 22, 1915, "Zeyouma, Philip," SIHSCF. Philip and Christina were married by Pastor G. M. Leigh of the Highland Park Baptist Church in California on October 8, 1913. Philip first worked at a water pumping plant in Bloomington, California. See "Eagle Rock," *Los Angeles Times*, October 12, 1913, 42.

86. Philip Zeyouma's obituary noted in part: "Mr. Zeyouma, who lived on McCabe Road, died Thursday in the Public Health Service Hospital here. Born in Mesa, he first came to this area as a scout for about 25 families of Mesa Hopis who subsequently settled here. He was a long distance runner in his youth, graduate from Sherman Institute in California and later worked as an electrician for the Bureau of Indian Affairs in Keams Canyon, Indian Wells and Winslow. He was an athletic coach for many years. Survivors include his son, Philip Jr., three daughters, Mrs. Gladys Perez of Santa Fe, N.M.; Mrs. Charlotte Byestewa of Parker; 15 grandchildren and 4 great grandchildren." See "Philip Zeyouma Sr., 87, Hopi Athlete and coach," *Arizona Republic*, February 16, 1969, 6-F. Also, in the 1960s, Zeyouma worked as chief of police in Parker, Arizona. See "Divers Hunt for Body of Youth," *Arizona Republic*, July 1, 1966, 15.

87. Perkinsman to D. H. Biery, exact date unknown, "Zeyouma, Philip," SIHSCF.

88. I write about this mythical race in Chapter 1.

89. Perkinsman to D. H. Biery, exact date unknown, "Zeyouma, Philip," SIHSCF.

90. The Sherman Indian Museum was originally the superintendent's office at Sherman Institute. For additional information, visit the Sherman Indian Museum website at http://www.shermanindianmuseum.org/history3.htm.

91. Angus, "Philip Zeyouma Will Run Again," III1.

92. Ibid.

93. Although he does not focus on athletes who returned to the reservation, Michael Coleman has written a fascinating account of the complex situations that Native students encountered when they came home from off-reservation Indian boarding schools. See Michael Coleman, *American Indians, the Irish, and Government Schooling* (Lincoln: University of Nebraska Press, 2009), 254–261.

94. Barbara Landis to Matthew Sakiestewa Gilbert, personal e-mail communication, June 16, 2009.

95. Landis to Sakiestewa Gilbert, personal e-mail communication, July 29, 2009.

96. For additional information on NAGPRA, see National Parks Service, Department of the Interior, National NAGPRA home page at http://www.nps.gov/history/nagpra.

97. Frank Roche, "Redskins Go on Running Path," *Los Angeles Times*, May 3, 1931, F3.

98. "Native Indian Athletes out to Beat Finns," *Fort Lauderdale News*, September 3, 1926, 9.

99. "Three Favored," *Arizona Daily Star*, June 25, 1932, 9. Issued by the Associated Press.

100. Ralph Hutson, "Suhu Wins Marathon," *Los Angeles Times*, May 24, 1931, 58.

101. First- and second-place finishers in the 1932 *Los Angeles Times* Pre-Olympic Marathon qualified to be on the US Olympic Marathon Team. See "Facts about the Marathon," *Los Angeles Times*, June 25, 1932, 7. Although Suhu came in second place, he did not have a strong finishing time (3 hours, 5 minutes, 14 seconds—more than 20 minutes slower than first-place Whitey Michelsen's time), which may explain why he ultimately did not qualify to be on the team. See "Marathon Run to Michelsen as Star Fails," *Los Angeles Times*, June 26, 1932, 61, and "Michelsen Wins Marathon Event," *Klamath News*, June 26, 1932, 7. A similar thing may have happened to Philip Zeyouma after winning the 1912 *Los Angeles Times* Modified Marathon, a victory that rightly earned him a spot on the 1912 US Olympic team. See Frank Conser to Moses Friedman, May 22, 1912, "Zeyouma, Philip," SIHSCF.

CHAPTER 6: FOOTRACES ACROSS AMERICA

1. "Hopis Win First Three Places in Annual Marathon Race: Winner Runs up Grade in 35 Minutes and 49 Seconds," *Colorado Springs Gazette*, October 11, 1926, 1. See also, "Indian Runners Win Mountain Marathon," *San Bernardino (California) Sun*, October 12, 1926, 20. Issued by the Associated Press.

2. "Mountain Race to Test White Man and Indian," *Amarillo Daily News*, September 28, 1926, 2.

3. In an article entitled "Hopi Indians Set Record in Mountain Climb," a reporter for the Associated Press noted the following completion times: Poho-

quaptewa, Hopi, 35:49 4-5; Honkuku, Hopi, 35:55 2-5; Quanohwahu, Hopi, 36:20 4-5; Sheka, Zuni, 36:52 1-5; Lino (Akoma) 36:52 2-5; Shack, Zuni, 44:06 1-5; Ever Green Tree, Pueblo, 44:52; Jack Phillipson, American, 46:50 3-5; Adolphus Stroud, American, 48:39 1-5; Allen Kinsman, American, 53:10 3-5; John Noe, Swiss, 57:38 2-5. See "Hopi Indians Set Record in Mountain Climb," *Arizona Daily Star*, October 11, 1926, 1. Issued by the Associated Press.

4. "Hopis Win First Three Places in Annual Marathon Race," *Colorado Springs Gazette*, 1.

5. Bloom, *To Show What an Indian Can Do*, xi.

6. Derderian, *Boston Marathon*.

7. For examples of Gordon Coola's running victories, see "Local Athlete Beats Time of Chicago Long Distance Runner," *Arizona Republican*, November 30, 1920, 8, and "Fanning," *Arizona Republican*, November 23, 1925, 7. In an article entitled "Speedy Pima Indian Runner Will Enter Gardner Marathon," a reporter for the *Arizona Republican* noted that "Azul is no stranger to the long runs, having competed in three big races and winning each event. Last year Azul won the Sweets trophy and on May 30, 1919, he won the 15-mile race and Business men's cup in the first annual meeting of the Los Angeles Athletic club at Ocean park. In 1915 Azul won the Sawtelle modified marathon over a nine-mile course against a field of 11 entries. The Pima running star is 23 years of age and has been developed under the guidance of the coach of the Sacaton Indian School." See "Speedy Pima Indian Runner Will Enter Gardner Marathon," 13.

8. "Few Indians Now in Sports," *Baltimore Sun*, December 5, 1926, 14.

9. Jared Farmer, *On Zion's Mount: Mormons, Indians, and the American Landscape* (Cambridge, MA: Harvard University Press, 2010), 160.

10. Richard E. Wood, *Here Lies Colorado: Fascinating Figures in Colorado History* (Helena, MT: Farcountry Press), 2005, 144.

11. "Sunshine State Indians Capture Marathon Event," *Albuquerque Journal*, October 11, 1926.

12. "Four Indians Arrive for Marathon Run; Balk at 'Ham and', So Will Cook Own Food," *New York Times*, May 9, 1927. See also, "Indian Runners Cook Own Meals," *Tampa Times*, May 9, 1927, 5. Other Hopi runners such as Louis Tewanima were indifferent at having their photograph taken. In an article in the *Ogden Standard*, the writer remarked: "Lewis was not strong for photographs. He was totally indifferent as to their being taken. He never asked for one himself no matter who took it. As the years rolled by and he accumulated prizes by the trunkful, it became necessary, in the usual course of events, that a photograph be taken. Lewis got into his running togs and all the medals, cups, watches, banners and plaques that he had won were placed in position. Then the photographer looked around with a worried expression. He was puzzled.

He scratched his head walked around the room several times, and then said: 'Now, where the deuce am I going to put that Indian?" See "Carlisle Runner Is Cool One," the *Ogden Standard*, September 25, 1912, 2. Also, in his book on the Atlantic City boardwalk in New Jersey, historian Bryant Simon noted that East Coast boardwalks tended to be places of "exclusion" where white middle-class Americans dressed in their finest clothes and pretended to be wealthier than they actually were. See Bryant Simon, *Boardwalk of Dreams: Atlantic City and the Fate of Urban America* (New York: Oxford University Press, 2004), 16–21.

13. In their children's book *Climbing Sun*, Marjorie Thayer and Elizabeth Emanuel note that on Hopi student Hubert Honanie's first Christmas at Sherman Institute in the late 1920s, he enjoyed eating the traditional Christmas food the school served, but he would have "preferred stewed rabbit or mutton and corn" prepared according to Hopi custom. See Marjorie Thayer and Elizabeth Emanuel, *Climbing Sun: The Story of a Hopi Indian Boy* (New York: Dodd, Mead, 1980), 60. For another example of a Hopi student at Sherman who missed traditional Hopi food, see Mischa Titiev, *The Hopi Indians of Old Oraibi: Change and Continuity* (Ann Arbor: University of Michigan Press, 1972), 16.

14. "Four Indians Arrive for Marathon Run."

15. Roberta Fiore, Carole Shahda Geraci, and Dave Roochvarg, *Long Beach*, Images of America Series (Mount Pleasant, SC: Arcadia Publishing, 2010), 41.

16. Bette Weidman and Linda Martin, *Nassau County, Long Island, in Early Photographs* (Mineola, NY: Dover Publications, 1981), 115.

17. Talayesva, *Sun Chief*, 416.

18. Cooper, *The American Marathon*, 70. See also "Indian Chief Wins Marathon from Star New York Field," *Washington Post*, May 16, 1927, 11.

19. "Indian Chief Wins Marathon from Star New York Field," 11.

20. Robert Edgren, "Finns May Find Indians Swift," *Baltimore Sun*, May 23, 1927, 16.

21. Weddell, "Famous Marathoners Beaten on the Desert," 29.

22. John Kieran, "Sports of Our Times," *New York Times*, May 13, 1927, 21.

23. Ibid., 21.

24. Stephen, *Hopi Journal*, 2: 780. See also Nabokov, *Indian Running*, 27, 28.

25. Lakota writer and religious thinker Vine Deloria, Jr., once remarked: "One of the most frequently reported feats of medicine men is their ability to change the weather. Newspaper reporters delight in covering stories where, after dancing, the Indians made it rain, and the Hopi snake dance has been written up many times by scholars who have observed this phenomenon." See Vine Deloria, Jr., *The World We Used to Live In* (Golden, CO: Fulcrum Publishing, 2006), 135.

26. In August 1926, George Hammond of the Auto Club of Arizona made mention

of this, saying: "Many newspaper men, magazine writers and scientists come from the east, west, north and south each year to witness the elaborate prayer for rain in which the Elder Brothers of the Snake and Antelope Clans must be part of." See George Hammond, "Snake Dance to Lure Many Motorists to Hopiland during Month of August," *Arizona Republic*, August 1, 1926, 22.

27. "The Hopi Drouth-breakers," *Democrat and Chronicle* (Rochester, New York), August 26, 1926, 14, and "Hopis Invoke Rain God," *Morning Register* (Eugene, Oregon), August 19, 1924, 1. In the 1920s, sometimes white individuals called on the "Hopi rain makers" to make it rain, and the Hopi produced meager results. An example here in the *Coconino Sun*: "Joe Lee, knowing the Knights had insured against rain during the celebration, offered one of the Hopi medicine men, famed also as a rainmaker, $5 for an inch of rain. As it didn't rain much and as the Indian thought he ought to get something anyway for his effort, Joe gave him a big watermelon." See "Hopi Rain-Maker Gets Watermelon for Rain," *Coconino Sun*, July 7, 1922, 1.

28. Bryan Field, "Blistered Feet Force Hopi Indian to Turn Down 3 More Marathons," *New York Times*, May 18, 1927, 22.

29. I thank Hopi scholar Sheilah E. Nicholas, a direct descendent of Nicholas Qömawunu, for this clarification.

30. Ibid.

31. The 1928 Summer Olympics took place in Amsterdam, Netherlands, from May 17, 1928, to August 12, 1928. See George Russell, *The Olympic Century: IX Olympiad, Amsterdam Netherlands, from May 17, 1928 to August 12, 1928* (Warwick, NY: Warwick Press, 2015).

32. See also "Indian Snake Priest Breaks American Marathon Record," *Binghamton (New York) Press*, May 16, 1927, 19.

33. "Hopi Runners Training Daily for Long Race," *Arizona Republic*, July 10, 1927, 4.

34. "Indian Snake Dancer Outstrips Big Field in 26-Mile Marathon," *News-Journal* (Mansfield, OH), May 16, 1927, 10. Issued by the Associated Press.

35. "Hopi Indians Defy Tarahumara Tribe," *Los Angeles Times*, May 25, 1927, B2.

36. "Manager Wants to Bet $10,000 on Hopi Runners," *Bluefield (West Virginia) Daily Telegraph*, June 8, 1927.

37. Damon Runyon, "Runyon Says," *Evening News*, January 13, 1927, 19, and Damon Runyon, "Runyon Says," *Monroe (Louisiana) News-Star*, January 4, 1927, 6.

38. "249 Participants 'Shove Off' in Start of C. C. Pyle's Transcontinental Race," *Pittsburgh Post-Gazette*, March 5, 1928, 14.

39. "Oraibi Indian Runner Enters Big Marathon," *Winslow (Arizona) Daily Mail*, February 16, 1928.

40. James, *Pages from Hopi History*, 115, 116.

41. See Sakiestewa Gilbert, *Education beyond the Mesas*, 2010.

42. "Indian Has His Rivals Worrying: Pyle's Gallopers Try to Figure Some Way to Stop Quomawahu," *Los Angeles Times*, February 23, 1928, Part III, 4.

43. Known as one of the "great dirt tracks of America," the Legion Ascot Speedway in Southern California became especially popular with race car enthusiasts in the 1930s. See John Heitmann, *The Automobile and American Life* (Jefferson, NC: McFarland, 2009), 116.

44. "Pyle's Bunion Derby Starts across Nation," *Honolulu Advertiser*, March 5, 1928, 1. Issued by United Press.

45. "275 Starters in Pyle's Marathon," *Wilmington Morning News*, March 5, 1928, 9. Issued by the Associated Press.

46. Kastner, *Bunion Derby*, 38.

47. "Still Leads in Bunion Derby," *Evening News*, March 6, 1928, 21.

48. Jim Powers, "Arizona Hopi Indian Leads Pyle Marathon as Runners Leave for Lap to Barstow," *Santa Ana (California) Register*, March 7, 1928, 10, and "Indian Leads in Footrace," *The News Leader* (Staunton, VA), March 7, 1928, 3, issued by the Associated Press.

49. Maxwell Stiles, "Indian Runner," *Cincinnati Enquirer*, March 7, 1928, 16.

50. "Gardner Victor in Fourth Lap of Derby," *Los Angeles Times*, March 8, 1928, B2.

51. "Negro Heads Bunion Derby in 4th Lap," *Los Angeles Times*, March 8, 1928, 18.

52. A newspaper writer noted that at the time Mojave Wells consisted only of a water tank and two nonresident railroad workers. See "Englishman Leading Pyle's Derby over Mojave Desert," *Klamath News*, March 9, 1928, 2.

53. "Sports: Veteran Shows Way to Rivals," *Los Angeles Times*, March 9, 1928, B3.

54. James Powers, "Racers Reach Bagdad under Blazing Sun," *Arizona Republican*, March 10, 1928, 11.

55. "Englishman Leading Pyle's Bunion Derby over Mojave Desert," 2.

56. The nearest hospital was most likely in the town of Bagdad ten miles away. See Powers, "Racers Reach Bagdad under Blazing Sun," 11.

57. Russell J. Newland, "Newton Again Leads Hoofers," *Los Angeles Times*, March 11, 1928, 19.

58. "Newton Continues to Increase Lead," *Daily Boston Globe*, March 11, 1928, A18. Reprinted in Newland, "Newton Again Leads Hoofers," 21.

59. "Canadian Outfoots Newton on 8th Lap," *New York Times*, March 12, 1928, 25.

60. James Powers, "Arthur Newton Has Good Lead in Bunion Trot," *News-Herald*, March 12, 1928, 10. Originally published by the United Press.

61. Kastner, *Bunion Derby*, 51

62. James S. Powers, "Rhodesian Leads in Pyle's Race," *Plainfield (New Jersey) Courier-News*, March 13, 1928, 21.

63. Ibid.

64. "Newton Nabs Eleventh Lap in Pyle Marathon," *Los Angeles Times*, March 15, 1928, B3.

65. "Charlotte Runner in Bunion Derby," *Greenville (South Carolina) News*, March 14, 1928, 11.

66. "Lloyd Johnson Forced Out of Cross Country," *Santa Ana Register*, March 18, 1928, 8.

67. Russell J. Newland, "Quomawahu, Hopi Indian, Not to Enter Marathon," *Arizona Daily Star*, June 12, 1928, 5, issued by the Associated Press.

68. "Pyle Derby into Bad Roads, Cold," *Lincoln Star Journal*, March 16, 1928, 10.

69. Harry Carr, *Los Angeles Times*, March 20, 1928, A1-A2.

70. Leland C. Lewis, "Runners in Hopi Indian Country," *Daily Republican* (Rushville, Indiana), March 19, 1928, 3. Issued by the International News Service.

71. Bryan Field, "Boston A.A. Run on Thursday to Be First of Series of Marathon Tests," *New York Times*, April 15, 1928, 164.

72. Prior to the Bunion Derby, officials of the American Olympic Committee urged Qömawunu not to run in the Derby. They instead wanted him to retain his amateur status and compete for the 1928 US Olympic team. See Theon Wright, "Hopi Sees Career Fade as He Drops Out of Derby," *Oakland Tribune*, March 13, 1928, 40. The same article has a photograph of Qömawunu in his running attire entitled "End of the Trail."

73. "Ray Outruns Crack Field in Marathon," *Boston Daily Globe*, May 20, 1928, A1.

74. A Karuk (Karook) California Indian named "Flying Cloud" won the 482-mile race in 167 hours and 51 minutes. The Hopi runners, who had been sponsored by Lorenzo Hubbell, did not finish among the top competitors in the race. See "San Francisco Marathon Lead Goes to Indian," *Iola (Kansas) Daily Register*, June 15, 1928, 8; "Flying Cloud Is Winner in Marathon," *Courier-Journal* (Louisville, KY), June 22, 1928, 18; and "Thirty-Entries Received for Indian Marathon," *Petaluma (California) Argus*, May 24, 1928, 8.

75. "Marathon Star Will Not Start," *Los Angeles Times*, June 12, 1928, B1.

76. Hopi runners Ray Honkuku (Honokuku) and Burton Quayangyamptewa also competed in this race. See "Olympic Marathon Tryouts Will Start Downtown at 9 A.M. Today," *Arizona Republican*, April 14, 1928, 10.

77. "Zuni Indian to Have Olympic Trial in East," *Arizona Republican*, April 15, 1928, 22.

78. Ibid.

79. "Greenway Day Marathoners Quit Olympics," June 11, 1928, 11. See also "Hopi and Zuni Runners Refuse Olympic Honors," *Messenger* (Athens, OH), June 1, 1928, 2

80. "Sees Hope for U.S. in Distant Races," *Boston Globe*, May 17, 1927.

81. A newspaper writer who observed the race remarked: "Simon Polingyumtewa, lean, supple Hopi from the Winslow country, galloped 15 miles on pavement and dirt track in the excellent time of 1 hour 30 minutes and 30 seconds, to win the Indian day marathon yesterday from 22 leather-lunged redskin run-

ners. The race, a feature of Indian day at La Fiesta de los Vaqueros, began at the West Congress street bridge and finished 20 laps around the track at the rodeo grounds. Climaxing a smooth, steady pace with a spectacular sprint at the finish, Polingyumtewa was more than a lap ahead of his nearest rival when he crossed the tape." See "Hopi Runner Is Easy Winner of Indian Gallop," *Arizona Daily Star*, February 24, 1934, 11. See also "Hopi, Papago, Racers," *Arizona Republic*, February 24, 1934, 1. Issued by the Associated Press.

82. "Hopi Indians to Appear at Wilson, Jefferson," *Evening Republican* (Columbus, Indiana), October 22, 1940, 2. For a photograph of "Little Eagle," see "Call of the Wild Comes to Hoosiers," *Indianapolis Star*, March 10, 1940, 29.

83. I am not suggesting that Hopis never won another race, or even a marathon. I am only suggesting that between 1937 and the immediate decades that followed Hopi runners did not appear to win a major American running event. Had they done so, news of their victories would have likely been reported in American newspapers.

84. "New Road into Hopi Indian Area Reveals Native Life to Buick-Marquette Scout," *Santa Ana Register*, December 1, 1929, 15.

85. One of the better-known examples of this took place nearly a decade before when a mathematics professor named Carey Melville with his wife, Maud, and their three children traveled to Hopiland in their Model T Ford from their home in Worcester, Massachusetts, in the summer of 1927. See Carolyn O'Bagy Davis, *Hopi Summer: Letters from Ethel to Maud* (Tucson: Rio Nuevo Publishers, 2007), and Lea S. McChesney, "On the Road with the Melvilles," in *Hopis, Tewas, and the American Road*, ed. Willard Walker and Lydia L. Wyckoff (Middletown, CT: Wesleyan University, 1983), 15–27. For a detailed road map to the Hopi Reservation during the mid 1920s, see "Highways Leading to Hopi Dances," *Arizona Daily Star*, August 8, 1926, 3. In August 1939, non-Indian Navajo trader Roman Hubbell (likely a relative of John Lorenzo Hubbell) recommended a specific route for visitors to take who wanted to see the Hopi Snake Dance on the reservation. See "Hubbell Advises Short Cut Road," *Gallup (New Mexico) Independent*, August 10, 1939, 1.

86. Older Hopi people would lament about this for years to come. In an article in the *Arizona Republic*, Norm Frauenheim remarked: "In 1968 and '69, there was some concern that the Hopi had lost interest in long distance running. Many villages abandoned the sport, and the young Hopi quit using his feet as the only mode of transportation. 'You see a lot of hitchhikers,' complained a member of the Hopi Athletic Commission. 'You don't see much running or even walking anymore, except for the older people who still walk from their homes on the mesa to their fields down in the valley." See Norm Frauenheim, "Hopi Legend," *Arizona Republic*, May 27, 1979, 23 (D1).

87. J. H. Nylander, "The Hopi," *Kerley News*, Kerley Trading Post, Tuba City, AZ,

July 6, 1936, 2, in A. F. Whiting *Ethnographic Notes and Papers, Hopi 34, History 2*, ed. P. David Seaman (June 1988): 196–217. Northern Arizona University Cline Library Special Collections, Flagstaff, AZ.

CONCLUSION: CROSSING THE TERRAIN

1. John Branch, "Two Hopi Traditions: Running and Winning," *Santa Fe New Mexican*, November 9, 2015, B4. Originally published in the *New York Times*, https://www.nytimes.com/2015/11/05/sports/hopi-high-school-cross-coun try-running.html.

2. Hopi runner Leonard Talaswaima once explained that winners of ancient Hopi races received "sacred eagle feathers which they planted in the fields as offerings for rain and a bountiful harvest." See Paul Brinkley-Rogers, "Racing Youths Revive Practice," *Arizona Republic*, November 11, 1995, A1, A21.

3. Even in the early 1900s, visitors to Hopiland still commented on the ability for Hopis to outrun horses: "Several times white men on horses have endeavored to follow these Indians in their races; but in the deep sends [*sic*] the horses have easily and quickly been distanced." See "Hopi Indians Are Runners," *Belleville (Kansas) Telescope*, October 31, 1902, 3.

4. Archie MacMillan, "De Mar, Marvel of Marathon Meets, Hopes to Capture Olympic Crown," *Abilene Reporter-News*, August 7, 1927, 38.

5. See Weideman, "Drawing Down Rain from the Devil's Claw," ZO51.

6. In his article on Jemez Pueblo runner Steve Gachupin, historian Brian Collier makes a similar connection between Gachupin and his people: "For Gachupin running is a way to connect with the traditions of the Pueblo and to remember those people from the community who ran before him and those who will run after him; it is part of the continuity of life's cycles." See Brian Collier, "To Bring Honor to My Village," 66.

EPILOGUE: STILL RUNNING

1. Scott Harves, *Run Hopi*, ESPN SportsCenter. https://vimeo.com/179251785. Accessed August 14, 2017.

2. John Branch, "Enduring Tradition," *New York Times*, November 5, 2015, B13, and "Two Hopi Traditions: Running and Winning."

3. Mario Kalo, "Hopi High Wins 26th Consecutive Cross Country State Title," *ArizonaCentral Sports*, November 7, 2015. http://www.azcentral.com/story /sports/high-school/2015/11/07/hopi-high-wins-26th-consecutive-cross -country-state-title/75171818/, accessed on August 14, 2017.

4. Harves, *Run Hopi*, ESPN, 12:29-50

5. Rodney Harwood, "Hopi High School Cross-Country Team Carrying on Proud Tradition," *Indian Country Today*, January 16, 2016. https://indiancountry

medianetwork.com/culture/sports/hopi-high-school-cross-country-team-carrying-on-proud-tradition/. Accessed August 14, 2017.

6. Crystal Dee, "Hopi High School Boys Win 26th Consecutive State Cross Country Championship Title," *Hopi Tutuveni*, November 17, 2015, 1.

7. Crystal Dee of the *Hopi Tutuveni* explains that in high school boys cross country, "The first five runners for each team are counted toward the final score; points are counted in the place they finish. First place: one point, 5th place: five points and 10th place: 10 points. The team with the least points wins." See Dee, "Hopi High School Boys Win 26th Consecutive State Cross Country Championship Title," *Hopi Tutuveni*, November 17, 2015, 1.

8. Dee, "Hopi High School Boys Win 26th Consecutive State Cross Country Championship Title," 1.

9. "Team of Hopi Indian Runners," *Gallup (New Mexico) Independent*, August 15, 1957, 4.

10. Tino (Celestino) Youvella ran for coach Bill Cordes at the Phoenix Indian School in the late 1950s. In 1959, he established a school record for the mile in 4 minutes and 38 seconds. He is known on and off the reservation for his remarkable Hopi kachina doll carvings. See Jerry Eaton, "Hopi Runners Please Cordes," *Arizona Republic*, April 5, 1959, Section 3, 2.

11. "Hopi Runners Sweep State Meet," *Hopi Action News*, December 27, 1967, 5. The newspaper article describes the runners as being from the following villages: Alfonso Gash of Old Orayvi, Clyde Nasafotie of Second Mesa, Merrill Hoyonwa of Ho'atvela, Gary Joshevama of Old Orayvi, Lauren Koinva of Second Mesa, Alde Monongye of Second Mesa, Lawrence Namoki of Polacca, and Ronald Takala of Ho'atvela. Originally published in the *Phoenix Redskin*.

12. "Hopi Runners Sweep State Meet," 5.

13. "Kingman Harriers Lose," *Kingman Daily Miner*, October 27, 1975, 8.

14. Herman Senayah was Arvis Myron's teammate on the Tuba City Cross Country Team. In 1979, Coach Davis had such a high opinion of him as a runner and believed that he had a "great chance at making the 1980 Olympic team." See Norm Frauenheim, "Basket Race Revives Hopi Desire to Run," *Arizona Republic*, May 27, 1979, 27 (D5). Also, in an article entitled "XC Legacy Big-15 National Rankings" by Aron Taylor and David Taylor, Senayah remarked: "I attended Tuba City from 1975–1978 and was pretty successful. During the three years I was on the team we were state champions. It was good work to be part of and that's what all high school teams strive is to be state champions. It took allot [sic] of hard work and discipline, we worked together as individuals and teams. The main reason I went to Illinois State was because [of Tuba City High School Cross-Country] Coach Bud Davis. He inspired me for more." See Aron Taylor and David Taylor, "XC Legacy Big-15 National Rankings," July 31,

2009, 6. http://www.milesplit.com/articles/24444/xc-legacy-1982-national
-xc-rankings. Accessed May 8, 2018.

15. "Graduate Record 1980 Illinois State University" (Marceline, MO: Walsworth Publishing, 1980) 40.

16. Arvis Myron, "Hopi Running at Illinois State University," Personal e-mail correspondence with the author, August 22, 2017.

17. At this time there was a handful of Hopis competing at different colleges in the United States, including Terry Honeyestewa and Wilbert Talashoma, who ran for Oklahoma Baptist College in Oklahoma City. See Frauenheim, "Basket Race Revives Hopi Desire to Run," 27 (D5).

18. Myron, "Hopi Running at Illinois State University," August 22, 2017.

19. Sharon Garcia, "Indian Forerunner," *Santa Fe New Mexican*, August 3, 1980, 15.

20. Juan Rios, "Message Run," *Santa Fe New Mexican*, August 6, 1980, 1.

21. Garcia, "Indian Forerunner," 15. For a map depicting the complete route of the run, see Nabokov, *Indian Running*, 34, 35.

22. Nabokov, *Indian Running*, 174.

23. Susan Kroupa, "At Age 58, Cooka Hasn't Allowed Life to Run Him Down," *Arizona Republic*, October 13, 1988, E8.

24. See also Crystal Dee, "Hopi Runner Sekaquaptewa Sets Sights on Boston Marathon," *Hopi Tutuveni*, February 18, 2015, 5.

25. Caroline Sekaquaptewa, "Caroline Sekaquaptewa's Boston Marathon Experience," We Run Strong, 2016. http://www.werunstrong.com/boston-mara thon/19-caroline-sekaquaptewas-boston-marathon-experience.html.

26. LaFrenda Frank, "Hopi Runner, Juwan Nuvayokva Signs with Saucony," *Navajo-Hopi Observer*, March 17, 2009. https://www.nhonews.com/news/2009 /mar/17/hopi-runner-juwan-nuvayokva-signs-with-saucony/. Accessed September 24, 2017.

27. Ibid.

28. Connie Koenenn, "New Hopi Chairman Tries to Bridge Two Worlds," *Albuquerque Journal*, June 16, 1994, C3. Originally published in the *Los Angeles Times*.

29. When operational, the Peabody Energy Company pumped two thousand gallons of water per minute from the Navajo Aquifer. See Leroy F. Aarons, "Destroying the Land," *Capital Journal* (Pierre, South Dakota), June 25, 1971, 23. Issued by the *Los Angeles Times–Washington Post* Service.

30. Judd Slivka, "Hopi Runners Deliver Plea on Aquifer," *Arizona Republic*, August 15, 2001, B4.

31. "Running in Honor of World's Water," *Arizona Republic*, March 4, 2006, B29.

32. Chris Hawley, "Hopis' Trek to Tell World about Water," *Arizona Republic*, March 2, 2006, B1.

33. Ibid., B2.

34. Ibid., B1.

35. See Martin Padget, "Hopi Film, the Indigenous Aesthetic and Environmental Justice: Victor Mesayesva Jr.'s *Paatuwaqatsi*—Water, Land and Life," *Journal of American Studies* 47, no. 2 (May 2013): 363–384.

36. Stan Bindell, "Hopi Ends 27 Year Reign as Cross Country State Champs," *Navajo-Hopi Observer*, November 14, 2017, https://www.nhonews.com/news/2017/nov/14/hopi-ends-27-year-reign-cross-country-state-champs/.

37. Mark Brown, "Northland Stops Hopi Boys' XC Title Run," *Arizona Republic*, November 5, 2017, 12C.

38. Wes Judd has written an excellent article on the many physical and mental benefits of running. He states in part: "You don't need all-promising pills, diet hacks, or hours of tedious (and dubious) brain games to look and feel younger. All it takes is doing that thing you love: running." See Wes Judd, "The Real Miracle Drug," *Runner's World*, January/February 2018, 66–72.

39. Hopi High School Cross Country Coach Rick Baker once remarked that "running isn't just about exercise in Hopi culture, we've been doing it for thousands of years. . . . I think we have kids that really want to run. Since we have this tradition of running, they all want to be part of it." See Rodney Harwood, "Running Wild: 5 Native Track Teams of Champions," *Indian Country Today*, May 23, 2015. https://indiancountrymedianetwork.com/culture/sports/running-wild-5-native-track-teams-of-champions/. Accessed September 23, 2017.

40. Branch, "Two Hopi Traditions: Running and Winning," B4.

41. Harves, *Run Hopi*.

APPENDIX A: LOUIS TEWANIMA, HOPI (1882–1969)

1. Matthew Sakiestewa Gilbert, "Marathoner Louis Tewanima and the Continuity of Hopi Running: 1908–1912"; *Western Historical Quarterly* 43 (Autumn 2012): 325–346; Copyright ©2012, Western History Association.

2. "History and Culture: Boarding Schools"; American Indian Relief Council.

3. Gilbert, "Marathoner Louis Tewanima and the Continuity of Hopi Running: 1908–1912."

APPENDIX B: "ARE MOQUI RUNNERS WORLD BEATERS?"

1. "Are Moqui Runners World Beaters?," *San Francisco Chronicle*, October 5, 1902, A3.

APPENDIX C: CARLISLE TOWN COUNCIL RESOLUTIONS

1. "Council Acts on Carlisle Triumph in the Olympiad," *Carlisle Evening Herald*, July 26, 1912, 1.

Bibliography

ARCHIVAL COLLECTIONS

Cline Library Special Collections, Northern Arizona University, Flagstaff, Arizona

Colorado Plateau Digital Archives, Northern Arizona University, Flagstaff, Arizona

History, Philosophy, and Newspaper Library, University of Illinois at Urbana-Champaign, Urbana, Illinois

Hopi Cultural Preservation Office Collections, The Hopi Tribe, Kykotsmovi, Arizona

Labriola Indian Data Center, Department of Archives and Special Collections, University Libraries, Arizona State University, Tempe, Arizona

Missouri Valley Special Collections, Kansas City, Missouri

National Archives and Records Administration (NARA), Washington, DC, Records of the Bureau of Indian Affairs, 1793–1989, Record Group 75. Carlisle School Files (CSF)

National Archives and Records Administration, Laguna Niguel, California

Sherman Indian High School Student Case Files (SIHSCF)

Sherman Indian Museum, Riverside, California

NEWSPAPERS AND PERIODICALS

Abilene Reporter-News
Albuquerque Journal
Albuquerque Morning Journal
Allentown (Pennsylvania) Democrat
Alta (Iowa) Advertiser
Amarillo Daily News
Anniston (Alabama) Star
Arizona Daily Star
Arizona Republican/Arizona Republic
Asbury Park (NJ) Evening Press
(Athens, Ohio) Messenger
Atlanta Constitution
Augusta (Georgia) Chronicle
Baltimore Sun
Belle Plaine (Iowa) News

Belleville (Kansas) Telescope

Binghamton Press

Bluefield (West Virginia) Daily Telegraph

Bolton Journal and Guardian

Boston Daily Globe

Boston Globe

Boston Journal

Boston Post

Brooklyn Daily Eagle

Capital Journal (Pierre, South Dakota)

Carlisle Arrow

Carlisle Evening Herald

(Carlisle) Red Man

Chicago Daily Defender

Chicago Daily Tribune

Chicago Tribune

Cincinnati Enquirer

Coconino Sun (Flagstaff, Arizona)

Coleman (Texas) Voice

Colfax (Louisiana) Chronicle

Colorado Springs Gazette

(Colorado Springs) Gazette-Telegraph

Columbus Journal

Courier-Journal (Louisville, Kentucky)

Courier-News

Crittenden Press

Daily Review

Des Moines Register

Deming (New Mexico) Headlight

Democrat and Chronicle (Rochester, New York)

Detroit Free Press

Eau Claire Leader

El Paso Herald

Evening Kansas-Republican

Evening Sentinel (Carlisle, Pennsylvania)

Evening Standard (Ogden, Utah)

Evening Star (Washington, DC)

Fort Lauderdale News

Gazette-Telegraph (Colorado Springs, Colorado)

Gallup (New Mexico) Independent

Greenville (South Carolina) News

(Harare) Rhodesia Herald
Hartford Courant
Honolulu Advertiser
Hopi Action News
Hopi Tutuveni (Kiiqòtsmovi, Arizona)
Hutchinson News
Indianapolis News
Indianapolis Star
Indian Country Today
Interstate Manufacturer
Iola (Kansas) Daily Register
Kansas City Times
Kerley News (Tuba City, Arizona)
Kingman Daily Miner
Klamath News
Lincoln Star Journal
London Sporting Life
(London) Times
Los Angeles Herald
Los Angeles Times
Messenger (Athens, Ohio)
Missionary Review of the World
Modesto Evening News
Mohave County Miner (Mineral Park, Arizona)
Monroe (Louisiana) News-Star
Morning Call
Morning (Portland) Oregonian
Morning Register (Eugene, Oregon)
Morning Sun (Pittsburg, Kansas)
Muskogee Phoenix
Nanaimo Daily News
Native American (Phoenix Indian School)
Navajo-Hopi Observer
New Castle (Pennsylvania) News
(New Orleans) Times-Picayune
News-Herald
New York American
(New York) Evening World
New York Sun
New York Times
New York Tribune

News-Journal (Mansfield, Ohio)
Oakland Tribune
Ogden (Utah) Standard-Examiner
Olathe (Kansas) Mirror
Ottawa Daily Republican (Ottawa, Kansas)
Petaluma (California) Argus
Philadelphia Inquirer
Philadelphia Times
Phillipsburg (Kansas) Herald
Phoenix Redskin
Pittsburgh Daily Post
Pittsburgh Post-Gazette
Plainfield (New Jersey) Courier-News
Plain Speaker (Hazleton, Pennsylvania)
Reading (Pennsylvania) Times
Rhodesia Herald (Harare, Zimbabwe)
(Sacramento) Record-Union
Salt Lake City Deseret Evening News
Salt Lake Telegram
Salt Lake Tribune
San Bernardino (California) County Sun
San Bernardino (California) Sun
San Francisco Call
San Francisco Chronicle
Santa Ana (California) Register
Santa Cruz Sentinel
Santa Fe New Mexican
Saturday Evening
Saturday Evening Mail
Sherman Bulletin
Spokane Press
Star-Gazette (Elmira, New York)
St. Louis Post-Dispatch
Tampa Times
Times-Picayune
Terre Haute Evening Gazette
Trenton Evening Times
Washington Post
Washington Star
Washington Sunday Herald

Washington Times
Wilmington Morning News
Winslow (Arizona) Daily Mail
Winslow (Arizona) Mail
Weekly Journal-Miner
Weekly Republican-Traveler (Arkansas City, Kansas)
Wyandott Herald (Kansas City, Kansas)
Yuma (Arizona) Examiner

BOOKS AND ARTICLES

Aarons, Leroy F. "Destroying the Land." *Capital Journal*, June 25, 1971, 23. Issued by the *Los Angeles Times-Washington Post* Service.

Abshire, Danny, with Brian Metzler. *Natural Running: The Single Path to Stronger, Healthier Running.* Boulder, CO: VeloPress, 2010.

Adams, Amy G. "The Hopi Indian Runner." *Carlisle Arrow* 8, no. 40 (June 14, 1912): 3.

Adams, David Wallace. *Education for Extinction: American Indians and the Boarding School Experience, 1875–1928.* Lawrence: University Press of Kansas, 1995.

———. "More Than a Game: The Carlisle Indians Take to the Gridiron, 1893–1917." *Western Historical Quarterly* 32 (Spring 2001): 25–53.

Adams, E. Charles. *Homolo'vi: An Ancient Hopi Settlement Cluster.* Tucson: University of Arizona Press, 2002.

Anderson, James D. *The Education of Blacks in the South, 1860–1935.* Chapel Hill: University of North Carolina Press, 1988.

Anderson, Lars. *Carlisle vs. Army: Jim Thorpe, Dwight Eisenhower, Pop Warner, and the Forgotten Story of Football's Greatest Battle.* New York: Random House, 2008.

Angus, Howard W. "Philip Zeyouma Will Run Again." *Los Angeles Times*, December 25, 1914, III1.

Azuma, Eiichiro. *Between Two Empires: Race, History, and Transnationalism in Japanese America.* New York: Oxford University Press, 2005.

Bahr, Diana Meyers. *The Students of Sherman Indian School: Education and Native Identity Since 1892.* Norman: University of Oklahoma Press, 2014.

Baker, Rick. "Native American Runners." www.ncacoach.org/uploads/Baker1.pdf.

Bakken, Gordon M., and Alexandra Kindell, eds. *Encyclopedia of Immigration and Migration in the American West*, vol 1. Thousand Oaks, CA: Sage Publications, 2006.

Bale, John. "Kenyan Running before the 1968 Olympics." In *East African Running: Towards a Cross-Disciplinary Perspective*, ed. Yannis Pitsiladis, John Bale, Craig Sharp, and Timothy Noakes, 11–23. New York: Routledge, 2007.

Behm, C. A. "Stood Guard over Brigham with Major Powell in Grand Canyon." *Weekly Journal-Miner*, April 22, 1903, 2.

————. "Exploring with Powell." *Weekly Journal-Miner*, May 6, 1903, 3.

Berman, LeRoy. "Jim Thorpe's Teammate 'Doing Well' at Shongopavi.'" *Albuquerque Journal*, November 8, 1968, 34.

Bindell, Stan. "Hopi Ends 27 Year Reign as Cross Country State Champs." *Navajo -Hopi Observer*, November 14, 2017, https://www.nhonews.com/news/2017/nov /14/hopi-ends-27-year-reign-cross-country-state-champs/.

Bird, Owen R. "Many Entrants Received for Big Marathon," *Los Angeles Times*, March 10, 1912, 10.

————. "Starting the Big Marathon." *Los Angeles Times*, April 15, 1912, 19.

————. "The Marathon Starts Tomorrow." *Los Angeles Times*, April 19, 1912, Section 3, 1.

Bloom, John. *To Show What an Indian Can Do: Sports at Native American Boarding Schools*. Minneapolis: University of Minnesota Press, 2000.

Boyd, Wm. H. *Boyd's Directory of the District of Columbia*. Washington, DC: John Polhemus, 1881.

Boyle, Hal. "The Globe and Guys." *Santa Cruz Sentinel*, October 14, 1954, 19.

————. "Gotham's Tall Tepees Leave Tewanima Cold." *Star-Gazette*, October 14, 1954, 21.

Bradsby, Henry C. *History of Vigo County, Indiana with Biographical Selections*. Durham, NC: S. B. Nelson, 1891.

Branch, John. "Enduring Tradition." *New York Times*, November 5, 2015, B13.

————. "Two Hopi Traditions: Running and Winning." *Santa Fe New Mexican*. November 9, 2015, B4. Originally published in the *New York Times*. https://www .nytimes.com/2015/11/05/sports/hopi-high-school-cross-country-running .html.

Broder, Patricia Janis. *Shadows on the Glass: The Indian World of Ben Wittick*. Savage, MD: Rowman & Littlefield, 1990.

Brooks, James F. *Mesa of Sorrows: A History of the Awat'ovi Massacre* (New York: W. W. Norton, 2016), 126–141.

Brown, Toyacoyah. "4 Native Runners Finish Boston Marathon," *Powwows.com*, April 27, 2015, www.powwows.com/4-native-runners-finish-boston-mara thon/.

Bryant, John. *The Marathon Makers*. London: John Blake, 2008.

Burfoot, Amby. *The Runner's Guide to the Meaning of Life*. New York: Skyhorse Publishing, 2011.

Burich, Keith R. *The Thomas Indian School and the "Irredeemable" Children of New York*. Syracuse, NY: Syracuse University Press, 2016.

C, B. L. "The Indian as an Athlete." *Reading Times*, January 8, 1910, 5.

Callahan, Ralph W. "Morning Musing." *Anniston (Alabama) Star*, May 22, 1931, 14.

Canaday, Sage. "Scratch New Surfaces." *Runner's World*, May 2018, 9–11.

Carter, Caleb. "How the Nez Perces Trained for Long Distance Running, 1911." In

Recovering Native American Writings in the Boarding School Press, ed. Jacqueline Emery, 104–106. Lincoln: University of Nebraska Press, 2017.

Child, Brenda J., and Brian Klopotek. "Introduction: Comparing Histories of Education for Indigenous Peoples." In *Indian Subjects: Hemispheric Perspectives on the History of Indigenous Education*, ed. Brenda J. Child and Brian Klopotek, 1–15. Santa Fe, NM: School for Advanced Research Press, 2014.

Clark, E. S. "Report on the Moqui Pueblos of Arizona." In *Extra Census Bulletin: Moqui Pueblo Indians of Arizona and Pueblo Indians of New Mexico*, ed. Thomas Donaldson, 51–68. Washington, DC: US Printing Office, 1893, 50.

Clemmer, Richard O. *Roads in the Sky: The Hopi Indians in a Century of Change.* New York: Routledge, 1995.

Clover, Samuel Travers. *On Special Assignment: Being the Further Adventures of Paul Travers; Showing How He Succeeded as a Newspaper Reporter.* Boston: Lothrop Publishing, 1903.

Coleman, Michael. *American Indians, the Irish, and Government Schooling.* Lincoln: University of Nebraska Press, 2009.

Collier, Brian S. "'To Bring Honor to My Village': Steve Gachupin and the Community Ceremony of Jemez Running in the Pike's Peak Marathon." *Journal of the West* 46, no. 7 (2007): 62–71.

Collins, Mabel W. "Curious Customs of the Moqui Indians." *Democrat and Chronicle*, April 29, 1900, 13.

Cooper, Pamela. *The American Marathon.* Syracuse, NY: Syracuse University Press, 1998.

Courlander, Harold. *People of the Short Blue Corn: Tales and Legends of the Hopi Indians.* New York: Harcourt Brace Jovanovich, 1970.

———. *Hopi Voices: Recollections, Traditions, and Narratives of the Hopi Indians.* Albuquerque: University of New Mexico Press, 1982.

Coward, John. *The Newspaper Indian: Native American Identity in the Press, 1820–1890.* Urbana: University of Illinois Press, 1999.

Crawford, Bill. *All American: The Rise and Fall of Jim Thorpe* Hoboken, NJ: John Wiley & Sons, 2004.

Cresswell, Julia, ed. *Little Oxford Dictionary of Word Origins.* New York: Oxford University Press, 2014.

Davis, Carolyn O'Bagy. *Hopi Summer: Letters from Ethel to Maud.* Tucson, AZ: Rio Nuevo Press, 2007.

Dee, Crystal. "Hopi Runner Sekaquaptewa Sets Sights on Boston Marathon." *Hopi Tutuveni*, February 18, 2015, 5.

———. "Hopi High School Boys Win 26th Consecutive State Cross Country Championship Title." *Hopi Tutuveni*, November 17, 2015, 1.

Diaz, Vicente M. "Voyaging for Anti-Colonial Recovery: Austronesian Seafaring, Archipelagic Rethinking, and the Re-mapping of Indigeneity." *Pacific Asia Inquiry* 2, no. 1 (Fall 2011): 21, 26–27.

Dixon, Joseph K. *The Vanishing Race: The Last Great Indian Council and the Indian's Story of the Custer Fight.* Glorieta, NM: Kessinger Publishing, 1973.

Deloria, Philip J. *Indians in Unexpected Places.* Lawrence: University Press of Kansas, 2004.

Deloria, Vine, Jr. *The World We Used to Live In.* Golden, CO: Fulcrum Publishing, 2006, 135.

Dennis, Wayne. *The Hopi Child.* New York: John Wiley & Sons, 1965.

Derderian, Tom. *Boston Marathon: The History of the World's Premier Running Event.* Champaign, IL: Human Kinetics Publishers, 1994.

Detweiler, Meade D. *An Account of the Origin and Early History of the Benevolent Protective Order of Elks of the U.S.A.* Harrisburg, PA: Harrisburg Publishing, 1898.

Dilworth, Leah. "Representing the Hopi Snake Dance." *Journal for the Anthropological Study of Human Movement* 11, no. 4, and 12, no. 1 (Fall 2001/Spring 2002): 453–496.

Dixon, Joseph K. *The Vanishing Race: The Last Great Indian Council.* Glorieta, NM: Rio Grande Press, 1973.

Donaldson, Thomas. *Extra Census Bulletin: Moqui Pueblo Indians of Arizona and Pueblo Indians of New Mexico.* Washington, DC: US Printing Office, 1893.

Dyer, Braven. "Nurmi Thrills 45,000 Track Fans." *Los Angeles Times,* April 26, 1925, 47.

———. "Carter Conger May Run Again." *Los Angeles Times,* May 6, 1929, 11.

———. "Chauca Wins 'Times' Marathon Race.'" *Los Angeles Times,* June 16, 1929, A1.

Dyreson, Mark S. *Making the American Team: Sport, Culture, and the Olympic Experience.* Urbana: University of Illinois Press, 1998.

———. "The Foot Runners Conquer Mexico and Texas: Endurance Racing, Indigenismo, and Nationalism," *Journal of Sport History* 31, no. 1 (Spring 2004): 1–31.

Eaton, Jerry. "Hopi Runners Please Cordes." *Arizona Republic,* April 5, 1959, Section 3, 2.

Edgren, Robert. "Mexican Youths May Be World's Best Athletes." *El Paso Herald,* November 9, 1921, 6.

———. "Deerfoots on Cinder Path; Through Camera's Eyes." *El Paso Herald,* November 21, 1921, 6.

———. "Remarkable Endurance of Famous Finn Surprising." *Salt Lake Telegram,* January 18, 1925, 6.

———. "Finns May Find Indians Swift." *Baltimore Sun,* May 23, 1927, 16.

Eisen, George, and David K. Wiggins. *Ethnicity and Sport in North American History and Culture.* Westport, CT: Praeger, 1995.

Evers, Larry, ed. *The South Corner of Time.* Tucson, AZ: Sun Tracks, 1980.

Eyestone, Ed. "6 Rules to Determine How Many Miles a Week to Run." *Runner's World* (July 5, 2016): 228–229.

Farmer, Jared. *On Zion's Mount: Mormons, Indians, and the American Landscape.* Cambridge, MA: Harvard University Press, 2010.

Fear-Segal, Jacqueline. *White Man's Club: Schools, Race, and the Struggle of Indian Acculturation.* Lincoln: University of Nebraska Press, 2007.

Fewkes, J. Walter. "The Wa-Wac-Ka-Tci-Na, a Tusayan Foot Race." *Bulletin of the Essex Institute* 24 (1892): 113–133.

Field, Bryan. "Blistered Feet Force Hopi Indians to Turn Down 3 More Marathons." *New York Times*, May 18, 1927, 22.

———. "Boston A.A. Run on Thursday to Be First of Series of Marathon Tests." *New York Times*, April 15, 1928, 164.

Finn, Adharanand. *The Way of the Runner: A Journey into the Fabled World of Japanese Running.* New York: Pegasus Books, 2015.

Fiore, Roberta, Carole Shahda, and Dave Roochvarg. *Long Beach.* Images of America Series. Mount Pleasant, SC: Arcadia Publishing, 2010.

Fitzgerald, Matt. *Run: The Mind-Body Method of Running by Feel* (Boulder, CO: VeloPress, 2010).

Fixico, Donald L. *"That's What They Used To Say": Reflections on American Indian Oral Traditions.* Norman: University of Oklahoma Press, 2017.

Fixx, James F. *The Complete Book of Running* (New York: Random House, 1977).

Fogelberg, Ben. "Sal Halyve, Forgotten Hopi Marathon Champion." *Colorado Heritage* 26, no. 4 (2006): 36–47.

Frank, LaFrenda. "Hopi Runner, Juwan Nuvayokva Signs with Saucony." *Navajo-Hopi Observer*, March 17, 2009. www.nhonews.com/news/2009/mar/17/hopi-runner-juwan-nuvayokva-signs-with-saucony/. Accessed September 24, 2017.

Frauenheim, Norm. "Basket Dance Race Revives Hopi Desire to Run." *Arizona Republic*, May 27, 1979, 27, D5.

———. "Hopi Legend." *Arizona Republic*, May 27, 1979, 23, D1.

———. "Legends of the Land Are Long-Running." *Arizona Republic*, June 16, 1991, D1, D11.

———. "Lewis Tewanima: Running for a Reason, Hopi Legend's Rain Cloud Had Silver Lining." *Arizona Republic*, December 1999, C3.

Freeman, William H. *Physical Education, Exercise, and Sport Science in a Changing Society*, 8th ed. Burlington, MA: Jones and Bartlett Learning, 2013.

Furber, Henry J., Jr. "A New Era for Athletics." *Crittenden Press*, February 27, 1902, 6.

Garcia, Sharon. "Indian Forerunner." *Santa Fe New Mexican*, August 3, 1980, 15.

Gems, Gerald R. *The Athletic Crusade: Sports and American Imperialism.* Lincoln: University of Nebraska Press, 2006.

Genetin-Pilawa, Joseph. *Crooked Paths to Allotment: The Fight over Federal Indian Policy after the Civil War.* Chapel Hill: University of North Carolina Press, 2014.

Gianelli, Frank. "Happy Hopi Lends Hand." *Arizona Republic*, June 27, 1964, 52.

Gotaas, Thor. *Running: A Global History*. London: Reaktion Books, 2009.

Gram, John R. *Education at the Edge of Empire: Negotiating Pueblo Identity in New Mexico's Indian Boarding Schools*. Seattle: University of Washington Press, 2015.

Guttmann, Allen. *From Ritual to Record*. New York: Columbia University Press, 1978.

Guttmann, Allen, and Lee Thompson. *Japanese Sports: A History*. Honolulu: University of Hawai'i Press, 2001.

Guy, George H. "Mastering the Moqui." *Los Angeles Times*, January 27, 1895, Part 2, 17.

Hammond, George. "Snake Dance to Lure Many Motorists to Hopiland during Month of August." *Arizona Republic*, August 1, 1926, 22.

Harjo, Suzan Shown. "Fighting Name-Calling: Challenging 'Redskin' in Court." In *Team Spirits: The Native American Mascot Controversy*, ed. C. Richard King and Charles Fruehling, 189–207. Lincoln: University of Nebraska Press, 2001.

"Harry M'Lean for Celebration Races." *Arizona Republican*, September 18, 1911.

Harvey, Byron S., III. *Ritual in Pueblo Art: Hopi Life in Hopi Painting*. New York: Museum of the American Indian, 1970.

Harvie, Robin. *The Lure of Long Distances*. New York: Perseus Books Group, 2011.

Harwood, Rodney. "Running Wild: 5 Native Track Teams of Champions." Indian Country Today, May 23, 2015. www.indiancountrymedianetwork.com /culture/sports/running-wild-5-native-track-teams-of-champions/. Accessed September 23, 2017.

———. "Hopi High School Cross-Country Team Carrying on Proud Tradition." *Indian Country Today*, January 16, 2016. www.indiancountrymedianetwork.com /culture/sports/hopi-high-school-cross-country-team-carrying-on-proud -tradition/. Accessed August 14, 2017.

Haslam, Oliver H. "Amongst the Indians in Arizona." *Bolton Journal and Guardian* (May 10, 1907): 5, 6.

Hawley, Chris. "Hopis' Trek to Tell World about Water." *Arizona Republic*, March 2, 2006, B1, B2.

Haynes, Henry W. "Early Explorations of New Mexico." In *Spanish Exploration and Settlements in America from the Fifteenth Century*, vol. 2, ed. Justin Winsor, 473–497. Boston: Houghton Mifflin, 1886.

Heinrich, Bernd. *Why We Run: A Natural History*. New York: HarperCollins Publishers, 2001.

Heitmann, John. *The Automobile and American Life*. Jefferson, NC: McFarland, 2009.

Hermequaftewa, Alfred. *The Hopi Way Is the Way of Peace*. Santa Fe, NM: Friendship Press, 1953.

Hill, Kenneth C., Emory Sekaquaptewa, and Mary E. Black, eds. *Hopi Dictionary Hopìikwa Lavàytutuveni: A Hopi-English Dictionary of the Third Mesa Dialect*. Tucson: University of Arizona Press, 1998.

Hinckley, Jim. *Backroads of Arizona: Your Guide to Arizona's Most Scenic Backroad Adventures*. St. Paul, MN: Voyageur Press, 2006.

Hokowhitu, Brendan. "Tracking Māori Masculinity: A Colonial Genealogy of Savagery and Sport." *Contemporary Pacific* 16 (Fall 2004): 259–284.

Holliday, Wendy. "Hopi Prisoners on the Rock." https://www.nps.gov/alca/learn/historyculture/hopi-prisoners-on-the-rock.htm.

Honahnie, Daniel. "After 1000 Years Hopi We Stand: An Overview of Hopi History." In *Hopihiniwtipu: Significant Events for Hopi People*, ed. Anita Poleahla and Kristin Harned, 121–124. Polacca, AZ: Mesa Media, 2012.

Hough, Walter. *The Moke Snake Dance*. Chicago: Passenger Department, Santa Fe, 1901.

———. *The Hopi Indians*. Cedar Rapids, IA: Torch Press, 1915.

———. "Biographical Memoir of Jesse Walter Fewkes, 1850–1930." In *National Academy of Sciences of the United States of America: Biographical Memoirs, Volume 15—Ninth Memoir*. Washington, DC: National Academy of Sciences, 1932.

Howell, John. *The Life and Adventures of Alexander Selkirk*. Charleston, SC: Bibliolife, 2009. Originally published in 1829.

Howes, Harry Bartow. *History of Missouri: A Compendium of History and Bibliography for Ready Reference*, vol. 3. New York: Southern History Company, 2006.

Hoxie, Frederick E. *Parading through History: The Making of the Crow Nation in America, 1805–1935*. New York: Cambridge University Press, 1995.

——— ed. *Talking Back to Civilization: Indian Voices from the Progressive Era*. Boston: Bedford, 2001.

Hutson, Ralph. "Suhu Wins Marathon." *Los Angeles Times*, June 25, 1932, 7.

Imada, Adria L. *Aloha America: Hula Circuits through the U.S. Empire*. Durham, NC: Duke University Press, 2012.

Irvine, Heather Mayer. "How I Broke Twenty Minutes in the 5K (and Why I Wanted To)." *Runner's World*, May 30, 2017, https://www.runnersworld.com/5k/how-i-broke-20-minutes-in-the-5k-and-why-i-wanted-to.

Iverson, Peter. "The Enduring Hopi." In *Hopi Nation: Essays on Indigenous Art, Culture, History, and Law*, ed. John R. Wunder, 144–154. Lincoln: Digital Commons, University of Nebraska–Lincoln, 2008.

Jacobs, Margaret D. "A Battle for the Children: American Indian Child Removal in Arizona in the Era of Assimilation." *Journal of Arizona History* 45 (2004): 31–62.

James, George Wharton. "Are Cruel Savages: The Seri Indians and Their Pacific Island Home. Physically They Are Superiors of All Other American Aborigines—Unequaled as Hunters and Runners." *Phillipsburg (Kansas) Herald*, February 8, 1900, 6.

———. "The Indian and the Artist." *Belle Plaine News*. January 29, 1903, 3.

James, Harold L. "The History of Fort Wingate." In *Guidebook of Defiance-Zuni-Mt. Taylor Region Arizona and New Mexico*. Albuquerque: New Mexico Geological Society, Eighteenth Field Conference, 1967.

James, Harry C. *Pages from Hopi History.* Tucson: University of Arizona Press, 1994.

Jenkins, Sally. *The Real All Americans: The Team That Changed a Game, a People, a Nation.* New York: Doubleday, 2007.

Judd, Neil M. "Walter Hough: An Appreciation." *American Anthropologist* 38, no. 3 (1938): 471–481.

Judd, Wes. "The Real Miracle Drug." *Runner's World,* January/February, 2018, 66–72.

Kalo, Mario. "Hopi High Wins 26th Consecutive Cross-Country State Title." *ArizonaCentral Sports,* August 14, 2017. www.azcentral.com/story/sports/high -school/2015/11/07/hopi-high-wins-26th-consecutive.cross-country-state -title/75171818/. Accessed August 14, 2017.

Kastner, Charles B. *Bunion Derby: The 1928 Footrace across America.* Albuquerque: University of New Mexico Press, 2007.

Katovsky, Bill. *Tread Lightly: Form, Footwear, and the Quest for Injury-Free Running* (New York: Skyhorse Publishing, 2012).

Kawamura, Yuniya. *Sneakers: Fashion, Gender, and Subculture.* New York: Bloomsbury, 2016.

Kieran, John. "Sports of Our Times." *New York Times,* May 13, 1927, 21.

King, C. Richard, ed. *Native Athletes in Sport and Society.* Lincoln: University of Nebraska Press, 2005.

———. *Native Americans and Sport in North America: Other People's Games.* New York: Routledge, 2014.

King, C. Richard, and Charles Fruehling, eds. *Team Spirits: The Native American Mascot Controversy.* Lincoln: University of Nebraska Press, 2001.

Koenenn, Connie. "New Hopi Chairman Tries to Bridge Two Worlds." *Albuquerque Journal,* June 16, 1994, C3.

Kroupa, Susan. "At Age 58, Cooka Hasn't Allowed Life to Run Him Down." *Arizona Republic,* October 13, 1988, E8.

Kuwanwisiwma, Leigh J. "Why Were Hopi Men Sent to Alcatraz Prison?" In Anita Poleahla and Kristin Harned, eds., *Hopihiniwtipu: Significant Events for Hopi People.* Polacca, AZ: Mesa Media, 2012.

———. "The Collaborative Road: A Personal History of the Hopi Cultural Preservation Office." In *Footprints of Hopi History: Hopihiniwtiput Kukveníat,* ed. Leigh J. Kuwanwisiwma, T. J. Ferguson, and Chip Colwell, 3–15. Tucson: University of Arizona Press, 2018.

Larson, Robert W. *Red Cloud: Warrior-Statesman of the Lakota Sioux.* Norman: University of Oklahoma Press, 1997.

Lewis, Leland C. "Runners in Hopi Indian Country." *Daily Republican,* March 19, 1928, 3.

Loughlin, Caroline, and Catherine Anderson. *Forest Park.* St. Louis: Junior League of St. Louis and University of Missouri Press, 1986.

Lummis, Charles F. *Bullying the Moqui.* Prescott, AZ: Prescott College Press, 1968.

Lutz, Richard L., and Mary Lutz. *The Running Indians: The Tarahumara of Mexico.* Salem, OR: Dimi Press, 1989.

Lyons, Patrick D. *Ancestral Hopi Migrations.* Tucson: University of Arizona Press, 2003.

Lyons, Scott Richard. "Migrations to Modernity: The Many Voices of George Copway's Running Sketches of Men and Places, in England, France, Germany, Belgium, and Scotland." In *The World, the Text, and the Indian: Global Dimensions of Native American Literature,* ed. Scott Richard Lyons, 143–182. Albany: State University of New York Press, 2017.

MacMillan, Archie. "De Mar, Marvel of Marathon Meets, Hopes to Capture Olympic Crown." *Abilene Reporter-News,* August 7, 1927, 38.

Mallon, Bill. "Louis Tewanima." In *Native Americans in Sports,* vol. 2, ed. C. Richard King, 296. Armonk, NY: Sharpe Reference, 2004.

Mallon, Bill, and Ian Buchanan. *The 1908 Olympic Games: Results for All Competitors in All Events, with Commentary.* Jefferson, NC: McFarland, 2000.

Mallon, Bill, and Ture Widlund. *The 1912 Olympic Games: Results for All Competitors in All Events, with Commentary.* Jefferson, NC: McFarland, 2002.

Malotki, Ekkehart, and Ken Gary. *Hopi Stories of Witchcraft, Shamanism, and Magic.* Lincoln: University of Nebraska Press, 2010.

Masayesva, Victor, Jr. *Husk of Time: The Photographs of Victor Masayesva.* Tucson: University of Arizona Press, 2006.

Masayesva, Victor, Jr., and Erin Younger, eds. *Hopi Photographers: Hopi Images.* Tucson: Sun Tracks & University of Arizona Press, 1983.

McArdle, William D., Frank I. Katch, and Victor L. Katch. *Essentials of Exercise and Physiology.* Baltimore, MD: Lippincott Williams & Wilkins, 2006.

McCarty, Teresa L., and Sheilah E. Nicholas. "Indigenous Education: Local and Global Perspectives." In Marilyn Martin-Jones, Adrian Blackledge, and Angela Creese, *The Routledge Handbook of Multilingualism.* New York: Routledge, 2012, 145–166.

McChesney, Lea S. "On the Road with the Melvilles." In *Hopis, Tewas, and the American Road,* ed. Willard Walker and Lydia L. Wyckoff, 15–27. Middleton, CT: Wesleyan University, 1983.

McDougall, Christopher. *Born to Run: A Hidden Tribe, Superathletes, and the Greatest Race the World Has Never Seen.* New York: Vintage, 2009.

McDowell, Edwin. "Famous Hopi Runner Louis Tewanima, Olympic Medal Winner, 'Doing Fine.'" *Arizona Republic,* September 8, 1968, 6.

McNickle, D'Arcy. *Runner in the Sun,* illus. by Allan Houser, 3rd printing. New York: Holt, Rinehart and Winston, 1962.

Medina, William Oscar. "Selling Indians at Sherman Institute." Ph.D. diss., University of California, Riverside, 2007.

Momaday, N. Scott. *House Made of Dawn.* New York: Harper Perennial, 2010.

Moorehead, Warren King. *The American Indian in the United States, Period 1850–1914*. Andover, MA: Andover Press, 1914.

Moran, Relman. "The Start, the Finish, and the Winner of the First Pre-Olympic Marathon." *Los Angeles Times*, June 16, 1929, A1.

Moses, L. G. *Wild West Shows and the Images of American Indians, 1883–1933*. Albuquerque: University of New Mexico Press, 1999.

Murray, Arthur, and Wesley Merritt. *Instructions for Courts-Martial*. Saint Paul, MN: Headquarters Department of Dakota, 1891.

Myrick, David. F. *Railroads of Nevada and Eastern California*. Berkeley, CA: Howell-North Books, 1963.

Nabokov, Peter. *Indian Running: Native American History and Tradition*. Santa Fe: Ancient City Press, 1981.

Nash, Casey Aaron. *The Olympic Glory of Jesse Owens: A Contribution to Civil Rights and Society*. Master's thesis. East Tennessee State University, 2012.

Nelson, David M. *The Anatomy of a Game: Football, the Rules, and the Men Who Made the Game*. Newark: University of Delaware Press.

Nequatewa, Edmund. *Truth of a Hopi: Stories Relating to the Origin, Myths and Clan Histories of the Hopi*. Flagstaff, AZ: Northland Press, 1994.

Newcombe, Jack. *The Best of the Athletic Boys: The White Man's Impact on Jim Thorpe*. Garden City, NY: Doubleday, 1975.

Newland, Russell J. "Quomawahu, Hopi Indian, Not to Enter Marathon." *Arizona Daily Star*, June 12, 1928, 5. Issued by the Associated Press.

Nicholas, Stewart. *Hopi Tutuveni*, August 31, 2006, 3.

Nylander, J. H. "The Hopi," *Kerley News*, Kerley Trading Post, Tuba City, AZ, July 6, 1936, 2, 10. In *A. F. Whiting Ethnographic Notes and Papers, Hopi 34, History 2*, ed. P. David Seaman, 196–217. June 1988, Northern Arizona University Cline Library Special Collections, Flagstaff, AZ.

O'Shaughnessy, Christine Forshaw. "Joseph Forshaw, Marathon Runner." *Journal of Olympic History* 12 (May 2004): 10–19.

Oxendine, Joseph B. *American Indian Sport Heritage*. Lincoln: University of Nebraska Press, 1995.

Padget, Martin. "Hopi Film, the Indigenous Aesthetic and Environmental Justice: Victor Masayesva Jr.'s *Paatuwaqatsi*—Water, Land and Life." *Journal of American Studies* 47, no 2 (May 2013): 363–384.

Parezo, Nancy J., and Don D. Fowler. *Anthropology Goes to the Fair: The 1904 Louisiana Purchase Exposition*. Lincoln: University of Nebraska Press, 2007.

Pitsiladis, Yannis, John Bale, Craig Sharp, and Timothy Noakes, eds. *East African Running: Towards a Cross-Disciplinary Perspective*. New York: Routledge, 2007.

Plymire, Darcy C. "The Legend of the Tarahumara: Tourism, Overcivilization and the White Man's Indian." In *Native Americans and Sport in North America: Other People's Games*, ed. C. Richard King, 17–29. New York: Routledge, 2014.

Pope, Steven W. *Patriotic Games: Sporting Traditions in the American Imagination, 1876–1926.* Knoxville: University of Tennessee Press, 2007.

Porter, Robert P. *Report on Indians Taxed and Indians Not Taxed in the United States (Except Alaska) at the Eleventh Census, 1890.* Washington, DC: US Census Printing Office, 1894.

Powell, Clement. "The Powell Expedition." *Chicago Tribune,* February 23, 1873, 2.

Powell, John Wesley. *The Exploration of the Colorado River and Its Canyons.* New York: Dover Publications, 1961.

Powers, James S. "Hopi Indian Now Leading Bunion Derby." *Atlanta Constitution,* March 7, 1928.

———. "Racers Reach Bagdad under Blazing Sun." *Arizona Republican,* March 10, 1928, 11.

———. "Arthur Newton Has Good Lead in Bunion Derby." *News-Herald,* March 12, 1928, 10.

———. "Rhodesian Leads in Pyle's Race." *Courier-News,* March 13, 1928, 21.

Qoyawayma, Polingaysi, as told to Vada F. Carlson. *No Turning Back: A Hopi Indian Woman's Struggle to Live in Two Worlds,* 9th printing. Albuquerque: University of New Mexico Press, 1996.

Reyhner, Jon, and Jeanne Eder. *American Indian Education: A History,* 2nd edition. Norman: University of Oklahoma Press, 2017.

Reynolds, Charles B. *The Standard Guide, Washington: A Handbook.* Washington, DC: Foster & Reynolds, 1898.

Rios, Juan. "Message Run." *Santa Fe New Mexican,* August 6, 1980, 1.

Robinson, C. M., III, ed. *The Diaries of John Gregory Bourke, Volume 5.* Denton: University of North Texas Press, 2013.

Robinson, Roger. *Running in Literature: A Guide for Scholars, Readers, Runners, Joggers, and Dreamers.* Halcottsville, NY: Breakaway Books, 2003.

Roche, Frank. "Redskins Go on Running Path." *Los Angeles Times,* May 3, 1931, F3.

Roosevelt, Theodore. "The Hopi Snake Dance." *Outlook* 105 (October 1913): 364–373.

Roznowski, Tom. *An American Hometown: Terre Haute, Indiana 1927.* Beverly, MA: Quarry Books, 2009.

Runyon, Damon. "Runyon Says." *Evening News,* January 13, 1927, 19.

Russell, George. *The Olympic Century: IX Olympiad, Amsterdam, Netherlands, from May 17, 1928 to August 12, 1928.* Warwick, NY: Warwick Press, 2015.

Sakiestewa Gilbert, Matthew. *Education beyond the Mesas: Hopi Students at Sherman Institute, 1902–1929.* Lincoln: University of Nebraska Press, 2010.

———. "Hopi Footraces and American Marathons, 1912–1930." *American Quarterly* 62, no. 1 (March 2010): 77–101.

———. "Marathoner Louis Tewanima and the Continuity of Hopi Running, 1908–1912." *Western Historical Quarterly* 43, no. 3 (Autumn 2012): 324–346.

_____. "A New Foreword to the Second Edition." In Don C. Talayesva, *Sun Chief: The Autobiography of a Hopi Indian*. New Haven, CT: Yale University Press, 2013, x–xv.

_____. "A Second Wave of Hopi Migration." *History of Education Quarterly* 54, 3 (August 2014): 356–361.

Schwilling, Lyle. "Indian Runs Mile in 4:22.8." *Evening Republican* (Columbus, Indiana). May 7, 1957, 10.

Scott, Danny W., and William H. Miller. *Equine: Dermatology*, 2nd ed. Philadelphia: Saunders, 2010.

Scott, Julian. "Report on the Moqui Pueblos of Arizona." In *Extra Census Bulletin: Moqui Pueblo Indians of Arizona and Pueblo Indians of New Mexico*, ed. Thomas Donaldson, 60. Washington, DC: US Printing Office, 1893.

Seaman, P. David, ed. *A. F. Whiting Ethnographic Notes and Papers*, Hopi 34, History 2, June 1988, Northern Arizona University Cline Library Special Collections, Flagstaff, AZ, 1–240.

Sekaquaptewa, Emory. "One More Smile for a Hopi Clown." In *The South Corner of Time: Hopi, Navajo, Papago, Yaqui Tribal Literature*, ed. Larry Evers, 14–17. Tucson: University of Arizona Press, 1980.

Sheehan, George. "Running." In *Runners on Running: The Best Nonfiction of Distance Running*, ed. Rich Elliot, 7–8. Champaign, IL: Human Kinetics, 2011.

Sheridan, Thomas E. *Arizona: A History*. Tucson: University of Arizona Press, 1995.

_____. *Empire of Sand: The Seri Indians and the Struggle for Spanish Sonora, 1645–1803*. Tucson: University of Arizona Press, 2016.

Sheridan, Thomas E., Stewart B. Koyiyumptewa, Anton Daughters, Dale S. Brenneman, T. J. Ferguson, Leigh J. Kuwanwisiwma, and Lee Wayne Lomayestewa. *Moquis and Kastiilam: Hopis, Spaniards, and the Trauma of History, Volume 1, 1540–1679*. Tucson: University of Arizona Press, 2015.

Silvius, Ray. "Aged Hopi Runner Enters New Era." *Arizona Republic*, October 10, 1954, Section 4, 3.

Simon, Bryant. *Boardwalk of Dreams: Atlantic City and the Fate of Urban America*. New York: Oxford University Press, 2004.

Simpson, Ruth DeEtte. *The Hopi Indians*, 3rd ed. Los Angeles: Southwest Museum, 1971.

Skinner, John E. "An Historical Review of the Fish and Wildlife Resources of the San Francisco Bay." Water Project Branch Report No. 1. Sacramento, CA: Department of Fish and Game, June 1962, 23–55.

Slivka, Judd. "Hopi Runners Deliver Plea on Aquifer." *Arizona Republic*, August 15, 2001, B4.

Smith, Bert C. "Red, White, Black Lads Mix in Dressing-Room." *Los Angeles Times*, April 20, 1913, Part 7, 10.

Smith, Watson. *Kiva Mural Decorations at Awatovi and Kawaika-a: With a Survey of Other*

Wall Paintings in the Pueblo Southwest. Cambridge, MA: Peabody Museum Press, 2006.

Spicer, Edward Holland. *Cycles of Conquest: The Impact of Spain, Mexico, and the United States on the Indians of the Southwest, 1533–1960.* Tucson, Arizona: University of Arizona Press, 1976.

"Sport." *Nanaimo Daily News,* April 30, 1907.

Stephen, Alexander M. *Hopi Journal,* 2 vols. Mansfield Centre, CT: Martino Publishing, 2005.

Steward, Julian H. "Notes on Hopi Ceremonies in the Initiatory Form in 1927–1928." *American Anthropologist* 33, 1 (March 1931): 56–79.

———. *Theory of Culture Change: The Methodology of Multilinear Evolution.* Urbana: University of Illinois Press, 1955.

Stoler, Ann, ed. *Haunted by Empire: Geographies of Intimacy in North American History.* Durham, NC: Duke University Press, 2006.

Strout, Erin. "The 6 Reasons You Need to Do Speedwork." *Runner's World,* June 29, 2017.

Sullivan, James E., ed. *Olympic Games: Stockholm 1912.* New York: American Sports Publishing, 1912.

Talayesva, Don C. *Sun Chief: The Autobiography of a Hopi Indian,* 2nd ed. New Haven, CT: Yale University Press, 2013.

Taylor, Aron, and David Taylor. "XC Legacy Big-15 National Rankings." www.ut .milesplit.us/articles/24444. Accessed August 15, 2017.

Thayer, Lee L. "The Hopi Indians and Their Religion." *Missionary Review of the World,* July 1917, 509.

Thayer, Marjorie, and Elizabeth Emanuel. *Climbing Sun: The Story of a Hopi Indian Boy.* New York: Dodd, Mead, 1980.

Thomas, David Hurst. *Skull Wars: Kennewick Man, Archaeology, and the Battle for Native American Identity.* New York: Basic Books, 2000.

Titiev, Mischa. "Hopi Racing Customs at Oraibi, Arizona." Papers of the Michigan Academy of Science, Arts and Letters, vol. 24, part 4 (1939): 33–42.

———. *The Hopi Indians of Old Oraibi: Change and Continuity.* Ann Arbor: University of Michigan Press, 1972.

Tobitt, Bill. "Chaca Takes Suisun—Vallejo Marathon." *Oakland Tribune,* December 23, 1929, D19.

Trafzer, Clifford E., Matthew Sakiestewa Gilbert, and Lorene Sisquoc, eds. *The Indian School on Magnolia Avenue: Voices and Images from Sherman Institute.* Corvallis: Oregon State University Press, 2012.

Trennert, Robert A. *The Phoenix Indian School: Forced Assimilation in Arizona, 1891–1935.* Norman: University of Oklahoma Press, 1988.

Troutman, John W. *Indian Blues: American Indians and the Politics of Music, 1879–1934.* Norman: University of Oklahoma Press, 2009.

Tsakaptamana. "The Racers at Tsikuvi." In *Hopi Voices: Recollections, Traditions, and Narratives of the Hopi Indians*, ed. Harold Courlander, 78–91. Albuquerque: University of New Mexico Press, 1982.

Uckert, Sandra. *Cold Application in Training & Competition: The Influence of Temperature on Your Athletic Performance*. Indianapolis: Meyer & Meyer Sport, 2014.

Udall, Louise. *Me and Mine: The Life Story of Helen Sekaquaptewa*. Tucson: University of Arizona Press, 1969.

Vandever, C. E., to Commissioner of Indian Affairs. "Report of Moqui Pueblo Indians, Navajo Agency." Fifty-Ninth Annual Report of the Commissioner of Indian Affairs to the Secretary of the Interior. Washington, DC: Government Printing Office, 1890, 167–172.

Viola, Herman J. *Diplomats in Buckskins: A History of Indian Delegations in Washington City*. Norman: University of Oklahoma Press, 1995.

Voth, Heinrich R. "The Oraibi Summer Snake Dance Ceremony." *Field Columbian Museum Publication* 3, no. 83 (1905): 324.

Walker, Andrew J. "The Aesthetics of Extinction: Art and Science in the Indian Sculptures of Hermon Atkins MacNeil." In *Perspectives on American Sculpture before 1925*, ed. Thayer Tolles, 96–115. New York: Metropolitan Museum of Art, 2003.

Ward, Michael. *Ellison "Tarzan" Brown: The Narragansett Indian Who Twice Won the Boston Marathon*. Jefferson, NC: McFarland, 2006.

Warden, Albert F. "Long Distance Running Growing in Popularity." *Salt Lake Tribune*, June 25, 1916, 3.

Waters, Frank. *Book of the Hopi: The First Revelation of the Hopi's Historical and Religious World-View of Life*. New York: Ballantine Books, 1963.

Weddell, Al G. "Famous Marathoners Beaten on the Desert." *Los Angeles Times*, November 19, 1912, Section 3, 3.

Weideman, Paul. "Drawing Down Rain from the Devil's Claw." *Santa Fe New Mexican*, August 18, 2006, ZO51-52.

Weidman, Bette, and Linda Martin. *Nassau County, Long Island, in Early Photographs*. Mineola, NY: Dover Publications, 1981.

Wexler, Laura. "The Fair Ensemble: Kate Chopin in St. Louis in 1903." In *Haunted by Empire: Geographies of Intimacy in North American History*, ed. Ann Stoler, 271–296. Durham, NC: Duke University Press, 2006.

Whalen, Kevin. *Native Students at Work: American Indian Labor and Sherman Institute's Outing Program, 1900–1945*. Seattle: University of Washington Press, 2016.

Whiteley, Peter M. *Deliberate Acts: Changing Hopi Culture through the Oraibi Split*. Tucson: University of Arizona Press, 1988.

———. *The Orayvi Split: A Hopi Transformation, Part 2: The Documentary Record*. New York: American Museum of Natural History, 2008.

Wilcox, Ralph C., "The Shamrock and the Eagle: Irish Americans and Sport in the

Nineteenth Century." In *Ethnicity and Sport in North American History and Culture*, ed. George Eisen and David K. Wiggin, 55–74. Westport, CT: Praeger, 1995.

Williams, Geoff. *C. C. Pyle's Amazing Foot Race: The True Story of the 1928 Coast-to-Coast Run across America*. New York: Rodale, 2007.

Witmer, Linda F. *The Carlisle Indian Industrial School: Carlisle Pennsylvania, 1879–1918*, 3rd ed. Carlisle: Cumberland County Historical Society, 2002.

"Wonderful Hopi Runners." *Indian's Friend* 16, no. 2 (October 1903): 10, 11.

Wood, Richard E. *Here Lies Colorado: Fascinating Figures in Colorado History*. Helena, MT: Farcountry Press, 2005.

Worster, Donald. *A River Running West: The Life of John Wesley Powell*. Oxford: Oxford University Press, 2001.

Wright, Barton. *Clowns of the Hopi: Tradition Keepers and Delight Makers*. Walnut, CA: Kiva Publishing, 2004.

Yamamoto, Eriko. "Cheers for Japanese Athletes: The 1932 Los Angeles Olympics and the Japanese American Community." *Pacific Historical Review* 69, no. 33 (August 2000): 399–430.

Yava, Albert. *Big Falling Snow: A Tewa-Hopi Indian's Life and Times and the History and Traditions of His People*, ed. Harold Courlander. Albuquerque: University of New Mexico Press, 1992.

Younger, Erin. "Changing Images: A Century of Photography on the Hopi Reservation." In *Hopi Photographers: Hopi Images*, ed. Victor Masayesva, Jr., and Erin Younger, 13–39. Tucson: Sun Tracks & University of Arizona Press, 1983.

Index